Tristan Jones

SAGA OF A WAYWARD SAILOR

SHERIDAN HOUSE

Other books by Tristan Jones
published by Sheridan House

Adrift
Aka
Dutch Treat
Encounters of a Wayward Sailor
Heart of Oak
Ice!
The Improbable Voyage
The Incredible Voyage
One Hand for Yourself, One for the Ship
Outward Leg
Seagulls in My Soup
Somewheres East of Suez
A Steady Trade
To Venture Further
Yarns

First paperback edition
published 1995 by
Sheridan House, Inc.
145 Palisade Street
Dobbs Ferry, NY 10522

Printed in the United States of America

ISBN   0-924486-79-1

Contents

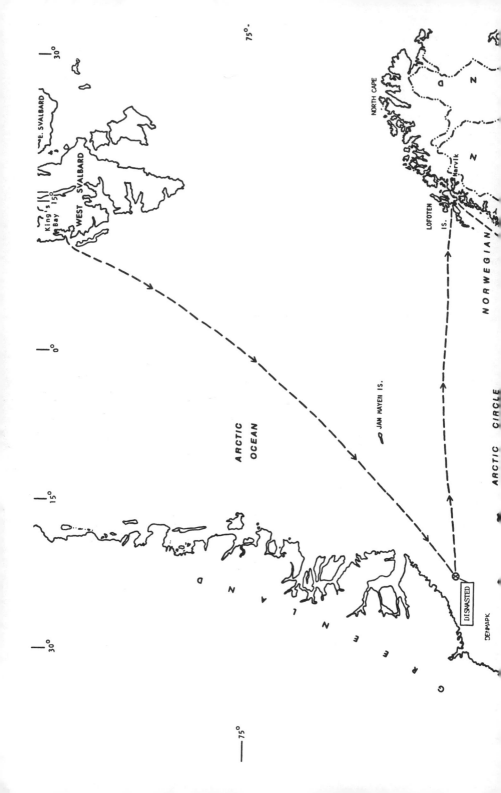

"SAGA OF A WAYWARD SAILOR"

SHOWING ROUTES DESCRIBED

→ TRACK OF "CRESSWELL"

To
the women of this world
without whom there would
never have been any voyages,
in memory of Megan Roberts,
who gave me life.

And to:
Neils Arblom of Lofoten,
Karl Boehm of Düsseldorf,
Paul Condamine of Bordeaux,
Alex Fougeron of Paris,
Simon Godolphin of London,
Jean-Pierre Berton of Brest,
Bob Perko of Santa Barbara, California,
Ruy Vidal Molinharo, Commander, Portuguese Navy,
Steve Llewellyn of London,
Mr. Ballcock, Chief Engineer, Harrods, London, and
Milt Johnson, Bill Karr, and Keith Miles, of the Boat Loft, Edmonds, Washington, who faithfully guarded *Sea Dart* while I wrote this book.

Apology to my British, Dutch, French, German, Spanish or Portuguese readers: my nursery was Wales, my school was the Royal Navy lower-deck; my language-colleges were the sailing boats and dock-side taverns of the world; my university was the sea; my apology is for any slight error I may have made in reporting colloquial speech.

Tristan Jones
London, Antarctica, and Manhattan
Easter, 1976—New Year, 1979

Foreword

My arctic voyage, 1959 to 1961, as described in the previous book of this trilogy, *ICE!*, was probably among the most futile of expeditions. It was made for the wrong reasons, with the wrong boat, meager finances and unsuitable equipment. It was a classic example of how *not* to tackle such an effort. *Or so it seemed at the time*, before the realization that I had been exploring *human limits* finally dawned on me.

The first leg of this voyage took me into the Baltic, on a futile detour of two thousand miles or so, to find a Finnish girl friend. I eventually found her, well married. I have not dwelt on this. Some parts of a man's life are his and his alone. To complain is not my function.

Be patient with a simplistic survivor at the start of this tale. Persist; endure with me; try to see things as I saw them then. See how time, although it may not quickly heal all wounds, at least puts *pain into perspective*. See how freedom demands sacrifice.

Nelson was a Labrador retriever, at the start of this saga about fourteen years old. His right foreleg and his left eye were missing, lost before I inherited him from his previous master (my first sailing skipper twenty-four years previously), Tansy Lee.

Cresswell was an ex-Royal National Lifeboat Institution sailing rescue craft, built in London in 1908. She served in that capacity for many years, until I bought her for $700 and converted her into a rough and ready cruising ketch. Her engine was an old ex-London Fire Brigade trailer-pump from the "Blitz." Her dimensions were 36 feet long by 6 feet 6 inches wide and she drew 2 feet 9 inches of water when fully loaded. When this story starts she carried 620 square feet of sail. Her construction was grown Portuguese oak frames, with double diagonal West African mahogany planking. She had twin, shallow, bilge keels and, being double-ended, an outboard hung rudder, which could be removed when going aground. At the start of this tale she was 54 years old. I was 38. Therefore the combined age of myself, Nelson, and *Cresswell* was 106. Our combined resources were about ten dollars a week plus what I could earn from occasional yacht deliveries; my wits and Nelson's loyalty.

The sequel to this account, the third book of the trilogy, *The Incredible Voyage* (Andrews and McMeel, 1977) has justified itself time and time again, in the letters I have received from people in hospitals and prisons and in situations where they imagined themselves to be at the "end of their tether." If this book, too, can help as well as amuse, then I shall be content— and I shall feel that our voyages, my reader's and mine, have been well worthwhile.

PART I

Let's Go!
July 1961-November 1963

Sweet are the uses of adversity,
Which, like the toad, ugly and venomous,
Wears yet a precious jewel in his head;
And this our life, exempt from public haunt,
Finds tongues in trees, books in the running brooks,
Sermons in stones, and good in everything.

William Shakespeare
As You Like it (act 2, sc. 1)

Yes our hearts to you are bounded,
Dearest Fatherland,
On the mountains songs are sounded,
On the sea-girt strand.
Legends in the forest linger.
Dreams of olden days,
Every bard-like wandering singer,
Sounds our Norway's praise,
Every bard-like wandering singer,
Proudly sounds our Norway's praise!

Norwegian National Anthem
(Translated by Tristan Jones)

1

Hell and High Water

The storm struck out of the southwest on August 3. It developed rapidly, in a matter of hours: from a steady blow to a howling rage of shifting cloud, rain, and wind, and the four cardinal points of the horizon galloped at me like the horsemen of the Apocalypse. And me in the middle of them. Waiting, vulnerable, patient.

"Hold onto your hat, old lad, we've got some fun and games coming," I said to Nelson, my three-legged Labrador retriever, as I watched the sky turn first into somber gray, then menacing blackness, with sheets of lightning electrifying the whole heaving, gray-green watery curve of the world. *Cresswell* plunged on, away from the Arctic Circle, which she had passed over only the day before. By the time the gale freshened to a full storm, I was exhausted.

I had set out on July 10, 1961, from Svalbard for Iceland, 800 miles away to the southwest. With the prevailing wind against me, this distance was doubled.

I thought I had recovered my strength and wits during the days in Svalbard, and *Cresswell* was again sound. I first headed due south to latitude 71, so as to avoid any ice floes which might have broken loose from the main pack; then I headed due west for Jan Mayen, with the idea that if anything went amiss, I could shelter in those lonely islands. But the wind shifted to northwest and I was forced away to the south; so I missed Jan Mayen entirely.

By July 25 I was 180 miles due north of the northeast tip of Iceland. With the northwest wind I had a close reach, and the boat was making fast time. I aimed to reach Cape Farewell, the southern tip of Greenland, not later than August 30. From there, with the Greenland Current helping me westward until it joined the southerly running Labrador Current, it was around 800 miles to St. John's, Newfoundland. If my luck held out, I should reach there by the end of September. I would have to push it, because my margin of safety, foodwise, was narrow indeed—only three weeks.

On July 31 I was in the Denmark Strait, heading southwest on a broad reach over the heaving waters, sometimes sighting Icelandic and British fishing vessels over the white-silver-topped, flashing green seas. Now came August, and with it the end of the short Arctic summer.

In the Arctic for almost two years, my diet had consisted mainly of rice, seal blubber, fish, and corned beef, and I was down to a wiry 120 pounds. Besides, I was suffering from what I call Arcticitis, a kind of lassitude which slows you down. Everything is slow motion, though you are unaware of it until you encounter someone who hasn't got it. It's something like a man from the mountains plodding along at his pace for years, nice and easy and perfectly normal to him. Then he goes to New York and immediately there's a difference in time, almost a time warp. After two years alone in the Arctic, even the mountain man would seem like a big-city tycoon.

Anyway, it blew seven bells and the sea worked up into monsters. I had been hove to under reefed mizzen only, when suddenly this great mountain of water, out of nowhere, crashed down onto *Cresswell*. I had not much fear of the hull giving way, for she was double diagonal mahogany on grown Portuguese oak frames with oiled canvas between the mahogany planks, which were beautifully laid with copper fastenings. The deckhouse I had added myself, continuing the original hull specifications all around. The masts were stepped on deck, in galvanized iron tabernacles. This was mainly for ease in dropping the masts when they were in danger of icing up too thick.

The sea that came on board was heavy and strong enough to bend the tabernacle, which was made of ½-inch-thick galvanized iron. This put such a strain on the starboard chain plates that they ripped right out of the hull. Amazing, for they were fixed through the side with ¾-inch-diameter phosphor-bronze bolts, six to each chain plate. Of course, as soon as the shrouds on the starboard side twanged away, over went the mast to port. At the same time the whole boat was lifted up and flung I don't know how far, then slammed onto the leeward seas with such a shock that it broke the engine loose from its bed. The engine started to dance around, and it was all I could do to lasso the thing and secure it with a Spanish windlass. If it tore the shaft out of the stern tube, I would have had a long, cold row in the dinghy to Iceland, about 300 miles to the southeast. But my luck was in and after a hard struggle I got the engine secured.

When I went aloft, the sight that met my eyes was enough to make a bloody bishop burn his Bible. The mainmast was splintered like a banana peel as far as the houndsbands (where the head of the mainsail luff reaches). It was dangling over the side and there was a forest of tangled shroud wires and wrecked, torn sails all over the topsides.

In the roaring gray twilight, with the hounds of death screaming in my ears all the way from Cape Farewell, I slowly and patiently cleared away the mess. The shrouds I chopped off with an ax, which I kept razor sharp for this very purpose. Then I set to work on the mainmast. Finally I managed to heave the whole rig over the side, for it had been threatening, with violent motions, to stove in the side. It was a relief to get rid of it. At least *Cresswell* would now be one entity and not a dozen, all working against each other.

I crawled back down below to size up the situation. I was still under reefed mizzen, which was holding her head up against the seas. Even if she broached to, I wasn't too concerned, for she was built like a barrel and, mastless, would probably just roll right over.

I decided to wait until the storm subsided, then rig a forestay from the top of the mizzen to the bow and try to make for Reykjavik or Hunafloi in Iceland. Then, once I was safely at anchor, I could clear up the mess and plan repairs.

It proved impossible, under that rig, to make Iceland, and I was forced to head for Norway, 1,000 miles away on the other side of the Arctic Ocean. It took me from August 3 until October 18, 76 days, during which I endured gale-force winds and stronger for 49 days.

My galley stove was useless, since the pipe which fed the kerosene to the burners had snapped and there was no spare. It contained a needle mechanism to regulate the kerosene supply, and I could not manage a jury rig, so I ate cold food all the way—dried fish and porridge mixed with a bit of water.I still had a good supply of nuts, which kept me going for a couple of weeks. Nelson went on short rations—that is, half a day's food every other day. By the time I reached the Norwegian fishing fleet and had some potatoes, ready cooked, and bread passed to me, I was even considering eating Nelson.

I encountered Norwegian herring boats about 200 miles west of Narvik. When they saw my predicament, they dropped supplies in a barrel over the side, for the seas were too rough to chance coming alongside me. Then the Norwegian Air Force sent a plane out twice a day to check that I was all right and guide me into the Westfjord and Lofoten Island. By the time I got in I was ready for a good meal and a couple of beers.

So there I was, as the old saying goes, "fed up and far from home," with my boat in a shambles, the old fire-pump engine off its bed, no mainmast, two tins of corned beef in the galley locker, and five pounds of Lipton's tea carefully wrapped in a spare oilskin. Lofoten in September isn't exactly like the South of France or Miami Beach, what with a cold fit to freeze the balls off a brass monkey and the stink of fish permeating everything. But at least the vessel was safe and that was the main thing.

Cresswell was tied up alongside a fishing wharf, subsidiary and remote to the main one, which was agog day and night with noise and activity. Being Welsh and, to the Norwegians, obviously stark raving mad, I had been relegated to an unfrequented corner of the harbor, rife with derelict fishing boats and not much else. Topsides, the sleet pattered down with gentle threats of another hard winter ahead. Below, although I had done what I could do to make things shipshape, *Cresswell* looked like a Port Said bumboat—ragged, tattered sails, ragged, tattered blankets smelling to high heaven, and a ragged, tattered skipper thanking his lucky stars he still had some tea left. My lame old dog sadly resigned himself forward, while all around us the snow-topped hills resigned themselves to winter.

I set to making tea, boiled spuds, and gravy. I'd save my corned beef for an emergency. Luckily I still had kerosene for the lamp and stove, so the cabin soon warmed up.

I was just dishing out the grub (which meant taking the lid off the pan—no fancy stuff like plates on the old *Cresswell*) when there was a knock on the doghouse roof. I replaced the lid on the pan, sealing off the delicious aroma of British boiled potatoes, and called, "Right-o, old chum, be right up!"

Outside the companionway hatch, it was pitch black and wetly cold. All I could see was a shadowy figure.

"Evening, mate," I said, "what can I do for you?"

A bulky, thickset man, wearing a long raincoat and a fedora hat, stood on the dock. He was chubby and clean-shaven, a fair-haired man around 45 with a worried expression.

"Gut evenink," he said. "I vas valking past your boat und saw der British flag and vonder vot you are doing here."

His accent was strange, much more guttural than a Norwegian speaking English.

"Well, come down below. It's far too cold to stand around up here. Have a cup of tea."

We passed down the companionway—me first, him following. He was unaccustomed to small craft, and it was with some clumsiness that he eventually settled onto the port berth, which is what I called the rough wooden plank which ran the length of the cabin. During the long bitter months *Cresswell* had been locked in the ice and the days when she had been disturbingly becalmed in the Denmark Strait, I used it to sit on when I played myself chess.

"I am Karl Boehm," he said, "from Hamburg."

"Tristan Jones—Liverpool, Yokohama, New York and all points west," I replied jocularly. If a fellow ever needed cheering up, this one did. He looked like a wet Sunday night in Aberdeen.

"Weather getting you down?" I went on, as we halved the potatoes and sipped the bitter tea, for I was out of sugar weeks back.

"Ach, no, it is not the veather, it is business."

"What do you mean? What business?"

"Vell, you see, I represent a firm in Germany which constructs very up-to-date fish-canning machinery, but in Norway I can do nothing. Ever since the var they hate the Germans. Their canning plants are old and out of date, but they vill not make deals vith us. I have been here for a month. Always they are very nice, always a glass or two of schnapps, but never an order." His tale of woe continued for a good half hour.

"Look, cheer up, Karl. I'll tell you what: if you like, tomorrow I'll put on my best bib and tucker and come with you."

"Good idea, Tristan, and if ve make a sale I vill make sure you get some commission."

"There's only one snag."

He looked at me quizzically. "Vot's that?"

"I don't know a thing about fish-canning machinery. It takes me all my time to keep that damned diesel fire-brigade engine of mine working, and even now, after three years of tinkering around with it, all I know it does is suck-squeeze-bang-blow. How the hell am I going to sell anything as complicated as your gear?"

"Sit down and I vill tell you about it. Maybe this vill help you understand better."

He pulled a bottle out of his pocket. Schnapps! And I hadn't had a wee drappie for almost three months! Holy smoke, for a half bottle of schnapps I'd have sat down with Hitler!

So we sat, into the small hours of the morning, with the wind and sleet increasing in the Arctic night outside, cozy, warm and schnapps-cheered, while Karl instructed me on the finer points of German technology and I eyed the slow, sad, outgoing tide of the schnapps bottle. Finally after effusive handshaking, he left to return to his hotel and I turned into my tatty bed to dream of green fields, church clocks, cricket, and English pubs flowing with ale and hospitality.

The following morning, though very cold and foggy, was at least dry. I tumbled out of bed, as usual fully clothed except for my seaboots. In the Arctic, although often tempted to fall into the slack ways of foreigners and "lesser breeds without the law," I made it a rule never to sleep in my seaboots except when the rigging was frosting up. Then it was a case of getting up every two hours or so, climbing topsides, and clambering up to the crosstrees to knock the black ice off the masts and rigging wires.

Breakfast was tea and one of the cigarettes that Karl had kindly contributed to my commissary the night before. I dripped two drops of water into the empty schnapps bottle, swirled it around as carefully as the head barman in the Waldorf-Astoria preparing cognac flambé, and poured it down my throat. Then I was set for the day.

Karl appeared at 9 o'clock sharp, as arranged, and together we set off for the town and the fish-canning factories, with Nelson. Despite his size, Karl walked as spritely as a boxer.

"Have you had breakfast, Tristan?"

"Cup of tea and a cigarette—mariner's breakfast."

He smiled, then patted my shoulder, his 200 pounds almost dislodging the shoulder of my 120-pound frame.

"Then ve shall go for coffee and a good breakfast. You English . . . "

"Welsh!"

"Ja, I beg your pardon. You Velsh like kippers, I believe?"

"Scrumptious. Let me at them!"

We entered a small restaurant and were soon replete with kippers and coffee, with crispy Norwegian bread and cheese, served by very pretty but stern-faced waitresses, who obviously knew Karl's origin. They even looked at me as if I'd blown in under the door; but I was accustomed to that, even at home. No bottom-pinching here, I thought, as I finished the first good meal I'd had in three months.

From the cafe we made our way to the main fish-canning plant. I had made an appointment by telephone with the chief engineer's secretary and, having been received by suspicious-looking underlings, finally arrived at his office. Karl waited outside.

I walked in to find a thin, ascetic-looking man wearing rimless spectacles and almost completely bald except for a fringe of ginger hair over his ears.

"Good morning, sir, I've come to chat about the fish-canning plant for which you are receiving tenders."

"Steady on," he replied in a broad Scottish accent, eyeing me closely. "Steady on . . . don't I know you from somewhere?"

"I suppose it could be. I've knocked around quite a bit."

"Wait a minute. By jumping Jehosaphat . . . yes, Tristan . . . Tristan Jones! I know you; we were on the old destroyer *Chieftain* together, for Crissake, in 1942. Convoys from Seydisfjord to Russia. Don't you remember me?" He jumped up from his chair and grabbed my hand.

For a few seconds I was puzzled, then it dawned on me that this was an old shipmate. "Yes . . . wait a minute. Yes, I've got it. Ewan McTavish, mechanician first class! Yes, by Crikey, Jock. I remember you now. How are you, old mate?" I grabbed his shoulder and laughed.

"Sit down old chap. Sit down and tell me what I can do for you."

I told him the truth—that my boat was a shambles, that I was broke, that the German salesman was the last straw to a drowning man, that I didn't know a damned thing about fish canning, that the German had offered me a commission on the sale, which if it came off would look after me for a whole winter and refit *Cresswell*, and would he please put an order in? Ewan by this time was laughing like blazes.

"I'll fix it, Tristan. We've a board meeting tomorrow. I know the plant is good. It's just that the Norwegians are very wary of Germans since the rough time they had during the fracas, but I'll put my weight on it. Dinna fash y'sel', laddie, we'll have that commission for you yet."

"Ewan, you know what this means to me?"

"Of course I do. Don't worry. And come round to my place for dinner tonight, and bring your friend with you. Seems like a decent sort to me."

"Yes, he's a good bloke. I don't give a tinker's damn if he's German, Eskimo, or a bloomin' Scotsman even, as long as he's all right." (Nothing like hard voyaging for bringing out the democrat in a man.)

Outside, Karl was glumly shuffling papers.

"Karl, *mein freund*, we've done it! We've done it!" He looked at me in disbelief.

"Vot? How? It's not possible. You have been in there only 15 minutes. How is this so?"

I explained to him what had happened and his face brightened. "Ve must go and drink to your great success on your first attempt at salesmanship, Tristan."

"Yes, and my last, too!" I replied.

By the time we had seen off a good deal of schnapps, Karl was becoming sentimental in the German way. Finally I asked him straight out what was bugging him.

"Tristan, I did not tell you. During the var I was in the *Deutscher Kriegsmarine*, the German Navy."

I grabbed his arm. "Come on, Karl, let's have another bloody schnapps!"

Two months later, after the fish-canning plant was installed, I was on my way south to winter over in the comfortable Norwegian port of Stavanger before heading into the Baltic. On board I had a new mast and six months' supply of food.

Oh as I was a-walking down Lime Street one day . . .
Hey! Weigh! Blow the man down!
A pretty young maiden she happened my way . . .
Give me some time to blow the man down!

I said to my folly "Oh how d'ye do?" . . .
Hey! Weigh! Blow the man down!
Said she "None the better for seeing of you" . . .
Give me some time to blow the man down!

"For sailors is tinkers and tailors is men" . . .
Hey! Weigh! Blow the man down!
"And I hope that I never will see you again" . . .
Give me some time to blow the man down!

So we'll blow the man up and we'll blow the man down . . .
Hey! Weigh! Blow the man down!
We'll blow the man up unto Liverpool Town . . .
Give me some time to blow the man down!

Capstan shanty, mid-nineteenth century
(To "blow the man down" meant to hoist the mainsails)

2

Pennies from Heaven

To the east of Lofoten, in the town of Narvik on the mainland of Norway, the local shipbuilders made me a beautiful mainmast of spruce, hollowed out and scarfed in three sections, with hounds, or pads of wood over which the loops of the standing rigging are supported, of *lignum vitae*, or ironwood. This was imported especially for the job by a Narvik shipowner who had heard of my plight and for some strange reason seemed to sympathize with me. But bless him, he paid for the whole job, and by the end of October 1961 *Cresswell* had a brand new mainmast, with six coats of varnish, sitting in the tabernacle.

On a gaff rigger the mainsail is fitted with a parrell on the head of the luff. This is a tough iron hoop strung with wooden balls, enabling the throat of the mainsail to be hauled up with ease. Getting hold of wooden balls was a headache, so I made do with Ewan McTavish's golf balls drilled through the middle. They served admirably. The new mainsail I made from a hatch awning, heavy canvas, donated by one of the Lofoten trawler skippers, while the new standing rigging was cut and spliced from trawl wires, one inch in diameter. These I coated with a mixture of gasoline and linseed oil. The gas acts as a vehicle for the oil to penetrate the galvanized strands and the hemp core, thus preserving the cable.

Treated like this every six months, galvanized wire will last for years and stay flexible.

My commission on the fish-canning plant deal from the German manufacturers had come to just over $300, which in those days was a small fortune, enabling me to buy charts for the Baltic, two 50-kilo sacks of rice and one of sugar, 30 pounds of tea, cocoa, flour, and porridge, a barrel of dried fish (which I called "yellow peril"), and a big sack of beef bones for Nelson.

The end of November is not the ideal time of year to be sailing around in the Norwegian Sea in a 36-foot, 53-year-old, gaff-rigged, seven-foot-wide, shallow-draft ex-lifeboat, and by this time I had been almost three years in the Arctic and felt it was time to thaw out a bit. So I decided to have a shot at getting into the Baltic, either to Sweden or Denmark, where there would perhaps be better prospects of finding a job ashore to tide me through the winter. Once in the Baltic, I could head for Finland.

I started the 800-mile run south to Göteborg at the beginning of December and, pushing as hard as the old girl would manage, arrived there at the end of that month. We crossed the very rough Vestfjord, where the southwesterly prevailing winds from the North Sea roar in fit to blow your ears off and the seas are short, choppy, and *vicious* at that time of year. Once inside the mainland leads, the going was easier, and for much of the passage I sailed in the lee of islands off the shore. There was a lot of tacking but old *Cresswell*, when she got a wind, soon had a bone in her teeth, and the sails balanced so she would steer herself going to windward, giving me time to make hot tea and dish up a pan of hot "burgoo."

Burgoo is the old standby of European Arctic sailors and fishermen. It is made by slowly filling an old, cleaned-out fish barrel with porridge. Every two inches or so put in a layer of dried herring or mackerel, which is soaked in whiskey or schnapps, or whatever other cheering potion is to hand. It is kept on deck, lashed to the mainmast or mizzen tabernacle, thus keeping it frozen. Whenever you feel hungry, whatever the weather, you nip topsides, dollop some of the burgoo in a pan, heat it up, and five minutes later there you are with a fine nutritious meal. A barrelful would last about two weeks. In very bad weather, when it's impossible to go below and cook, you can just grab a handful and eat it cold.

Even old Nelson loved his twice daily dollop of burgoo, and I don't think he ever had an illness in his life. He was still the terror of all the male dogs and the light in the eyes of every bitch on the coast of Norway. Three years later, on the coast of Spain, I had a letter from Ewan McTavish, still in Lofoten, which said that the dog population of that hospitable island had increased enormously and that many of the newcomers bore a remarkable resemblance to Nelson.

The voyage down the coast of Norway was fascinating, despite the darkness, cold and snow, the rough outside passages, and the frequent gales and storms. I cannot imagine a more delightful cruising ground for a summer expedition. There are hundreds of long inlets which drop back through the mountains for scores of miles, all deep, all with good safe anchorages, while the country people every-where are friendly and very honest, which is more than I can say for many other parts of the world. Even in the frequent snow storms it was exhilarating to sail through the meander-ing leads, behind long islands which shielded us from the North Sea boisterousness.

Cresswell called at two big towns on the way south, Trond-heim and Stavanger, both busy fishing ports. From Sta-vanger, having heard a favorable weather report from the BBC broadcasts, I hightailed it over the Skagerrak, the 80-mile-wide strait which separates Denmark from Norway. I wasn't too anxious to visit Denmark, as I had been charged outrageously high port dues in Iceland which I had been unable to pay. The administration of Iceland was at that time closely tied up with that of Denmark, and as I didn't want any bureaucrats clomping onboard to tie me up with paper, I de-cided to give that country a miss and head up through Sweden to the Baltic by way of the Göteborg Canal.

This was great fun, which, after the rough passage down

from the north of Norway, I enjoyed very much, chugging along the canal in calm water and drinking illegal home-made schnapps with the farmers and their families in the evenings. As it was easy to raise and lower the mainmast, which was stepped ondeck in a tabernacle, I sailed over the two big lakes on the canal passages.

Every boat going to the far north should have a tabernacle-stepped mast which can be lowered easily. When at anchor and the black ice threatens to capsize the boat, you can lower the top hamper and so minimize the risk. If you encounter a real snorter, you can again lower the sailing gear and ride it out ahull in comparative safety. However, for one man in a rough sea it's an almost impossible thing to do. For that reason *Cresswell* had lost her mainmast in the Denmark Strait, north of Iceland.

I took my time going through the Goteborg Canal, not the least because of ice and recurrent hangovers. The Swedish country folk are very hospitable, and I recommend the trip through Sweden to anyone who might be in jeopardy of losing faith in human nature. His spirit will be restored; but if he hits the ice and the schnapps like I did, it will take all his tenacity, obstinacy and single-mindedness to complete the course. The Swedish maidens, of course, are renowned worldwide; at no time during the whole run from Göteborg to Norrköping, a run of around 250 miles, which took me 30 days, was I ever alone for one minute, and I hardly steered the boat, or made a meal, the whole way. It was a sailor's dream come true, except for the weather and the long nights. But with company like that, who worried how long the nights were?

I managed to fetch Norrköping just in time, before the canal iced over solid. The Baltic was also icing over by this time, so I decided to winter over in Norrköping until March, when I would push on across the Baltic to Finland. I had a good amount of stores and kerosene for the lamps and the galley stove.

In March 1962 I slipped Norrköping, destination Helsinki via the Aaland Islands. I wanted to visit these islands, part of a very extensive archipelago, because they were the home of many of the old time square-sail-ship sailors. Sure enough, I found quite a few, in their seventies and eighties, and heard many a good yarn from them, for they all spoke English perfectly and remembered all the sailing terms. I stayed there a month or so, then headed on for Helsinki, where I arrived in May, and stayed for a month, visiting friends, seeing the country, and meeting the people. A beautiful country and the friendliest people.

I cleared Helsinki for Visby, on the Swedish island of Gotland, which I intended to make my first port of call. In the summer the Baltic is very often flat calm, with hardly any wind at all, so a good engine is a must if one wishes to make a fast passage. This was the case when I slipped from Helsinki. At first the old fire-pump diesel worked like a charm, even if it coughed and wheezed. I intended to motor on until I had cleared the Gulf of Finland, which is bordered on the southern side by the Soviet Union, Estonia to be exact. All day and night the engine pottered along, jerking on its bed like a Morris dancer; but finally, with a pitiful wheeze and an ominous clang, it stopped dead. I was lying in a flat calm. It was early morning, and I had been at the wheel for 24 hours solid; so before tackling an inspection to find out what was wrong, I went to sleep.

After three hours' kip and a dollop of burgoo, this time with bacon in it as well as dried fish and schnapps, I took off the cylinder-head covers of the Coventry Vixen twin-cylinder horizontally opposed London fire-brigade ex-trailer-pump diesel engine, to find that both big ends had finally given way. I'd no spares, for the engine was out of production by this time, and with an immense sigh of relief I concluded that this trip to Holland was going to be done under sail. Happily, I went back to sleep, for I was still becalmed. Nelson loped off topsides to keep a shipping watch. He had a box in the cockpit where he kept his bone of the day, so he could happily gnaw at it while keeping his one eye out for other craft.

Sure enough, after a while Nelson woke me. I reached for

my seaboots and jersey and, bleary eyed, climbed up the companionway. The roar of a powerful engine sounded not very far away.

A disturbing sight met my eyes. About 100 yards away to starboard was a Soviet destroyer, with all its guns pointed straight down my throat. On deck were a number of sailors, pointing machine pistols at *Cresswell*. A boarding party was being readied.

"Blimey!"

As they came alongside in a fast 30-foot motorboat, Nelson growled and got ready to repel boarders. "Quiet now, lad," I said; "let's see what these blokes are after."

A young officer clambered on board, followed by three sailors, all pointing guns at me. He shouted something in Russian and I shook my head. Then he used what was either Finnish or Estonian, who knows? It could have been Mandarin Chinese. I shook my head again and said "English!" He then shook his head, so I said *"Parlez-vous français? Sprechen Sie Deutsch? ¿Habla español?"* He again shook his head, all the while doing his best to look very stern and military. I could hardly keep from bursting out laughing. Then I shouted "Schnapps?"

"Da!" he replied.

I dove down below and brought up the bottle, which was passed round. Then the officer indicated by gestures that I was to be taken in to Tallinn, the old capital of Estonia.

The destroyer came up ahead and a long towing line was passed. Once we got into Tallinn, a motorboat was lashed alongside and *Cresswell* was ignominiously hustled into the navy yard, like a drunk being dragged into jail by the scruff of the neck. By this time I had resigned myself to the situation and was beginning, in fact, to enjoy this rather bizarre entry. I was not aware at the time that this was probably the first visit ever of a Western private vessel to the Soviet Union.

The boat was tied up securely along what appeared to be a destroyer in reserve, still under the watchful eyes of armed sailors. Eventually an English-speaking officer arrived.

"You and your vessel are under arrest!"

"What for?"

"You were in waters reserved for the exclusive use of the Soviet Navy! You will be investigated, and if we find you have been carrying out any kind of intelligence activity, you can expect to be in the Soviet Union for quite some time to come, my friend."

"Intelligence? What's that?"

"Don't try to be funny with me!"

"It *would* be rather difficult, wouldn't it?"

"Captain, tomorrow you will be moved to another berth. You will not be allowed ashore until it is decided what to do with you. Good day."

The following morning I was towed to a small jetty in front of the Naval Administrative Building. A guard was put onboard: four older men, obviously time-servers. They sat in the cabin glumly staring into space. I could not play my radio, for it had been taken ashore, but I got out the chessboard and challenged the most amenable-looking guard to a game. His eyes lit up and soon we were passing away the time on the late evening watch much more comfortably.

On the third day, he smuggled on board a bottle of vodka. He spoke a little German, having been in the Second World War. He told me he had five children and that he was a native of Tallinn. He was 55, serving out his last two years of navy time. Gradually he became more and more friendly, so that by the end of the fourth day we were laughing together and he was shaking my hand when he went off duty.

I racked my brain to think of a present I could give him. I had no chocolate or chewing gum, which were worth a small fortune in Tallinn. Then I hit on an idea.

In those days the English penny was a great copper and nickel coin about an inch across and a good sixteenth of an inch thick. With a Gripfast nail driven through a hole, they made the finest, most durable washers in the world, and I always kept a soapbag full of them for use in emergencies. So I delved into the locker where I kept my odds and sods and dug out four pennies, which I polished so they shone like new.

When Igor returned that evening, with his usual bottle, I handed him the pennies. When he saw them his eyes shone as bright as the coins. That night I let him beat me at chess again, but it was obvious something else was on his mind. Just before he went off duty at midnight he said to me, "These pennies, do you have any more?"

"About 200."

"My friend," he said, "we can make a lot of money! You polish them up, I will sell them to my friends. We can get maybe five roubles apiece!"

"Five roubles?"

I grabbed the soap bag and metal polish and by morning had 50 pennies all shining like they had just come out of the Royal Mint. Igor sold them as fast as I could polish them, and I ended the operation with a great roll of banknotes.

I spent two weeks under arrest in Tallinn, with the Russian Navy feeding me and interrogating me regularly. The sessions would go something like this:

"Now, my friend, we know that it is not possible for you to wander around at sea without someone paying you. We are sure it is British Naval Intelligence. No?"

"No. I get my invaliding pension, as I have told you many times—six dollars a week. That's the going Royal Navy rate. And I manage to make a bit on the side here and there, delivering other people's boats, for example. If you think I'm doing anything else, you're barking up the wrong tree!"

He glared a quiz at me.

"You are making wrong presumptions," I explained. "You have to be intelligent to work for British Intelligence, and what intelligent man in his right mind would go sailing around the north of Europe in a leaky old tub like this? I don't even have electricity, or an echo sounder. My chronometer is a seven-shilling job I picked up in Pettycoat Lane five years ago."

And so on and so forth, until eventually I was released. At the end of July I was towed 20 miles offshore, and with a good northerly breeze made the island of Gotland. In Visby, I sold the roubles to a Polish trawler skipper. Even though I only got half the going rate for them, I finished up with something like $200.

After a good night ashore with the Poles in Visby, I reckoned up. I'd had two weeks' free food from the Soviets and I'd made a clear profit of 200 bucks. I stored up some good Swedish ham and jellies, yeast (to make my own bread), and two cases of canned fish and corned beef. Then I was off, through the Kiel Canal and into the North Sea to Holland.

In Amsterdam there lives a maid
(Mark well what I do say)
In Amsterdam there lives a maid,
And she is the mistress of her trade;
I'll go no more a-roving with you, fair maid!

A-roving, a-roving, since roving's been my ru-eye-in,
I'll go no more a-roving with you, fair maid!

British seaman's song
early seventeenth century

Most seamen's songs and chanties, from the sixteenth century on, were highly "permissive" when read aright. They were much bowdlerised in the nineteenth century, and many lost their original honesty and delight. This one, innocent except to the seamen's ears, survived. ("To rove," is the sailor's term for the weft in canvas. It means "to insert"—"to pass through." "Trade," in English, has always had a sexual connotation.)

3

Say Cheese

With a clapped-out auxiliary engine and neither the time nor the cash to make an overhaul, I had to sail *Cresswell* down from the Swedish island of Gotland, in the Baltic, to Holland or England. I decided on Holland because I had arranged to pick up a job of delivering a new 40-footer from Van der Stadt's boatyard to the West Indies. But this could not be until December, when she was to be completed, and right now it was July 1962.

As I wished to avoid passing through Danish waters, it meant I would have to try to sail through the Kiel Canal. We had a three-day passage with good easterlies most of the way through the 65-mile canal passage. *Cresswell* was within 10 miles or so of the port of Marne, at the Elbe River end of the canal, before I succeeded in getting a tow from a barge.

From the canal exit at Marne I headed for the port of Cuxhaven, where I rested a week before traveling down to Düsseldorf to look up Karl Boehm, the fish-canning-plant salesman I had met in Lofoten almost a year previously. He was overjoyed to see me and vastly amused by my tales of the happenings in the Baltic. I left Nelson in charge of the boat with a bag of bones and a great pot of burgoo. He didn't enjoy traveling ashore much now, and anyway he couldn't stand Germans. His previous master, old Tansy Lee, had been sunk six times by them in two wars.

I returned from Düsseldorf by train, loaded down with
about 80 pounds of good German sausages, two huge hams,
and three bottles of Scotch whisky. Karl had looked after me
well, and I arrived back onboard like a Titan. Now it was
September and I wanted to reach Holland before the
equinoctial gales set in. So I cleared for Den Helder while the
going was good.

The passage from Cuxhaven to Den Helder was pleasant
despite the tricky navigation among the many shoals and
sandbanks and one day of blustery winds and heavy rain.
After five days of beating hard to windward against the prevailing southwester, I was off the Friesland Islands. As I
stood in to make the passage through the Vlie Stroom, one of
the main entrances to the Wadden Zee, between the islands
of Vlieland and Terschelling, I dearly wished the engine was
working for I had a girl friend, Marlieka, on the island of Vlieland. The tides were strong and the wind blustery but fair for
my passage to Den Helder, at the entrance of the Noord Ne-
derland Canal. So, dowsing my baser instincts, I girded my
loins, gritted my teeth, and stood in for Den Helder, 20 miles
to the southwest, which I fetched after dark. Once in the lee
side of the great harbor walls, I kicked the hook over the side
and fell asleep, to dream of windmills, tulip fields, pretty girls,
and cheroots.

At night in those days, on arrival at a haven I would heave
out the 60-pound yachtsman's anchor (fisherman's, we used
to call it), drop the gaff after letting go the mainsheet, leave
the mizzen standing and close hauled, put out a kerosene di-
optic lens anchor light, have a crap in my rubber bucket or
over the side, if there was no one around (in those days there
were few cruising yachts in Europe, and we knew each other
very well), grab a panful of burgoo and sausage, and settle
down below to eat the day's main meal. I kept the sausages
hanging on the mizzen boom (I had no refrigeration). I tied
the ensign on the mizzen backstay to stop it frapping away
during the night.

After an hour or so of boiling water for tea and frying brat-

wurst and smoking two or three pipes of Balkan Sobranie to-
bacco, the cabin would take on a smoky glow all its own, cozy
and dankly warm. (Then, we hadn't heard anything about air
pollution.) Nelson and I loved it, with the kerosene lamp
glowing on the mahogany cladding on the sides of the boat,
dripping with condensation droplets like slowly sinking
pearls, and all the books on the shelf, good companions which
had cheered many a cold, lonely Arctic night: Shakespeare,
Milton, Byron, Dickens, Mark Twain, Conrad, D.H. Law-
rence, Shaw.

There were five pictures in frames on the forward
bulkhead: Ernest Shackleton, the bravest Antarctic explorer
of them all, to the right; and impetuous Nansen and Robert
Falcon Scott, the most tragic one, to the left. Her Majesty the
Queen was in the middle, keeping a stern eye out to make
sure things never got too near the knuckle down below in
Cresswell. I had a good few souvenirs from the Arctic hanging
on the bulkheads, too: a walrus tooth, a Norwegian Air Force
plaque, a Soviet Navy quartermaster's badge, and two
beautiful Norwegian plates, picked up in Lofoten at a presen-
tation by the local trawler fleet. Besides this, I had two great
heavy brass gun-tampons—the covers they fit into the
mouths of the 4.5 inch guns on destroyers. These were from
H.M.S. *Cheviot* and H.M.S. *Chieftain*, in which I had served. I
had a cozy little home in *Cresswell.*

In the morning the great gates opened and *Cresswell* was
towed into the locks by a Dutch Navy tug. The water in the
lock dropped about 15 to 20 feet. And there we were, in a
Dutch canal, *below* sea level!

The Dutch canal and dike system is one of the wonders of
this world. About one-third of the country is below sea level,
protected from the North Sea fury by thousands of miles of
great dikes. These have been built up patiently over the centuries—a marvel of ingenuity and skill. ("God made the world
but the Dutch made Holland," the saying goes.)

In exchange for one of my bottles of whisky I arranged a
tow through the canal to the town of Alkmaar, about 20
miles or so from Den Helder, with a barge master. I didn't

lose on the deal, for when he cast off the lines he threw me a box of cheroots.

Passage through the Dutch canals is a delight. Everything is so clean and shipshape. All the little houses have window boxes of flowers and there are miles upon miles of flower fields. In those days many of the local men still wore baggy trousers and wooden clogs, and the lasses were fair and cleanly scrubbed. It was like being in a fairy story or a Disney film.

Upon fetching Alkmaar, the barge let go and chugged off to its wharf with a cheer from the crew. I slowly worked *Cresswell*, with the big sweep oar, down the canal, looking for a place to moor the boat for the winter. It had to be a good safe place because I would be away on the voyage to the West Indies for at least four months, possibly longer.

Halfway through the town, not far from the square, I saw a little offshoot from the canal, well protected by poplar trees on one side and what seemed to be a warehouse on the other. I worked my way in the calm grayish water, through a drizzle of rain (it was September), and dropped the kedge anchor astern on a 15-fathom line; then, as *Cresswell* slid to a graceful halt, I cast the heavy yachtsman's anchor ahead. After paying out the main anchor chain about 10 fathoms, I took in on the kedge anchor line, and she was moored.

In Western Europe, before the great yachting boom of the mid-sixties and seventies, you could moor a boat practically anywhere, and very rarely was a visiting foreign yachtsman charged mooring fees. You might have to show your passport upon entering a country, but that's all there was to it.

By now dusk was falling but I was content, for the Dutch are the most honest folk on earth, and I knew that by December I would have found someone who would keep an eye on *Cresswell* for me and feed Nelson. I made my supper—burgoo, bacon, bratwurst, and tea laced with a drop of fair Scottish sunshine. The drizzle had become heavy rain, so there was no point in going ashore, and I settled down to read a while before turning in. I had warped the boat over to the far end of the warehouse jetty and tied her up fore and aft with spring lines, the anchors holding her off the jetty about two feet or so.

Suddenly, through the patter of the rain on deck, I heard a slow, steady clomping noise: Clomp . . . Clomp . . . Clomp. I picked up my ears, just as Nelson did. The clomping stopped. Ten, 20 seconds later a voice hollered out, thin in the wind: "Haloo, Englander! Haloo!"

As Nelson growled from under the table, I groped my way into the drizzling darkness. Under the glare of the warehouse wharf lights I saw a figure straight out of Robert Louis Stevenson, wearing a woolen seaman's cap and an oilskin jacket down to his knees, or I should say *knee*. He had an honest-to-God wooden pegleg. On his good foot was a thigh-high seaboot. Obviously one of the "gentlemen of the coast," thought I as I pulled the boat in for him to step onboard.

He was a short, stocky fellow, around 50, looking for all the world like Long John Silver. Over one eye was a big black patch.

"Dirk Van Scheltema, ex-petty officer, Netherlands Navy. I am the night watchman in this warehouse."

"Tristan Jones, ex-petty officer, Royal Navy. Pleased to meet you, Dirk, have a drink."

Eventually, after he had fought the war over again and I had given my version, he stood up to go and make his rounds. As he clomped up the ladder he said to me in a half whisper, "Hey, Tristan, you like der cheese?"

"Like cheese? Of course I do, Dirk, I like anything that's edible!"

"Right, my friend. I bring you some cheese when I get back after midnight. O.K.?"

"Bloody O.K.! I'll be here, have no fear."

He clomped along the jetty and disappeared into the door of the warehouse, while I settled down to read once more. After about two hours I heard a loud rumbling noise, together with a clomp! clomp! I rapidly went topsides and the sight that met my eyes was *astonishing*.

Trundling along the jetty was a full-size Dutch railroad wagon, with Dirk shoving it along with his shoulder, going along fine, despite his one leg. The sight so amazed me that I just stood and stared until the wagon was alongside *Cresswell*. Puffing and blowing, Dirk grinned at me and waved a hand at the wagon.

"There you are, Tristan . . . bloddy cheese!"

"Jumping Jehosaphat!" I cried as I leaped upon the wagon and spied at least *two tons* of small, round, red-skinned Edam cheeses.

"What in the name of No-Nose Lil are we going to *do* with this lot?"

The watchman grinned up at me. "Get it onboard the boat, of course. I'll give you a hand."

And so for about two hours, in the pouring rain, Dirk threw Dutch Edam cheeses to me and I stacked them in the cockpit, and finally stowed them down below. I had cheeses in the forward dodger, cheeses in the bilge, cheeses in the lazarette, cheeses in the deckboxes, cheeses under the berths, cheeses in the lockers where I kept the oilskins and other clothes. I even filled the galley stove with cheeses. I must have taken onboard at least 200 Edam cheeses, each one about half the size of a soccer football. All in red skins. I even had cheeses stuffed around the defunct engine.

After a nightcap with Dirk, I returned to my berth, thinking I had enough cheese to keep me alive for the next 10 years. Months of semistarvation in the Arctic ice had given me a mania about sufficient food supplies. Whenever I looked at anything the first thing that went through my mind was: Is it edible? In Helsinki, where I visited the art museum, I had looked at a Matisse, for example, and thought to myself: *What bloody use would that be if there were no food around?*

The next morning I woke to find the boat permeated with the smell of cheese. I lit the small coke stove and made breakfast—Edam cheese, of course, and burgoo and tea, with a cheroot to follow. And I thought of all that food. I was like a man who had won a state lottery! Now I could sail forever. Then I heard a commotion ashore.

Looking through the doghouse porthole, I spied several gentlemen grouped on the jetty, wearing fedora and derby hats and raincoats down to their ankles. Nelson growled from his burgoo bowl.

"Pipe down, old son," I murmered. "If those aren't rozzers then I'm a Dutchman." I thought fast. There was no chance of sailing the boat out, and anyway, if I left in a hurry the game would be up.

I stoked the fire in the coke stove and poured on more fuel; then I got my seaboot stockings, which hadn't been washed since Helsinki, four months before, and draped them around the stove. By the time the detectives came onboard the temperature down below with the coke stove glowing, was up to about 120. The place stank like a stockyard drain. On top of that, I was smoking three cheroots at once.

One of the detectives, a huge fat man, clambered down the companionway, losing his derby hat in the process (which Nelson went for right away, chewing it into a wreck). The rozzer stood in his raincoat at the bottom of the hatchway, and in seconds was sweating like a coolie.

"We are looking for a quantity of cheese which was stolen from this warehouse last night. We are wondering if you might have seen or heard something?"

"It was raining last night," I said.

I too was sweating like a pig. The stove was almost taking off by now and the seaboot stockings were steaming like a locomotive. The stink was incredible.

"It was raining, and of course in a boat it's difficult to hear anything through that noise. I was tired and went to sleep."

By now the perspiration was rolling down the policeman's collar and he was obviously uncomfortable. I could see that he wanted to search the boat, but this would require the presence of a magistrate and also the British consul from Amsterdam, as *Cresswell* was *de facto* British territory and the Dutch police had no jurisdiction onboard her. With a *"Gott verdommer!"* he took off topsides, and as he stepped ashore I heard him mutter to one of his colleagues: *"Verdommdt Englander!"*

I chuckled and patted Nelson. Then we laid low for the day.

The following morning I let go the lines and tried to kedge *Cresswell* out of the warehouse canal. She had gone down a few inches with the extra weight of cheese, but now I found that she was well and truly stuck in the mud. So there I was, sunk in a Dutch canal with two tons of stolen cheese onboard and the place crawling with the law. Obviously, I would have to get rid of some weight so she would float. But what weight?

I couldn't bear the thought of throwing away edible food. I got out the spanners, unbolted the useless ex-London fire-brigade-trailer-pump-diesel engine, and after dusk hauled it up through the bridge-deck hatch. It weighed at least an eighth of a ton. Then I ditched that languishing hero of the Great German blitz over the side, to an ignominious end in the mud at the bottom of the Alkmaar Canal. This raised *Cresswell* just enough that I was able to kedge her out to the main canal. All was ready for a sailing getaway, before the police got permission to search the boat, and at dawn I was off, with a good northerly sweeping me in two hours to the North Sea Canal, which emerges at Ymuiden.

"Just off for the day!" I called to the Dutch customs boat as I passed through the great sea locks and into the gray North Sea. I stood well out beyond the treacherous sandbanks along the coast, standing to the north until sunset; then heading west, bowled along on a broad reach. I was reefed down, for a near-gale was blowing. Just before dawn of the following day I raised the North Foreland light.

I was tired, very tired, when I raised the light but I was exultant, for this was the first light of the British Isles that I had seen in almost four years. I had made it back home! After all the privation and suffering I had been through, I had made it back to British waters. What if it was blowing a bastard in Dover Strait—I was in home waters!

I looked at the light longingly. Then I hove to and made tea. I was well off the sands and could afford to drift a bit. Tomorrow I'd negotiate the Straits of Dover, in the dawn light of the morning.

The gale increased during the night but piped down next forenoon, when I was able to get a little shuteye, with Nelson keeping watch. Next day, as we plunged along through the straits, I determined to head for Alderney. This is one of the British Channel Islands, which are self-governing, and in those days were completely free of taxes and duties. Just the spot for a struggling naval pensioner like me.

I heard from Dirk about a year later, via my London letter drop. The Dutch police had eventually given up the case of the missing cheeses, being unable to prove anything. He still had his job and was looking forward to joining me for a cruise one day.

Breathes there the man with soul so dead,
Who never to himself hath said,
"This is my own, my native land!"
Whose heart hath ne're within him burn'd
As home his footsteps he hath turn'd
From wandering on a foreign strand?
If such there breathe, go, mark him well;
For him no Minstrel raptures swell;
High though his titles, proud his name,
Boundless his wealth as wish can claim;
Despite those titles, power, and pelf,
The wretch, concentred all in self,
Living, shall forfeit fair renown,
And, doubly dying, shall go down
To the vile dust from whence he sprung,
Unwept, unhonour'd, and unsung.

Sir Walter Scott
Patriotism (I. "In Nominatus")

4

Hit and Miss

Mid-September is not the ideal time to make a passage west through the Straits of Dover and down the English Channel. It's a boisterous stretch of water at the best of times, but during the equinoctial gales it is a 22-carat sod, with short, choppy, froth-spumed cross-seas, specially sent by the Almighty to keep eau-de-cologne, frogs' legs, and the bloody metric system out of the British Isles.

Of course, it's also a great help for the "gentlemen of the coast" on both sides, and there has always been quite a smuggling trade, with brandy and wine going north and cigarettes and whisky going south. Much of the trade was still carried on under sail in the early 1960s, and generally you could tell who was one of "the brethren." A right boozy lot they were, too, but always merry company, with a pithy wit.

The brethren hung around the waterfront pubs in the English Channel ports, waiting for full gales or moonless nights before making a run to France. They knew the Channel like they knew their old mother's wrinkles. In deep winter, they moored in the inner harbor at Ryegate, just to the east of Dover, usually drawing the dole. There would be about 50 boats there, all shapes and sizes, from Drascombe luggers to Bristol Channel pilot cutters, wonderful sea boats.

Each night one boat would cook a meal for all the others,

usually "bean pot," a great tureen of baked beans laced with bacon and scraps of mutton, potatoes, and carrots. After all these years, I can still smell the aroma of the steaming pans as they slowly simmered in the canvas shelter on the jetty, while all the idling, hungry, weathered, hard-fisted gentlemen hovered around, taking shelter from a bitter east wind, until a hammer was struck on the oil drum to signal that grub was up. If anyone had won on the horses or the football pools, he would chip in a ferkin of ale and someone would chime in with a mouth organ or banjo after the feast. It was a lively community, even though the east wind blew bitterly all the way out of Siberia.

As *Cresswell* lay hove to off the North Foreland, the southeast corner of England, in the lee of the cliffs, waiting for a southwesterly gale to blow itself out, I thought about all my old chums who had been tremendously helpful to me while I was fitting my boat out for the Arctic cruise four years previously. I wanted to join them, but as I was not entitled to any unemployment pay I had to husband my meager resources and head for the island of Alderney, where there were no taxes or duties and where I could hole up for the winter until the Dutch yacht for the West Indies was ready. So, reluctantly, I started for the Straits of Dover, away from the tempting lights of England.

By nightfall that day I was within sight of Dover Castle, slowly ghosting past the white cliffs (the Seven Sisters) on the tide, for the wind had dropped completely. Then the fog dropped, and just after nightfall I was becalmed. While the fog was thin, I took the opportunity of tuning the rigging, which I always kept fairly slack, and taking the winches apart to grease the innards. By midnight the sea was flat calm and the fog so thick that I couldn't see the mainmast from the cockpit. Tired, I lay down the toolbox and set to, dead-reckoning.

After finding my way around some very tricky waters, with small chance of celestial sights most of the time, I was proud of my instinct for navigational position. In fact I was getting far too cocky about it for my own good. I got out the

Channel tide tables in *Reed's Nautical Almanac* and hour by hour worked out my position. I was not the least bit concerned about tidal drift or currents. After the Norwegian leads, with their fierce tides, the English Channel was going to be a cakewalk.

Soon, by the noise of ships passing and hooting I realized I was drifting into the shipping lanes, so I started blowing my siren. This was an old Royal National Lifeboat Institution relic which had come with the boat. It had been—I can't say "manufactured"—it had been *constructed* about 1870, and it looked as if the builder had been Isambard Kingdom Brunel himself (the engineer who built the *Great Eastern*, the biggest iron ship of her time). It was a massive brass cylinder, about three feet high by six inches diameter, with a wooden-handle plunger that I had to bear down on with all my weight (I can't say "strength," for after a dozen plunges I didn't have much left). The noise that came out of the huge brass trumpet (something like an old-fashioned phonograph) was terrifying. It sounded like an old bull elephant dying in pain and rage. But at least it was heard, even if it almost busted my eardrums.

The fog lasted *five days*. For five days and nights I drifted around the busiest shipping lane in the world, with ships' engines thudding in every direction and their hooters sounding like the death dirges of a thousand wandering banshees all around me, and not a breath of wind, and no engine. By the second day I was exhausted with working that great monster of a Victorian siren, with my eyes hanging out red and blood-shot, Nelson half dead on the foredeck—at the same time trying to work out my position on the tide tables, taking into account that they were five years out of date. (The Channel is pitiless, with sandbanks all over the place. But if I grounded out on one I wouldn't worry too much, for *Cresswell* was a twin-keeled beaching boat. I'd put out the anchors and just sit out the fog.)

By the end of the fourth day of fog I worked out that I was somewhere off the French coast, probably in the vicinity of Cape Gris Nez. There was certainly less shipping about and I imagined I could hear the sound of the tide lapping the cliffs. After sounding with the lead, I found I was in six fathoms, so I was either somewhere near the French shore or near one of the offlying sandbanks. However, there are no offlying sandbanks on the French side. Right, I said to myself, then I must be off Gris Nez! I stayed awake, resorting to my old trick of propping my eyelids open with two matchsticks, checking the compass at intervals.

About midmorning on the fifth day, a slight breeze piped up, and by noon the fog began to clear. "Thank Christ for that!" I murmured to Nelson, who, like me, was hardly able to keep his eye open.

Then it cleared quickly, until I could make out, to starboard, a great high cliff, looming menacingly. Between me and the cliff was a small rowboat, manned by a little fellow wearing oilies and a black beret. I hailed him in French.

"*Hulloo. Bonjour, m'sieur! Comment s'appelle cette falaise là?* What's the name of that cliff?"

Back came the answer, loud and clear, which I shall never forget to my dying day—which I recall every time I think I'm getting too confident about a navigation problem: "You've got the wrong bloody country, mate. That's Beachy bleedin' Head!"

I had dumped the toolbox under the magnetic compass— the crowning sin at sea! I was 60 miles out on my reckoning! That's the Channel for you. "No wonder Napoleon and Hitler were scared shitless of tackling it. Treacherous, fickle, fierce, and downright perilous," I kidded myself.

I set off with a fair easterly breeze, picking up to 20 knots, chagrined and humbled, down the Channel, watching the cliffs slide by. When the sun shone, in the afternoon, I saw the green-green fields (there's no other green so green anywhere, not even in Ireland) rolling away behind the cliffs and the little cottages and grand manors and the castles above the towns. Past Seaford and Newhaven, until, toward 5 o'clock, I was fetching Brighton up ahead. This is a big seaside resort, the favorite watering place of Londoners; so I decided to tie up to the pier and stretch my legs ashore.

The watch on the English coast was lax, for this was before the illegal immigrants started pouring in. I just tied up a line on the leeward side of Brighton Pier and walked into the town past rows of slot machines. Past "What the Butler Saw" and "Print Your Own Name for Sixpence!" Past the Cockney kids, lively as sparrows, begging Mum to buy them an ice cream or a candy floss. Past the old folks dreaming of summers gone by and Edwardian elegance. I crossed the busy seafront road, walked into Woolworth's, and bought five pounds of potatoes with the few English pennies I had not been able to sell in Russia.

When I walked back to the boat, there was a crowd of kids staring at her. I was blithely unaware of what was to come (the biggest yacht marina in Europe is now at Brighton—an artificial harbor where you have to be the Aga Khan's brother to afford to stay). I clambered onboard, raised the gaff, slipped the line, and was off, bound for Alderney on the other side of the Channel. I had not been challenged by any-one, neither customs nor police nor pier officials, who had wished me good afternoon and a pleasant trip. That was the way cruising used to be.

Once I got clear of the coastal groundswell I hove to and made supper: sardines and french fries—a delightful change from burgoo and Edam cheese.

With an easterly wind, I made a fine direct passage to Al-derney, picking up the French light of Barfleur (where Henry V knocked the stuffing out of the French in the early 1400s). Then the Channel tide set against me. The remaining 40 miles took all day, but by nightfall Alderney loomed, low and humpy, off to the west. I hove to off Cherbourg because I didn't want to tangle with the seven-knot Alderney race at night.

Another plate of french fries, and burgoo for Nelson, who had been sulking all day—I couldn't take him ashore in Eng-land because of the strict quarantine laws. I put him topsides, with an admonition to be particularly careful of French fishing boats, which have only two speeds: full ahead and stop, and only two directions: the one the skipper orders and the one the helmsman steers. Usually straight through the nearest boat to hand. That's what come of drinking wine instead of good honest ale.

At dawn, the wind had swung round to the prevailing southwest, and it took me all day to beat into Braye Harbor, as the small bay with a pier is called. When I fetched the harbor the wind was slight, still southwesterly. I was in the lee of the island, so getting to the quay was a tricky business. I got within 30 yards or so, quickly dropped the gaff, and heaved my long throwing line at a local idling on the jetty. And he missed it! Splash it went in the water, just as the tide grabbed hold of *Cresswell* and moved her back out to the offing at all of a knot and a half! I was soon swooshing around the eastern side of the island, in a generally northern direction, back toward England.

"Damn and blast; he missed it! That lazy, idle, good-for-nothing scupper lizard missed the bloody heaving line!" I rehoisted the gaff.

By midnight, still in the grip of the tide race which sweeps at a great rate from the passage between Alderney and the French coast, I found by star sights that I was 25 miles northwest of the islands. Then, to top it all, early next day the wind turned southeast! This is about as frequent an occurrence as my being invited to a Buckingham Palace tea party. To get back to Alderney I would have to beat for hours at a stretch, if not days, and mostly against the race, and when the race *did* turn, against the wind. There would be a hell of a rough sea.

I traced a grubby finger over an even grubbier chart and made a decision: I would head for Plymouth, running free. I could probably make it by morning, although the weight of two tons of stolen Dutch cheese was making the old girl a bit more sluggish than normal. Instead of her usual stately dowagerlike progress, she was hobbling along like a doxy in the early morning after a fruitless night's patrol.

I sighted Prawle Point during the night following, and in the afternoon I fetched Hamoaze, where I kicked the hook over the side in the lee of Mountbatten Island and went to sleep.

In the morning the wind again was southwest, so I again took off, without going ashore, for Alderney. I had a nice broad reach all the way over the Channel, almost 200 miles of bouncing boisterousness, but there was no one around when I reached Braye Harbor; so I just drove *Cresswell* straight onto the beach, all sail standing. I had sailed 340 futile miles because of a missed heaving line.

Wearily, I headed for the Diver's Arms pub, carrying a cargo of Edam cheese which I bartered for 18 pints of good foaming ale from England. The pub was full of "brethren" islanders, who in those days were renowned as the aristocrats of the trade. More whisky was passing through the island, bound on moonless nights for the Contentin Peninsula in France, than was going by the legal trade routes.

The Channel Islands govern themselves, each one—Alderney, Guernsey, Jersey, and Sark—separately, for they are part of the old fiefdom of William the Bastard, duke of Normandy, who with the aid of 20,000 Normans conquered England in 1066 by stabbing at Saxon Harold, who was exhausted from fighting off the Danes in the north.

The Alderney men are fine seamen; they have to be, for most of the year in that part of the Channel there are gale conditions, if not worse. During the war, when the Germans occupied the Channel Islands, they converted the lighthouse on a notorious rock, called the Casquets, to a weather station. The Royal Navy recruited some of the islanders, all of whom had been evacuated, to man fast motor gunboats. Whenever there was a roaring gale, the boats sortied out of Plymouth, to lie to off the Casquets, which the locals (and only they) knew like the backs of their hands. Then a Royal Marine commando party raided the station and took off the garrison.

This happened regularly. There was nothing the Germans could do about it because, in those weather conditions, not being Channelers, they were frozen. Toward the end of the war, when things got tight for the Germans, their soldiers were volunteering in flocks for duty on the Casquets. They knew they would be taken prisoner, but that was far better than being sent to Russia.

They still tell the tale of one islander who, having escaped from Guernsey in a six-foot boat in 1941, a year after the Germans arrived, joined the Royal Navy. He was made petty officer-pilot of one of the commando boats, and one night an intelligence party was send to the south coast of Guernsey. While the boat, disguised as a fishing smack, lay at anchor, he donned an issue-blue raincoat over his uniform, put on his peak cap, and walked across the island to visit his old Mum in St. Peter Port. On returning, he thought he would visit the Crown pub, on the waterfront, for a quick pint. Upon entering the brightly lit public bar, he found that it was used as a German sergeants' mess!

Using the peculiar Alderney French-Norman patois, he convinced the Germans that he was a member of a visiting Italian Navy delegation. The German sergeants insisted on buying beer all night for their gallant ally, and the P.O. got back on board about 2 a.m., three sheets to the wind. He still managed to pilot the commandos back to Plymouth, though.

In the Diver's Arms, I made a deal with a Cherbourg trawler skipper. The next day the cheese (or most of it) was transferred to his boat, while 400 pounds sterling passed to me. Then a brand new Volvo-Penta MD2 two-cylinder darling of a diesel was ordered for me from Guernsey, brought up by one of the "fishermen," and with their aid and assistance it was installed. They even put in a battery and an electric light.

Having to scrape and clean the bottom, and bearing in mind that I would be absent from *Cresswell* for some months, I decided to neap her. That is, take her as high on the beach as I could on the highest spring tide and secure her. She would float for only a few minutes once a month; the rest of the time she would be beached and secure, with the brethren keeping their eye on her through the mullioned windows of the public bar in the Diver's Arms.

A local lady took custody of Nelson. Rather she promised to see he was fed, for no woman could take custody of him; he suspected them. I suppose that was something else he learned off Tansy, who used to say, in his gruff voice:

"Bloomin' women . . . brassiers in the head, knickers in the sail locker. All on top and nothin' handy. They're just like a midshipman's locker: bad luck onboard they are, me ol' son." But at 86 and a real storm-tossed hard case, what could you expect?

Personally, I think he'd once been very much in love after his wife died quite early in their marriage, but something happened and it came to nothing. However, he would never talk about it. Ashore, he was always most courteous to the ladies, not to say *gallant*, lifting his hat and complimenting the barmaids. With his habits, they were about the only females he ever came into contact with—though one old dear in Margate, every time we put in, would come down to the jetty with a nice steak and kidney pie and a bottle of Guiness. She was about 80, always dressed in a bonnet with flowers and a lace shawl. Tansy used to gruffly dismiss her, then go below and scoff half the pie, leaving the other half for me. I often wondered about that old girl.

I flew up to Holland just after Christmas, picked up the 40-foot yawl *Utterlo*, and sailed her to Curaçao, direct via the Canaries and Barbados (the Lady's Passage, we call it). I arrived in that hot place (in more ways than one) in April '63 and, having found nothing to sail back to Europe, flew back, arriving in Alderney to find dear old *Cresswell* still sitting there, pretty as a picture.

The night was drear and dark,
While our devoted ark,
There she lay . . . til next day,
In the Bay of Biscay, oh!

Old sailor's song, eighteenth century

5

Dismasted Again

For the *Otterlo* delivery I had earned close to a thousand dollars (U.S.), which was paid into my London bank account. I decided to head for the Mediterranean and, having seen that all onboard was Bristol fashion, took off bound for Vigo, on the northwest tip of Spain. This meant crossing the Bay of Biscay, which is just about the hairiest stretch of Atlantic, at that time of year, south of latitude 50 north and north of latitude 30 south.

The winds in the Bay of Biscay blow hard from the west, and five days out of 10 they are gale force or more. All the huge bay is over the shallow European continental shelf, so a wicked sea is set up. The traditional way from the Channel to Vigo, therefore, is to stand well out into the Atlantic, making a track on a semicircular course.

I left Braye Harbor, after a farewell party given by the "brethren" in the Diver's Arms. This slugged me with a hangover which could have felled an ox. I delayed my departure for 24 hours, before I set off into the windy Channel.

The BBC forecast on the day I left wasn't inviting: "Wind force six to eight, areas Fastnet, Plymouth, Wight, Dover, southwest"; but of course in those days they were not always accurate in the Meteorological Office, nowhere near as precise as nowaday. In fact, our method of deciding whether to sail or not was much more primitive. We would light a two-inch stump of candle in the bottom of a jam jar, walk to the end of the seawall, and if the wind didn't blow it out, we'd sail.

Off I went, and as the strong Alderney race was running five knots north, I followed it, or rather it grabbed hold of *Cresswell's* twin keels and dragged her north, past the notorious Casquets rocks. About three hours out, a great black cloud in the west promised a jolly time coming, so I handed the gaffed main (getting a smart tap from the wildly swinging gaff as it clattered down) and made a course north-west under working staysail and mizzen. By now the tide was running out of the Channel, so I wasn't worried about making too much leeway.

I had just got settled down, with the boat steering herself under lashed helm, when suddenly I spied, way out to the east, to my lee, what appeared to be a small power craft. I broke out the new Zeiss binoculars (lovely job, a present from Herr Boehm, the German fish-canning-plant salesman) and, balancing in the mizzen shrouds, took a look. She was a small craft, 18 feet long, with a deckhouse aft. Someone was stood up in the stern, waving what appeared to be an oar at me, though it was difficult to tell, what with the violent movement in the Channel chop and the distance between us, about two miles.

The seas were getting up so much that most of the time the small power craft was out of sight. She was obviously in distress, for she was making no way.

"Bugger it," I said to Nelson as I eased *Cresswell* off the wind to head east for the powerboat. Just my luck, I thought. Here I am, trying to pinch up to the west as much as I can, and now I'm going to lose two miles to leeward just because some silly fool has lost his flamin' starting handle!

But the law of the sea is immutable. Because a vessel was in distress, it was my bounden duty to go to her assistance. There would be too many mirrors to look into in the future, and the sea would be forever unforgiving if I should ignore a plea for help. There were no other craft around, and with the forecast weather piling up in the west it would be no less than manslaughter to ignore her.

Cresswell, off the wind, which by now was blowing a good 30 knots, bounded like a stag from one green sea to the next, straight for the power boat, and soon I had fetched up close alongside her, with the jib sheet let fly and the mizzen gaff lowered. Now was the time to try out my brand new Volvo-Penta. It worked like a charm, starting at first kick.

I eased up closer to the small craft and saw a sight I shall never forget as long as I live. In the cockpit of this tiny boat, which was staggering up and down in the chop like a maddened steer, was an elderly gentleman with a three-day growth of white whiskers, wearing spectacles, a bobble cap and a pea jacket, and *reading a newspaper* in the lee of the doghouse.

"Hello, there!" I sang out, all the while keeping an eye out that I didn't approach too close. The western horizon was ebony.

He peered over the bulwarks of his boat and gazed at me over the top of his spectacles. He was only five yards away, and the two boats were bouncing around with such a violent movement that it would have made Captain Cook himself go green.

"Hello, there!" I repeated, "Are you in trouble?"

"Hello, old chap, glad to meet you!" His thin, educated Oxford accent was carried over to me by the stiff Channel wind. "*Terribly* decent of you to drop by!"

"What's the problem?" I shouted.

"Actually, my engine's sort of *kaput*. It's one of those damned petrol-driven *internal combustion things*, and I've simply no idea why it refuses to start. I've pressed the sort of button *innumerable* times, but oh dear! I've never had much luck with these damned new-fangled *gadgets* (he pronounced it 'gejits')!"

"Do you have fuel in the tank?"

"Just a tick, old chap, I'll have a *shufti* (Indian Army slang for 'look'). These damned motors are so *complicated!*"

He was holding onto the doghouse roof. How he managed to keep his balance with that violent motion I'll never know.

"By the way, old chap, better *introduce* myself . . ."

"Jesus Christ Almighty," I muttered to Nelson. "What the hell do we have here, *introducing* himself, in the middle of a roaring gale!"

"Colonel Featherstone, retired. Royal Household Artillery!"

"Tristan Jones. Liverpool Deep-Sea Divers' Social Club! Now, sir, for God's sake *check your tank!*"

I was having great difficulty maintaining station alongside him, kicking the engine slow ahead one minute, slow astern the next, and all the while the jib flogging away like a machine gun.

The colonel staggered aft and fiddled around for a minute, then stood up, looking abashed.

"I say!" he sang out in his quivering voice, "*terribly* sorry, old chap, I've run out of *blasted naptha!*" (This was the term they used for gasoline in the 1880s!)

I shouted: "Do you want to come onboard? It will be risky and I advise against it. It will be better for me to pass you a line. I can get you in the lee of the Casquets in about two hours. I'll pass you two lines—one you make fast around your foredeck cleats . . . "

"What? What's that, old boy?" He had a hand cupped to one ear.

"That bit of wood up front."

"Oh, I see, sounds terribly *nautical*, eh?" he shouted, grinning.

"*Holy Jesus* (this low to Nelson). And pass the other line around your doghouse and back to the after cleat, but leave it slack."

"Right-o, old chap, you're in command. Navy wallah? You look it to me. Had a second cousin in the *Royal Naval Reserve* once . . . "

"Catch this line!"

I interrupted his family memoirs and heaved the line over, a difficult thing against the wind, but it caught, and soon he was under tow, very slowly, about two knots, heading south for the lee of Casquet rocks. We were now with the tide, so we would make the lee before nightfall. Several times I looked back and saw the old boy had gone back to the *Times*. When he saw me looking he stood up and waved, just like the Queen Mum.

By 5 o'clock we were well under the lee of the Casquets and in much smoother water, and at 6 o'clock I entered Braye Harbor once more. At the entrance to the harbor a "fishing" boat, heading in, took the colonel in tow and I slipped out to sea again. I hate returning in this way to a place I've already departed from.

As I handed the colonel over, the old boy was shouting: "*Awfully* kind of you, old chap. Such a *shame* you won't stay for a sort of noggin. Anyway, have an *awfully splendid* trip. Where are you going—Blighty (British Army slang for Britain) or foreign?"

"Spain!"

"Oh, dear. The wine's nowhere *near* as good as Madeira. I always get the sort of *tummy runs* there. The sanitation is simply *woggish*, y'know."

"Goodbye, Colonel. Good fishing!"

"Cheerio, old chap. *Do* come and see me when you tootle up again!"

"Toc H!" I replied, thinking I'd get one over on him, for it was British Army First World War slang for "all right."

"Awfully nice meeting you . . ." His voice faded into the distance and Nelson looked at me with his one eye gleaming.

I hauled up the mizzen gaff. By the time I got back into the offing it was blowing a gale, but under staysail and mizzen I made good way, and the following morning, very early, I sighted the light of Start Point, England, and came about. From there it was beat, beat, to the southwest for 400 miles, six days; and by the time I was at the point where I turned south the wind was down to about 25 knots, just right for a close reach to Vigo. I'd hoisted the main and *Cresswell* was flying along very well. The sight I obtained on the seventh day out put me at about 12 degrees west of Greenwich, 47 degrees north.

For two days the weather was perfect. Brilliant sunshine

through cirro-stratus clouds and a course which was about 70 degrees off the wind, heading straight for Cape Finisterre, Vigo, wine, and (hopefully) beauty. (Blast the music, as old Tansy Lee used to say.)

I got a BBC forecast on the ninth day, May 11, which gave "winds strong to gale force, area Biscay."

"Reef down your tail, Nelson," I said; "we're in for another dusting!"

By midnight on the twelfth, the sky was completely over-cast with black clouds, it was raining cats and dogs, and the wind was hammering at us all the way from Cape Hatteras. I'd reefed down the main and handed the mizzen. The main stay'sl was straining like a dray horse, while *Cresswell* thundered up and down, up and down violently, like a fiddler's elbow.

I was well lashed to the binnacle, in my oilskins, and hanging on for dear life. I wasn't too concerned, because I thought that if it blew any harder I'd hand the main and run to the east under stay'sl only. I had plenty of sea room, and if worse came to worst I could make for the lee of Belle Isle or even the port of St. Nazaire, both on the coast of France, about 400 miles away. That would be disadvantageous, though, for it would mean I'd have to beat all the way back out again.

I had shut the companionway hatch doors, so *Cresswell* was as tight as a drum. I never like doing this because when it's blowing a bitch it's such a comfort to be able to peep down below and see the oil lamp gleaming in a haven of peace and sanity. But this night I was taking no chances, for *Cresswell*, being an old beach-launched sailing lifeboat, didn't draw more than two feet nine inches, even with her bilge keels, and sometimes, in a blow, she would slide over alarmingly, threatening to capsize. It was a bit like trying to sail a gravy dish.

This time she did capsize, or very nearly. Suddenly a great monster of a growler came at her from the starboard bow, lifted her up, and before I had a chance to do anything, let alone ease the mainsheet, she was over on her side, with the mainsail in the sea to leeward. The main was reefed down to about one-third the total area, but this was enough to hold plenty of water, about 20 tons or more. She seemed to be on her side for a matter of minutes, and I thought she was going to capsize. I remember thinking: Thank God the kentledge (thin sheets of lead ballast, cut to fit between the frames in the bilge) is battened in, because if she does go over, chances are she'll right herself.

By this time I was up to my waist in cold water, hanging onto the port winch, although I was also lashed to the binnacle. The strange thing is that even with all the noise, with the sea and wind roaring away and everything clattering around, I still heard Nelson down below, barking. I thought to myself: Poor old boy; if she does go, he'd be much better off up here, to feel the wind before he kicks off.

Suddenly, with a jar that shook every bone in my body and flung me across the cockpit onto the starboard bulwark she righted herself. It happened in less than a second. For some reason (probably the trough of the growler passing under her), she just sat up bolt upright. Then, with a shudder, the weight of the water in the mainsail, plus the force of the wind on the starboard side, cracked the mainmast just above the tabernacle. It splintered like a matchstick. It was solid Norwegian spruce up to the houndsbands, and from there on up hollow to save weight aloft. Built by the finest craftsmen in Norway, of the strongest, best materials then available, it just carried away like it was made of paper. As the mast cracked, the starboard shrouds gave way with a zinging twang—two-inch-diameter galvanized steel wires. Both of them parted just below the hound upper splice. Over it went, with a crash loud enough to shake your teeth out.

The mainmast finished with the "top" end under the seas and, the "lower" end beating up and down on deck, threatening to stow the boat in. Just as I freed myself from the binnacle, in intense pain because of my bruised ribs, the foot of the mast smashed in the forward port corner of the doghouse roof. The mast was still fixed to the boat by the port shrouds, the forestays, and the running backstays.

The first thing I tried to do was haul the top end of the mast alongside by heaving in on the collapsed port shrouds, but this was far beyond my strength. The only thing left was to cut the mast adrift. In *Cresswell* the shrouds and other standing rigging wires were roved and spliced through deadeyes, so the only way to let go the wires was to cut them. I dove below for one of the two sharp axes I kept for that purpose; then I started to work on the wooden deadeyes. With a sharp ax I could splinter a deadeye in about six strokes. It would have been much better to cut the rigging at the head of the mast, so as to save the wire and the headsail, but the mast pounded around like a wild animal in that sea and threatened to stove in the boat's side. The vital thing was to keep the boat a single moving entity. Anything that worked against it must go, or at least be separated from it.

In four hours I had cut all the rigging wires, the mainsheet, and everything connecting the mainmast and boom to the hull. A very difficult and dangerous job, for the mast was hammering about like a horse's hind hoof. I had secured the mainsheet around the mast as high as I could; then I led the mainsheet forward, onto the knighthead cleats. Then, with an agony of pushing and heaving, I managed to get the mast over the lee side. Mast, gaff, reefed mainsail, stay'sl, the lot. The whole mess of gear, semisubmerged, floated off ahead, or rather it stayed put and the wind blew *Cresswell* away from it.

Now the wrecked gear was acting as an anchor, holding *Cresswell's* head up into the sea until I could get the mizzen up, which I finally managed to do, with one reef in. Close hauled, this acted as a weather cock, holding the bows up to the seas and against the wind, about 40 degrees off, which is ideal in a small vessel.

By the time I got the mizzen hoisted and took a look around, it was obvious that the wrecked mast and gear were slowly sinking, probably because the canvas mainsail was becoming saturated. Without hesitation I went forward and with one stroke of the ax cut the mainsheet. It was a great pity, almost a thousand dollars' worth; but I couldn't chance the weight of the sunken gear dragging *Cresswell's* head down, for if a sea broke onboard while she was in that condition it would probably flood her through the stoved-in doghouse roof.

Having lashed down the odds and ends safely, I pumped out what bit of water had entered through the stoved-in roof and set to blocking the hole, which I did with my mattress— jammed into the hole from *outside* and bashed in well and truly with the blunt side of the ax. Then I went below and made a cup of tea and some burgoo and sat down to think.

Nelson was unscathed, lying on the starboard (mattress-less) berth, looking at me as if to say, Well, you silly bugger, done it again, eh? He enjoyed a dollop of burgoo, too.

I had enough diesel fuel (four gallons), after towing the colonel in, to take me about 20 miles. The coast of France was 400 miles away to leeward, to the east. Therefore I would have to rig jury sails and make for St. Nazaire or Bordeaux. But first of all I would have to rest, for with everything now secured there was no hope of doing anything properly until the weather abated, and anyway the wind, now west-northwest, was slowly blowing *Cresswell* toward the French coast. I had food enough for another two weeks; there was no hurry. I fell asleep, jammed into the space between the stove and the end of my berth.

When I woke up it was around midforenoon next day. The movement of the hull was much gentler and the wind was diminishing slowly. By late afternoon it was down to about 30 knots, so I decided to wait another night and hung an oil lamp on the stern, in case I had drifted into a shipping lane. The wind and water were still *Cromwellian*; the clouds mar-bled-smoke.

Next day was bright sunshine, with a few cumulus clouds scudding overhead. The sea was settling down to a nice easy lob and the wind was down around its usual 20 knots. In fact, if I'd still had my mainmast I would have called it an ideal sail-ing situation. But the boat was in chaos.

I decided to rig a forestay on the mizzen. It would have a very shallow angle, but at least I would be able to catch more

wind and steer the boat much better. I did this by splicing together the two busted starboard shrouds which were still
onboard. I led the jury forestay forward and seized it onto the
knighthead bits. Then I handed on the sails and there we
were. She looked a bit like Nefertiti's barge, but there was a
noticeable increase in speed, from one knot to perhaps two,
course southeast. I got a sight, which put me 380 miles east-
northeast by east of Bordeaux, or at least the entrance to the
Gironde River. So I decided to make for there.

We made it, without further mishap, in a week. It was hard,
tiring work at the wheel, with heavy seas continually kicking
my unbalanced rig off course. About 10 miles off the mouth
of the Gironde River, having heard another dirty-weather
forecast, I started the engine and used all my precious fuel
pushing against the strong currents off the river and getting
behind the headland and into the anchorage of the port of
Royan. Safe.

The customs officer who entered *Cresswell* was a kindly
chap who, realizing my plight, changed the two English
pounds I had onboard into French francs and refused to take
the entry fee. The first thing I did when I stepped ashore was
cable my London bank. "Send $500. Urgent." Then I went to
a cafe for coffee. Back came the reply: "Exchange Control
Regulations effective as of May 1. Cannot send you more
than 25 pounds annually. As you have already drawn this regret cannot send $500."

Damn and blast! *Merde alors! Putain!* There I was, with a half-
wrecked boat, two days' supply of food, and no money.
Again! I sat down to think this one out.

If the British government knew of my plight, they would
probably stretch the law a bit and allow my bank to send *my*
money out; but that would take time, maybe several weeks.
Meanwhile I had to exist and, if possible, refit my boat. But
how? I couldn't stay in Royan; it is only an anchorage, open to
all winds but westerly. And anyway I had no dinghy.

I took out the atlas, for I had no chart of the area. It was
clear to me I would have to work my way upstream with the
tides going in, for my fuel had run out. And I would have to

try to reach Bordeaux, a fair-size city about as big as Baltimore. There might be prospects of work there, or at least a boat to work on, or to deliver perhaps, with the summer season coming on.

The following day, as the tide turned, I weighed anchor and with the help of the tide and the mizzen hoisted to catch the westerly wind, made my way to Bordeaux. At the end of the third tide I came to a bend in the river. It was raining and miserable and I'd had very little food. I worked my way close inshore, to where I spied a landing pontoon tied at the river's edge, close to a village. With lines ready, I made for the pontoon, let go the sheets, and hopped over as she floated on, bringing her up short with a quick 'round turn on a bollard. Then I worked *Cresswell* in, at high tide, alongside the pontoon.

By dusk it was still raining and I was still miserable. My French was not too good and the few people who came to look at the boat spoke with an outlandish accent and did not appear too friendly. I had hardly any food left and only one dry cigarette, and the rain was dripping into the cabin through the saturated mattress. As the old saying goes, "There I was, one foot in the gutter and the other on a bar of soap."

Just after nightfall the rain eased off and I decided to go ashore and have a look around Lormont, as the village was called. There was hardly a soul about. It was a typical French village after dark on a rainy night. I walked past the church, up the hill, and then, as it started to rain again, turned back and headed for the pontoon and my wounded boat. (Nelson was sniffing disdainfully at the lampposts: his old master, Tansy, couldn't abide Frenchmen, and this had rubbed off on the dog.) By the steps leading down to the pontoon was a bus stop and standing in the shelter was a little man in a beret, wearing a blue raincoat and carrying an umbrella. I took out my last dogend and asked him for a light.

"*Bon soir, M'sieur. Vous avez de feu, s'il vous plaît?*"

"*Oui, M'sieur. Vous êtes Anglais?*"

"*Oui, M'sieur . . . Gallois.*"

"Ah, I am very pleased to meet you. I am learning English."

"Really?"

"Yes," he replied. "Iz zat your boat down zere?"

"Yes, unfortunately, it is."

"Are you 'ere on 'oliday?"

"Sort of."

"You have had some damage?"

"Oh, a spot of bother, you know." I introduced myself.

"Paul Condamine. I live quite near. Iz zere anysing I can do for you?"

"Well, you might be able to advise me. You see, I need work very badly because I may have to spend some months here, to repair my boat, and I cannot get any money from England."

"Yes, I heard on the BBC. I lizen every night, to improve my Engleesh. It muz be very 'ard for you. Look, I work 10 kilometers away, at a factory. We print official forms for ze French government, and my boss is Engleesh, though now naturalized French. Why don't you go zere tomorrow? Maybe zey will help you. I will write ze name of ze personnel manager and ze address. You may tell 'eem I sent you."

"Thank you very much, *M'sieur*. If there's anything I can do for you . . . "

"Yes, zere is. My wife and I would like you to come each week to our houze for dinner, so we may practiz our Engleesh."

"I shall be delighted, *M'sieur* Condamine!"

The bus crunched up and the little Frenchman climbed onboard, after folding his umbrella.

The next morning, spruced up in my best Fair Island sweater, seaboots, clean new jeans, Channel Island blue fisherman's cap and oilskin jacket, Nelson and I walked the 10 kilometers to the factory. We arrived at 9 o'clock and I walked into the luxuriously decorated main foyer, with wall-to-wall carpets and beautiful modern furnishings everywhere. The receptionist was much more beautiful than even the furniture—so slim she looked as if a light breeze would blow her all the way to Paris. She seemed rather disturbed by my appearance, though I couldn't imagine why, for I'd trimmed my beard in Alderney, only three weeks before . . .

"Leave your name with me and I will pass it on to the personnel manager. You have an appointment to see him at 5 o'clock this afternoon."

"But *Mam'selle*, I have no money; I cannot go anywhere."

"I am sorry, you will have to wait. Please come back at five."

So Nelson and I went and sat under a dripping hedge, close by the gleaming new factory, waiting in the rain all day. It was one of the longest waits I can remember. It was a gray day, and we sat on the "inside" of the hedge so that we could not see the people passing in their cars, munching on French-bread sandwiches and smoking cigarettes.

Finally, guessing that it was near 5 o'clock, with poor old Nelson hobbling on his three legs, we made our way back to the factory and the reception desk. As I walked through the door the *commissionnaire* saluted and the receptionist broke into the most beautiful smile north of the Pyrenees and south of Dover.

"*M'sieur* Tristan!" She glided from behind her desk and grasped my hand, then led me to a sofa.

"Please sit down. The *managing director* wishes to speak to you."

In my dazed state, cold, wet, and hungry as I was, and dying for a smoke, I sat in silence. After a few minutes a man came bouncing down the wide, carpeted stairway from the executive offices. He was rather short and chubby, dressed in an immaculate gray suit with shining dress shoes and wearing what looked like an "old school" tie, stuck with a pin which had a pearl half as big as a baseball. He was rosy cheeked and obviously accustomed to the good life. He rushed to me and grasped my hand.

"You are Tristan Jones?" he asked in a very British accent.

"Yes, as a matter of fact, I am."

"Don't you know who I am?"

"No, can't say as I do," I replied, puzzled.

"This is fantastic!" He took my elbow and led me toward the stairs. "Do you remember, about three weeks ago you came across an old gentleman adrift in a small fishing boat in the Channel off Alderney?"

"You mean the colonel? But how do you know about that?"

He put his arm around my shoulder. "Tristan, *that man is my father!*"

Mr. Featherstone *fils* grabbed both my elbows. "Now tell me, and don't be shy: what in the name of God can I *do* for you?"

"Well, I'll be . . . "

"My name is Featherstone and I'm the managing director. What do you need? Condamine told me about you this morning, and of course my father told me about you earlier, but it wasn't until I saw your name on the personnel manager's appointment list that I realized who you are. Had a spot of bother, I hear. Need a job? I'll take you on, put you in charge of a laboring gang digging the foundations for our new extension. How's your French?"

"Bloody awful."

He laughed. "Doesn't matter, old chap. They're all Algerians anyway! Now, what do you need right away?"

"A cigarette and a week's advance, please!"

"Done. Here you are, 200 francs."

He turned to the receptionist, who was still smiling broadly. "Get the *M'sieur* some cigarettes—and something for the dog!"

Nelson looked at Mr. Featherstone with his one eye and, for the first time since he'd landed in France, wagged his tail.

Amazing though this may seem, it actually happened. In fact, the story was picked up by the French press and publicized at the time.

Although the father and son were 500 miles apart, *something* or *someone* had guided me, in my distress, straight to the one man in 48 million in France who was not only anxious to repay a debt but had the resources to do so.

Fate? Synchronistic destinies? I don't know. I prefer to think it was a guiding hand, the One who looks after fools, drunks, and sailors in distress. He certainly looked after all three that time!

Before the Roman came to Rye or out to Severn strode,
The rolling English drunkard made the rolling English road.
A reeling road, a rolling road, that rambles round the shire,
And after him the parson ran, the sexton and the squire;
A merry road, a mazy road, and such as we did tread
The night we went to Birmingham by way of Beachy Head.

G. K. Chesterton, "The Rolling English Road"

6

Lost and Found!

The next thing was to settle the boat in for the months it would take me to earn enough to refit. Luckily (again), it turned out that the mayor of Lormont, where the boat was moored, was a good friend of Mr. Featherstone; so it was arranged that I could moor *Cresswell* against the village landing stage for the length of my stay.

I kedged out two anchors, one forward and one aft, broadside to the boat so that they would hold her off the mooring stage, for there was a lot of heavy barge traffic which raised enormous bow waves, the wash from which, unless she was held off, would smash her against the stage. I continued to sleep onboard, and while I was at work Nelson guarded the boat. No one could come near, despite his having only three legs and one eye. He was a terror for his territory.

The job I had was interesting. I was put in charge of a gang of Algerian and Tunisian laborers who were digging the foundation ditches for the factory extension. Each morning I had a lift from Paul in his Citroën *"deux chevaux,"* a wheezing rattletrap of a conveyance which trundled along like a biscuit box on wheels.

The Algerians and Tunisians were a friendly lot and I soon started to relearn the little Arabic I had picked up in the Middle East years before. As they were on piece rates—so many francs per hundred meters of ditch—they worked like heroes. What with their fezzes and *djellabas* and my Fair Island sweater and seaboots, we must have looked a real motley gang. The surveying part of the job came easy to me; once again, it was just a matter of solving the triangle.

Mr. Featherstone came out to see me every couple of days, bringing wine and a picnic basket full of goodies, like roast chicken and *carnard à l'orange, potage au feu,* and all kinds of French food, which tasted good, even though they weren't boiled *à l'Anglaise.* The Arabs were friendly to me because I always shared the food—but not the wine, of course. They were Muslims, Allah be praised!

In the evenings and on weekends I slowly got *Cresswell* back in shape. Gradually, with scrimping and saving, I got enough money together to buy a new mast. This had to be built in, and brought down from, Brittany, which at that time was the only place in France where hollow spars were made.

One evening a week I visited Paul for dinner and "practiced" speaking English with him and his wife. One weekend a month I went to stay with Mr. Featherstone at his chateau, doing jobs on his estate that needed a sailor's skills.

By mid-June the ditches were ready for the foundations and my crew and I set to on the concrete mixers. We had a grand time, sloshing around in wet concrete. At the end of August, the new factory-extension building was roofed, a grand-opening celebration was arranged and Mr. Featherstone came to me one afternoon just as I was ready to go back to my boat.

"Tristan," he said, "I have a nice little moonlighting job for you, if you want it."

"What's that?"

"I need a barman at the opening ceremony, and—well, you know how it is in France . . . They think a British barman is the thing. *Très chic.* Think you can handle it?"

"When?"

"Next Saturday."

"You're on!"

"Good, there's 200 francs in it, and tips. And 'fringe benefits,' of course."

"What can I wear? I don't have anything but sailing gear, and most of that is buggered up with cement."

"That's all right. I'll hire a tuxedo for you."

"Jesus Christ! What would old Tansy say? O.K. I'll be there."

On the Saturday, Nelson and I turned up and I changed into barman's rig. I felt like a penguin, but what matter? For 200 francs I'd have gone naked. It would buy a new mainsheet. The room where the reception was held was a sailor's dream of heaven. There was a bar, about a hundred yards long, *stiff* with booze: whisky, gin, and brandy by the crate; liquers by the hundred; vodka; beers by the mountain; and, of course, enough wine to keep the French Navy going for the next 10 years.

"Mmm," I said. "Mmm . . . well, well!"

The reception commenced and for the next six hours I was dashing around, fixing drinks and being nice and friendly to everyone. Of course, this was dead easy, because for every six drinks I fixed for them I slugged one for myself. By midafternoon the place was jammed with about 300 men and women, all chattering away ten to the dozen.

Suddenly Mr. Featherstone turned up at the bar with another very well dressed gentleman in tow, rather taller than himself and splendidly outfitted in a very English Saville Row suit.

"Tristan, I want you to meet M. Chaban-Delmas, the mayor of Bordeaux. He is a very prominent sailor in these parts, and he has heard of your voyaging."

"Please to meet you, *M'sieur le Maire*," said I, shaking hands.

"I have heard and read about you," said he. "Tell me, where is your boat now? I would like to go for a sail with you soon, before the winter sets in." He spoke perfect English.

"Unfortunately, *M'sieur*, that will hardly be possible for she is lying dismasted at Lormont, and it will take me quite a while to get her fixed up."

"*Quel dommage!* What a pity! Well, if there is anything I can do for you, be sure to let me know."

With a handshake he passed on and Mr. Featherstone turned to me and said: "He's a very prominent man in France. He's going to Paris later today, but he'll be back next Thursday. Don't forget what he said."

"Right . . . hiccup . . . I'll remember . . . hey, wanna drink?"

The party went on into the night. Tired and indisposed by the final nightcap, I decided to sleep at the factory. In the morning, rerigged in my Fair Island sweater, I walked back to Lormont, for on Sunday mornings there were no buses. To my horror, when I arrived, bleary eyed and very hungover, at the landing stage, there was no *Cresswell!* Only Nelson, who whined and growled while I headed for the *gendarmerie*, the local copshop.

"*Mon bateau, ce n'est pas là!* My boat's missing!"

"Missing—how can that be? It was there on Saturday, at lunchtime. I saw it myself, *M'sieur!*" The sergeant's eyes were like opened oysters.

"Well, she's not there now. And she hasn't sunk at the moorings, because there's no ropes about and no sign of strain at the bollards."

"You mean she's been *stolen?*"

"What else?" My head was pounding with worry and the effects of the previous night's binge.

"*Mon Dieu!*" The sergeant dived for the telephone. "Give me *Bordeaux Gendarmerie Centrale!*"

Quickly he was connected through the police system, and after speaking very rapidly for about 10 minutes he turned to me and said, "We are setting up a search headquarters at the central *gendarmerie*. You go there with Officer Velieux"—he pointed with his chin at a young *flic* standing by a window— "and give them all the information about the boat you can. Don't worry, *mon vieux*, they will soon find her, if she is still afloat."

The officer, Nelson, and I piled into the police Citroën and in 20 minutes were at the headquarters of the *Sûreté Nationale* for the whole of southwestern France. I was interviewed by three burly detectives, a map of the whole area of the Gironde was conjured up, and *voilà!* a full-scale search was afoot. They detailed 5,000 cops to check every dock and mooring within 100 miles of Bordeaux. The French Air Force sent three helicopters to search the rivers and a sea-rescue flying boat to cover the Bay of Biscay to seaward off the mouth of the Gironde.

Throughout the day reports flowed in from every man and unit detailed to look for the missing *bateau anglais*. In the afternoon, several reporters from the local and national press showed up, and there were screaming headlines in the evening editions about "the mystery of the English ghost ship."

At nightfall, M. Bertiot, the detective in charge of the search, came to me and said: "All hope is not lost. Tomorrow we will continue the search for your *bateau très gallant*. But in the meantime I insist that you join my wife and me for dinner at the *Hôtel Central*." And so, in a charming Gallic way, M. Bertiot tried to cheer me up. The wine and cognac flowed freely, a fine revitalizer after the whisky consumed the day before. And that night I was given a luxurious suite in the Hotel Central—all at the expense of the *Sûreté Nationale*.

However, most of the night my worry was increased by telephone calls of commiseration from dozens of people I had never heard of. "Don't worry, *mon vieux*. We *Bordelaise* are not stupid; we will find your boat. Our police and air force are the best in the world . . . "

"*Merci, M'sieur,*" and so on all through the night, for the radio and television stations had picked up the story and it seemed to be the talk of the whole Midi of France. I watched on TV as "experts" gave their opinions as to the movement of the boat, while one radio station put out the story that "my companion," an English girl of astounding beauty, the errant daughter of a duke, with whom I had eloped from England, had been kidnaped by a gang of thugs hired by her father to recover "*cette petite rose Anglaise.*"

I had never heard so much nonsense in my life, but though I was sorely grieved at the thought of losing *Cresswell* (she was all I had in the world), I still had a good laugh at the antics of the media. Another story, put out by a television personality, claimed "the boat was used in the Great Train Robbery and contained 2 million pounds in British Treasury notes!" The British government supposedly had sent a commando team to sequester the boat from French waters and return the money *à l'Angleterre.* "No matter," continued this expert, "no matter what the boat contained, or what *Capitaine Ton-Ton* (my media alias) had done, this act of piracy by the government of 'perfidious Albion' would not for one minute be tolerated by any patriotic Frenchman" . . . etc., etc.

That was the one that amused me the most. Two million pounds? They'd be lucky if they found two bent pennies.

In the morning I was wakened by a *gendarme,* who was under instructions to take me to the *Café Grande Bretagne* for an "English breakfast."

Widened, the search went on all day Tuesday and the Bordeaux fire-brigade units of the French Army were brought in, while the French Navy at St. Nazaire and Brest sent two armed trawlers to search the northern areas of the Bay of Biscay. The whole thing was developing into what the French call a *cause célèbre.*

Every time I was escorted into the street (by two *gendarmes*) we were surrounded by a knot of people, all shouting encouragement and *Vive l'Angleterre!* Old ladies came to our table with paper bags containing woolen socks and scarves, truck drivers sent over foaming liters of *bière alsacienne,* and well-dressed gentlemen offered cigars. All I wanted was my *boat.*

On Tuesday night, during the dark hours, the search was called off while the searchers returned to their homes, their wives, their stewed tripe and their wine. I was specially invited by the worthies of the local businessman's club to a dinner in my honor, during which many speeches were made, most of them alluding to "courage in the face of irreplaceable loss" and the famous *flegmatique anglaise.*

That night, back in the Hotel Central, I heard on the radio that the boat had been "kidnaped" (*a*) by the IRA, (*b*) by Scots Nationalists (after which the "expert" went into a long account about Bonny Prince Charlie and how Scotland was France's oldest ally, so the search should be called off), and (*c*) by Spanish Basque gun runners. On television, "experts" from two channels were busy with maps, diagrams, and little flags. I went to sleep.

On Wednesday morning, after another mountain of an "English breakfast," with two glum *gendarmes* nibbling their *croissants*, I was again taken to the *gendarmerie*. M. Bertiot met me with tears in his eyes.

"*M'sieur le Capitaine*, it is with regret that I inform you that our search in the Bordeaux area has been called off. But farther north and south, in the Bay of Biscay, our navy will continue to search diligently for the next few days. In the name of the French people, all I can do is offer my sincerest regret," . . . etc., etc. Two other detectives were wiping their eyes. "Now, what can we do for you?" he asked.

"You could take me back to Lormont, please, so I can contact Mr. Featherstone. He lives in the big chateau there." Bertiot flicked his fingers at a sergeant: "*À Lormont!*"

I was whisked in a Citroën, with a motocycle escort, to Lormont, hardly able to think. All the same, I wasn't in a complete pickle! I had a job; I could work and save and build another boat. It might take three or four years, but all was not lost.

When we came to the little *estaminet* opposite the landing stage, I asked the sergeant if he and his companions would care to join me in a cognac with the *patron* for a farewell drink, for I would be moving closer to the printing factory and my work.

"*Mais certainement, M'sieur le Capitaine,*" said the sergeant, honking to bring the parade to a halt.

Like a funeral party, we went inside the dark little bar, with its whalebone ornaments and zinc top. The *patron*, Albert, was at the bar; he looked up at me as we entered. Bald head; blue, watery eyes; walrus mustache; blue-and-white-striped apron.

"*Bonjour, M'sieur* Tristan. But . . . " He gestured at the policemen. "But what is wrong, *mon vieux. Vous-avez des problèmes?*"

"*Bonjour*, Albert. No, it's nothing. These friends have been helping to find my boat. You know, she went missing."

"Missing? What do you mean, *missing?* She's behind the bar here, in René Latour's boatyard."

"*Quoi?*" shouted the sergeant.

"*What?*" I shouted.

"*Quoi?*" echoed the *gendarmes.*

"Yes, René was in here last night. He said he got orders from some bigwig to haul your boat out and start refitting the topsides. And whoever it was said he was ordering a boatyard in Brest to send someone to measure for a new mast." Albert opened both hands, palms out, and stared at me, eyes bulging. "Didn't you know?"

"*Merde!*" I said.

"*Merde!*" said the sergeant and the other *gendarmes.*

The sergeant grabbed my elbow in a vice lock. "Come on," he said, and we traipsed out behind the *estaminet.* There, in René's yard, was *Cresswell,* sitting as perky as a peacock. Carpenters were hard at work sawing and hammering. I was dumbfounded. The sergeant, glaring at me with steely blue eyes, adjusted his gun holster.

"Up you go!" he said.

I climbed ondeck.

"Go inside!"

I descended the companionway hatch.

"Give me the keys," the sergeant told René. Then he locked the hatch and shouted at me: "Stay there until I contact Bertiot!"

Of course, the whole *affaire* was quickly hushed up, and when I was released from my "prison" later that day, René, the boat builder, told me what had happened.

"On Saturday afternoon, while you were playing barman, we got a message from the mayor of Bordeaux to haul your boat at his expense and to order a new mast and refit the deck and topsides; so we hauled her with the crane that evening."

"But didn't you hear and see the radio and television? Didn't you read the newspapers, all making a hell of a din about *Cresswell* being missing?"

"Well, you know, Tristan, we *Girondaise*—especially us river folk—we don't take much notice of all that government crap. It's mostly lies, anyway. We have only one *téléviseur* in Lormont, and that's broken. And, well, you know, we have our wives and the boats and the *estaminet*. What more do we need, *mon cher marin?*"

"*Merde!*" I said, thinking of those hundreds of men out searching for two full days. But nothing further was said by the authorities. Bertiot came to see me, of course, and when I told him what had occurred, he laughed. Featherstone was away in London; so he didn't know about it until his return.

Three weeks later the boat was completely refitted and half the celebrities of Bordeaux turned up to see her re-launched. Mr. Featherstone was there with his family, together with most of the staff and workers of the printing factory. He looked the boat over carefully, noting the gleaming varnish and the repair, hardly noticeable, to the coach roof, which had been half destroyed during the storm in the Bay of Biscay. He tapped the brand new spruce mast and smiled.

"One good turn deserves another, eh, Tristan?"

"What can I do for *you* in return?"

"You've already done enough, in the Channel," he replied. "But if you'd like to take my family and me for a sail one weekend, of course we'd be delighted."

"How about next Saturday? And bring the mayor along."

"Right-o, old chap!" he said. "I'm sure he'll love that!"

By the following Saturday I had *Cresswell* looking like a Royal Navy admiral's barge, all the varnishwork polished, all the brass cleaned and gleaming and shining like a fire engine. When my guests arrived they were impressed, and that, of course, was ample reward for a week's hard work.

We sailed to Royan, about 35 miles, where I anchored, and they spent the night in a hotel. We all returned to Lormont on the Sunday, after a glorious sail with plenty of wind and sun, and the food and wine they had brought along. As we sailed, I entertained them with yarns from the Arctic, from Ireland, from the Baltic, from the West Indies and the Pacific— some hair raising, some sad, some funny.

As we pulled along the Lormont landing stage on that

balmy September Sunday afternoon, with everyone aglow after an ideal weekend, M. Chaban-Delmas (who was later to become the prime minister of France) said to me, "Tristan, thank God you're not a Frenchman!"

"Why's that, *M'sieur?*"

"Because if you were, *you* would be mayor of Bordeaux!"

"Well, if I was, I'd be highly suspicious of any British yachts that went mysteriously missing!"

"*Touché!*" He clapped my shoulder and stepped ashore.

Nelson wagged his tail and panted over a fresh ham bone.

PART II

ALLONS!

November 1963—May 1965

And gentlemen in England now abed
Shall think themselves accursed they were not here
And hold their manhoods cheap while any speaks
That fought with us upon Saint Crispin's day.

William Shakespeare
Henry V (act 4, sc. 3)

As I was walking down Lime Street,
A fair young maid I chanced to meet,
She said "Hello, how do you do,
Would you like to play with . . .
My ringer-rahnger-roo?"

She took me to her father's cellar,
She said "You are a nice young feller!"
She gave me wine and whisky too,
All the while I played with . . .
Her ringer-rahnger-roo.

Her dad came home, kicked down the door,
He said, "You are a bloody whore,
Get out of here, I've had enough of you,
Get out and live on . . .
Your ringer-rahnger-roo!"

She went to town, became a whore,
And hung a sign upon the door,
"Ten shillings down, nothing less will do,
And you can play with . . .
My ringer-rahnger-roo."

Now the fellers they came, and the fellers they went,
And the price went down to twenty pence,
From sweet sixteen to ninety-two,
She had to live on . . .
Her ringer-rahnger-roo.

Now sailor lads give ear to me,
When you return fresh home from sea,
Drink your full fill and eat well too
But stay away from . . .
The ringer rahnger-roo!

Liverpool merchant-seaman's song (19th century)

7

"Blue to the Mast,
True to the Last!"

(British sailor's method of identifying the French tricolor
[vertical stripes: red, white, blue] among similar ensigns)

In November of 1963 I contracted to deliver the newly built
ketch, *Rose d'Archachon*, from La Rochelle to Martinique. I had
met the owner of the vessel through Mr. Featherstone and it
was arranged that I would join the craft in April 1964 for sailing trials in the Bay of Biscay, then get her to the West Indies
as soon as could be, before the hurricane season commenced
in August.

By this time *Cresswell* was once again back in the water, with
a new mainmast, new sails, a complete paint job, and the
engine refitted at a yard far away inland, at Lyons (the city of
Lugd, the Celtic god of light). At the beginning of December
the groundworks for the printing-factory extension were
completed, and, with a couple of hundred dollars in the kitty
it was time for me to move on.

During my time at Lormont I had heard vague rumors of a
small gathering of British and French yachts wintering over
at Toulouse, about 200 miles southeast of Bordeaux on the
Canal du Midi, which cuts through France from the Biscay

coast to the Mediterranean. The west coast of France can be very cold in winter, and I'd had quite enough cold during the past five years. The city of Toulouse, on the Mediterranean side of the country, has a much milder climate. So I decided to make for Toulouse and leave *Cresswell* there during the time I would be away in *Rose*.

For the first and only time in my voyaging career, I adjusted my departure date so that friends and acquaintances could see me off. The day was Saturday, and it poured. Nevertheless, practically the whole working crew of the factory turned up, from Mr. Featherstone in his Rolls-Royce to the Algerian laborers in their *djellabas*. I doubt if a more motley crowd had gathered in Bordeaux since the *Girondaise* marched for Paris to take over the French Revolutionary Assembly. The well wishers, who arrived in the pouring rain, brought bottles of wine, cheeses, bread, fruit, cooked dishes and, in the case of the Muslims, a live chicken. They also brought a reporter from the Bordeaux press.

In the pouring rain, I let go of the moorings and, with the boat crowded with friends, made for Bordeaux, 10 miles upstream, to obtain the necessary permits for the passage through the French canal system. All the way along the river, as we neared the boats tied up, there were cries:

"*Halloo! Regardez! C'est le bateau perdu!*" "*Ho! le bateau célèbre anglais!*"

Kids scampered and hollered along the cobblestone waterfronts as the boat, painted and polished, new varnished masts gleaming, chugged by, with Nelson standing on the foredeck like a figurehead, gluttering his tongue, exalted at being underway again.

I waited in Bordeaux the weekend, until the canal authority offices opened. All weekend it rained; it simply poured down in sheets. I spent most of the time entertaining and gossiping with friends from all walks of city life: from the mayor's office, the police, the fire brigade, the navy, the army, and the air force. They all turned out to see *le bateau très mystérieux Anglais*. The necessary forms to navigate in the interior of France were quickly prepared on Monday, and the prefect himself carried them to the boat.

"*Bonjour, M'sieur l'Anglais!*" he shouted streaming with rain as he shook his umbrella on deck. He was surprisingly young.

"*Bonjour, M'sieur le prefect; mais je suis Gallois!*" I threw my hands up, like a *Bordelaise.*

"*Ah, oui, c'est vrai; mais nous ne connaissons pas la distinction!*"

"*C'est très simple, M'sieur. Les Anglais sont très distingués; les Gallois sont très 'extingués'!*"

He laughed and patted my shoulder. (In his lapel he wore the tiny ribbon of the Resistance.) He lit a cigarette, then turned to me, frowning. "Do you know, *M'sieur le Gallois*, that there is very serious flooding on the river Garonne?"

"Yes. I have read about it in the papers. But that shouldn't affect me much. I can't drown—I was born with a cawl on my head!" I had trouble explaining what I meant by "cawl," but finally he nodded in comprehension.

"Really? *C'est vrai?*" He raised his eyebrows.

"Yes, and upside down. I was a breech birth, and we say that if you are born feet first you will be hanged—not drowned!"

"Well, *mon ami*, it may be more serious and dangerous than you suppose. If I were you I would wait here for a week or so and let the floods pass. The Pyrenees Mountains are sending snow in avalanches onto the plains, and the snow is melting, and the river . . ."

"Ah, what's a bit of snow? Besides, I'm used to it. I'll be all right, *M'sieur*, never you fear. Besides, I really want to get to Toulouse. I have an old friend there. You may have seen him pass through about a year ago."

"*Comment s'appelle?*" he asked, draining his teacup.

"Dod Orsborne."

"Ah, the famous, irrepressible Dod! Of course I met him. *Quel type!* But he is so old?"

"About 80, and I hear he's in a bad way. I want to go down and cheer him up a bit before he croaks."

"Well, *M'sieur le Gallois*, that's good. Also, don't forget that Wales is playing rugby at Toulouse next month."

"That, too. And I hear we have a good team this season, all

piss and vinegar." The prefect laughed as I translated the phrase literally into French.

"*Oui*, that's good: *la pisse et le vinaigre!* So you think it will be another Waterloo, eh, *mon ami?*"

"For sure, and a Crécy, and an Agincourt, and if it's raining a Trafalgar, too!"

"*Merde!*" He turned to go up the ladder. At the top, he turned again. "*Bien, mon cher marin, bonne chance!*"

"Mercy buckets, M'sieur. See you next time."

I started the engine, the prefect cast off my lines, and I was off, into the flooded Garonne River. The floods and *Cresswell* met at the first stop on the river route to the canal, at the town of Langon. I arrived there at dusk and, sighting a cozy-looking *estaminet* along the waterfront, headed for the mooring berth, just outside the door, and tied up. There was not a soul about. The door was shut but not locked; I opened it, stepped inside, and shouted, but no answer. I stepped outside again. Then I heard a noise, a soft rumble at first, then louder. Then I heard a shout. I looked up to the roadway on the hill above the long, cobblestone jetty, where two *gendarmes* were waving their arms and shouting at me.

"Take your boat away to anchor! Get out in the river!"

Then I saw it: a wall of water, about eight feet high, driving straight down the river, about two miles away.

I dove onboard, scrambled for the long stormline, and made it fast on the knighthead. With the other end secured to the ringbolt on the jetty, I cast off all the other lines and let her go. The boat immediately started to scrape her way stern first down the long jetty, but in two shakes I had the engine started and was heading the bows out into midstream. Once there I ran forward, as the boat swung wildly in the fast current, heaved the anchor over the bow and let all the line go. When the anchor bit, the bows were head-on to the current, with the engine running at full speed; and so she was held against the flood.

The wall of water, when it arrived, was just that. It was almost vertical. Brown, muddy water topped with gray foam. It ran straight over the boat. For a minute or so *Cresswell* was, or seemed to be, completely under water. A ton of cold water sluiced into the cabin—the cabin I had spent weeks cleaning and varnishing and making shipshape. I cursed like a trooper. I was shit-scared, but angry at my bad luck.

As soon as he saw the waterbore speeding down on us, Nelson hightailed it aft for the cabin, and I grabbed the steering wheel and locked both arms around it, but the force of the water, when it hammered onto the boat, nearly tore me away. For a minute or two *Cresswell* heeled over onto her starboard side, then swung back and heeled over onto her port side, then swung back and heeled over onto her starboard side, with the freezing water from the snows of the Pyrenees pouring over her in a brown, muddy cataract. Then the anchorline snapped.

"Holy Moses!" I gasped, wet through. Nelson managed to crawl topsides.

Back went the boat, with the heavy stormline tied to the submerged jetty, with the engine still running, but in neutral. Back she went, at a tremendous rate, until the full length of the stormline was snapped taut. Then she swung with a crash, wildly, into the river bank, over the top of the waterfront roadway which was now six feet under water, and whooshed right over the flooded church graveyard.

As the side banged against the church wall, I scrambled forward, grabbed the snapped anchorline, tied a bowline into the broken end, and lassoed one of the church gargoyles. Thank God it did not snap off under the weight of the wildly weaving boat! I did all this automatically; then I set to bailing the boat out. Tons of mucky, filthy, oily water.

When the first rush of the flood passed, the water continued to rise, until it was around 16 feet above the normal level of the river. Broken trees, wooden sheds, animals, driftwood, barrels, and the flotsam of half the farms in the Midi swirled by. And there I was, tied up to a village church! And there I stayed, with the waters rushing past, with the rain pouring down, for three days, until the flood started to subside. For most of the two days the side of the boat was fended off just below a great stained-glass window. I cleaned out the muck, cursing the whole time.

On the second day, with the current down to about two knots, I started the engine, let go of the gargoyle, motored to a spot above the jetty ringbolt, cast off the coiled-up storm-line, weighted, and, following a small French police launch, cruised around the town, picking up people stranded in attics and on the roofs of flooded houses and ferrying them to a spot on the side of the hill. We must have had well over 200 passengers that day.

The flood was so high that most of the town was inundated, and *Cresswell* was able to pass the length of the main street. At each house I approached to rescue the folk, a great cheer went up as the boat, a veteran of so many storms and hazards in the oceans, cruised sedately around above the streets of a French town 70 miles inland!

We picked up people of all shapes and sizes and gave them hot tea and sandwiches. Old ladies clutching bundles, men and boys in blue overalls, teenagers and kids (enjoying the whole thing immensely, now that the weather had cleared up), and tiny tots and babies.

Nelson got excited only when babies and other dogs came onboard. A gentle kick subdued him when female dogs were around, a curse when he growled at the male dogs. He fussed over the babies and was fed bits of cooked meat by the mothers and kids, who in turn fussed over him.

By the end of the third day, everyone who'd been stranded was safe and dry on high ground. The rain stopped, the water level rapidly decreased, and the flood speed diminished. A French Navy craft arrived to anchor before the town, and *Cresswell* was tied up alongside her while frogmen gallantly recovered my main anchor and stormline. By the end of the week the river was almost back to its normal level, and so I pressed on eight miles upstream and entered the lock gates of the Canal du Midi, where the boat would be safe from further floods.

Many of the British think that the first modern lock-controlled canal was the Bridgewater Canal, near Manchester, constructed about 1780. This is not so. During the 1600s the great French cardinal, Richelieu, ordered the building of the Canal du Midi, from the Atlantic coast of France to the Mediterranean, in order that small French vessels could carry cargoes, and especially cargoes of war materials, between the two coasts of France without having to pass through the Straits of Gibraltar or the British Navy blockades. For that time, it was a magnificent engineering feat, rising over the highlands of the Haute Garonne. As far as Toulouse, much of it has been modernized, especially in Napoleonic times, but south of Toulouse long stretches of the canal are in the original state, as it was built 300 years ago.

The passage from Langon to Toulouse was peaceful and calm. When the weather was kind it was a great pleasure to chug along at an amiable rate over the graceful viaducts, sometimes 300 feet in the air, as they pass over valleys and farms. I would sometimes stop the boat and gaze over the side of the brick water-bridges and watch the flooded Garonne with its tributaries as they rushed down to Bordeaux and the sea. But I could not linger long, as the canal was icing up.

The passage through Toulouse by canal was delightful. We passed through the busy center of the great city, along Richelieu's canal, through old worn-brick, rosy-colored tunnels, with creepers from back gardens hanging over the ancient walls. The contrast, when the boat emerged into the roar of the city center—with all the traffic and the people in the early morning rush to work at the aircraft factory (where the *Concorde* supersonic plane had been started)—was like a time warp to my senses.

Dod Orsborne was at the boat basin, biding his time between the local *estaminet* and a friend's boat. It was obvious he was ailing despite his oxlike constitution.

"Hello, Dod, I've heard so much about you. It's a pleasure to meet you!"

"H'lo, where've you come from?"

We sat in the pub on the waterfront and spun yarns that wet day, and it was good to see how Dod's eyes lit up when I told him of my adventures in the north.

Dod was spare and lean, with a bronzed face, Van Dyke beard (now pure white), and dazzling blue eyes under shaggy brows; he wore an old peaked cap and pea jacket. A living, walking, laughing legend, Dod had been the skipper of the English herring trawler *Girl Pat* back in 1936.

One fine day he and his crew decided they'd had enough of the Arctic; so he just upped nets and made for the West Indies! After a tremendous, gale-tossed passage through the middle of the hurricane season, their small 40-footer had arrived at the then British island of Trinidad and Dod was arrested and sent back to England, where he became the last man to be tried at the Old Bailey Courthouse on the charge of *barratry*. This is the crime committed by a skipper who makes away with the vessel under his command without permission of the owners. But the story told by Dod and his crew was so innocent and funny and courageous that the charge was dismissed; it was laughed out of court.

Having made contact with Venezuelan revolutionaries, Dod went to South America in the late thirties and was engaged in gun running there. During World War II he was commissioned into the Royal Naval Reserve as the skipper of a minesweeper-subchaser in the North Sea. Then he transferred to running commandos to the coast of Europe, which of course was just up his alley, and had several bloody run-ins with the German forces in *Festung Europa*.

On D Day of the Normandy invasion, Dod was among the first ashore on the British Army beaches. With his gungy seaman's cap at a swashbuckling angle, he charged up the beach, waving a cutlass.

But apart from this, he could *write* about his adventures. His two books, *Danger Is My Destiny* and *Skipper of the "Girl Pat,"* did quite well in the postwar years, enabling him to live modestly in his boat and cruise the coast of Europe. But now, at age 80, he was slowly sinking, though merrily, for his intake of French wine was a wonder even to the Frenchmen.

I felt highly privileged to sit with him, stranded in a French town far from his beloved northern waters. Many a yarn was spun, with laughter, with sorrow, with joy. We knew full well that some of life's rare moments were at hand.

One fine though chilly evening, Dod and I were returning to our boats along the cobblestone canal waterfront, still chatting and reminiscing. Across the canal, against a grassy bend, several French craft were moored, mostly pleasure craft, both sail and power. Onboard a 40-foot sailing craft, lights were shining brightly and the music and laughter floated to us above the roar of the traffic crossing the canal bridge nearby.

"Noisy blighters," said Dod, clomping his walking stick on the cobbles. Under the dim lamplight near *Cresswell*, a black shadow moved suddenly and Nelson came hobbling toward us, his tail wagging. I'd just bent over to pat him when there was an almighty bang. The party boat had *blown up!* The whole doghouse went sailing through the crisp night air, landing on the jetty only a few feet away from us. The doghouse top was accompanied by bodies, half a dozen of them, that came crashing down into the murky canal waters. With a sickening thump, one of the bodies landed head first on the cement edge of the canal. It was a woman, whose head was smashed in like a melon.

"Get a boat!" shouted Dod—now, in an emergency, his old self. Like a young man, he sprang into a canal cleaner's dory, tied up against the jetty. I followed him, and soon we were picking people out of the water. Two men were unconscious but still alive. Then we went after the screaming men and women who were still in the water, floundering around in panic. Soon we had them onboard the dory and landed them, crying and moaning, onto the jetty.

The other people in the boat basin had heard and seen what was happening. Soon first-aid was being rendered by various onlookers, while I dashed to *Cresswell* to make a big pot of hot, strong tea. (The local *gendarmerie* and fire brigade merely waved their arms in the air and started writing on thick pads.) Soon the tea had the survivors, all five of them, in a calmer mood.

The butane-gas cooking stove of the sailing boat, which had disappeared into the canal waters, had leaked deadly gas into the bilge. A cigarette had been lit, and whoosh! the whole shebang had gone up. Explosions like this cause more deaths in small craft than any other type of accident.

Later, after he had recovered from his shock, the owner of the craft, *Monsieur* DuPont, came over and introduced himself to Dod and me. While drying his clothes in *Cresswell's* cabin, he told us he was married to a doctor and he had been in the French Resistance. (In France, practically everyone claimed this, but in M. DuPont's case it was true; he had been a leading light in the Midi Resistance movement.) He was now the French agent of an American medical equipment manufacturer, and there and then gave Dod and me the job of salvaging the boat. We told him we'd salvage his boat for nothing and would arrange for a friend of ours, an itinerant Manxman, a fishing-boat carpenter, whom we'd met in the pub, Joe by name, to repair his boat.

In this way did I meet M. DuPont and his good lady, who for the whole winter entertained Dod, Joe, Nelson, and me at their house on Sundays for a slap-up meal. And in France that is enough to last an Arctic hand a week!

M. DuPont later introduced us to the faculty of the University of Toulouse. Every Thursday night, Dod and I put on our best bib and tucker and attended the university's English-culture course to show the sprightly lads and lively lassies (about 200 graduates) how to make tea correctly. We also gave talks on soccer and cricket, fish and chips, the "pub culture" (this alone took a month), and British courting routine, which of course is very different from the French way, the latter being surprisingly restrictive (women did not come of age, in those days, until age 28!).

We enjoyed these evenings tremendously. After classes, Dod sat in the *Café Pensez-Y*, opposite the university entrance, surrounded by a great crowd of young worshipers, telling his salty takes of derring-do, while I hovered to one side learning about the latest Beatles music, which was a craze among young French people at the time. Dod, Joe, and I were plied with glass after glass of Alsatian (bock) beer, and Joe and I made them laugh with his attempts at French in our Manx and Liverpool accents. Outside the brightly lit, warm cafe, with its walrus-moustached, long-aproned waiters and cheery madam (who at the age of 90 still had a sparkle for Dod), the snow and rain twinkled and sprinkled.

In March 1964 I resecured *Cresswell's* mooring lines, opened all the cupboard doors, closed all the hatches, showed Joe and Dod where the bilge-pump key was and where they should leave Nelson's food, gathered my sextant, sea clothes, sleeping bag and navigation tables, and caught the train for St. Nazaire.

I was off to deliver the 38-foot ketch *Rose d'Archachon* to the Antilles, then bring back the yawl *Quiberon* from Cayenne to Marseille.

I left *Cresswell* in the care of Nelson. I left Nelson in the care of Dod. I left Dod in the care of Joe. And I left Joe in the care of *M'sieur* DuPont, who in turn was very ably supervised by his charming lady-doctor wife. So all was well and I headed for St. Nazaire with a good conscience.

At the 'B' International Match the Wales rugby team beat France hollow, which was good for free drinks from all around before I left Toulouse.

When I was a youngster I sailed with the rest,
On a Liverpool packet bound out for the west;
We anchored that night in the harbour of Cork,
And we set sail next mornin' for the port of New York.

For thirty-two days we were starvin' and sore,
The winds they did lash and the gales they did roar,
'Til at Battery Point we did anchor at last,
With the jib-boom stove in and the canvas all fast.

The boarding-house masters were out in a trice,
Shoutin' and promisin' all that was nice,
And one fat old crimp that caught on to me,
Said "Young man, you're foolish to follow the sea."

The next thing I mind was I woke up next morn,
In a three-skysail-yarder bound south of the Horn,
With an old pair of seaboots and two pairs of socks,
A busted in nose and a dose of the pox.

Now all you young sailors all listen to me,
Just mind what you drinks when the likker is free,
And pay no attention to runner nor whore,
When your hat's in your hand and your foot's on the shore!

Chorus: *Singing ho, row, ho row, ho row, ho bullies, ho,*
The Liverpool gullies have got us in tow!

"The Liverpool Gullies"

(Sung to the tune of "The Wild Rover," this was a
"pulley-hauley" song [mid-19th century]. The "gullies"
were the seabirds in Liverpool Bay, which were supposed
to help the square riggers on the last few miles home
after an ocean crossing [the thought of the "ladies"
waiting in the red-light district, the "holy ground," also
helped]. The verses were sung by the ship's fiddler; the
chorus was sung by the deck watch
as they heaved the braces.)

8

A Classic Passage

My train pulled into St. Nazaire on the last day in March, 1964. As usual in that part of France at that time of year, it was raining, but after a couple of glasses of *cassis* in the station bar the town began to take on a better aspect. I had some spare francs in my pocket, so I took a taxi to the yacht club, where I met the owner of *Rose d'Archachon*, M. Alex Fougeron, a friend of Mr. Featherstone. He grasped my hand and shook it vigorously in the French way.

"We will have lunch together and then go down to look over the boat; then later this afternoon you will meet your crew. There is Jean-Pierre; he is by all accounts an excellent sailor, from Brest. Jacques is from Paris. He will be the cook."

He made the French gesture for excellence, bringing his first finger and his thumb together in a circle and pursing his lips and making an explosive *pouf*!

As we sat down at a spotless table, he continued, "You will eat well on this voyage, my friend. I have laid out 50,000 francs to provision the boat."

"Any porridge and kippers?" I asked him, jokingly.

"*Hein?*"

"Doesn't matter. I know we'll eat well: *on toujours mange bien dans les bateaux Français.*"

"How long do you think the voyage will take?" Alex asked

me as we delved into the delicious *carnard à l'orange* and the yacht club waiter, immaculate in his white jacket, refilled the wine glasses with a very good Bordeaux red.

"Well, let's see. She's 38 feet, right?"

He nodded.

"Then, given a good beat out to Vigo . . . That's the only stretch where we can count on contrary prevailing winds . . . allow a week for that . . . a week down the coast of Spain and Portugal, with a day in Lisbon and perhaps one day in Tangier . . . "

Alex looked at me questioningly. "Why do you intend to call there?"

"To replenish water and fresh food. Also, to break the length of the voyage. Don't forget, *M'sieur*, a bored sailor is a bad sailor."

Alex nodded.

"Let's see, we figure two and a half weeks to Tangier, right?"

"That brings you to the end of April, if you leave here next week."

"Right, and that means that the winds at the beginning of May off the coast of Morocco and around the Canaries will be less strong, but still hard enough to move *Rose* well," I speculated.

"*Et après Tanger?*"

"To Lanzarote, the easternmost of the Canary Islands."

"But why not sail direct for Tenerife? Surely that's much shorter?" he said, splaying out his palms.

"In distance, yes," I replied, "but the Portugal Current carries on down the coast of Morocco at a good rate, about one and a half knots. That will give us an extra 36 miles a day, or 180 'free' miles over five days. From Lanzarote to Tenerife, with the winds blowing almost always westward from the Sahara, is only one day's sail. If we go direct from Tangier to Tenerife, outside the current, with a quartering wind blanketing the main most of the way, it will take us nine to 10 days. This way it will be only six days."

"That makes good sense, Tristan." Alex ordered coffee.

"I shall stay in Tenerife two days, long enough to pick up water and fresh supplies, then head direct for Martinique."

"How long do you think that will take?" He lighted a *Gauloise*.

"With normal, average wind conditions for late May, say about 30 days. But I am going to allow for 50 days, just in case we lose the wind and are becalmed."

"That means you will be in Martinique in mid June?"

"Yes, with a good margin of six weeks or so before we can expect the hurricane season to commence. But the sooner we are over the Atlantic the better, for you never know when an odd, early hurricane might break out."

"That means two months for the whole voyage. I will order the charts today. Do you need anything special: ocean charts or great-circle course charts?"

"All I need is the exit from the River Loire, the coast of Spain from Cabo Ortegal south, and Portugal—just general, small-scale charts, you understand. The entrances to La Coruña, Vigo, Lisbon, Tangier, the coast of Morocco—again, just general: as far south as Agadir; a general chart of the Canary Islands, with the entrances to Lanzarote and Santa Cruz de Tenerife—a general, small-scale chart of the islands of Martinique and Guadeloupe, together with the entrance to Fort de France. That's all."

"What about ocean charts?" Alex asked.

"Not necessary. I work out my great-circle courses from the computed navigational tables. I can do that in the log—in fact, on the back of a cigarette packet, if need be."

Alex smiled. "Come on, let's look the boat over. She's just out of the yard—brand new. I have her insured for $45,000 with Lloyds of London."

"That's a good Welsh name," I said, grinning at him.

"*Ah, merde, les Gallois!*" Alex moved his portly frame toward the bobbing forest of masts in the yacht basin. He was still a youngish man, about 42 or so. Like M. DuPont in Toulouse, he had been active in the Resistance during the German occupation, and since the war had carved out a chemical distributing empire for himself. Now he was beginning to enjoy the fruits of his toil.

Rose d'Archachon was a ketch. She was 38 feet in length and 10 feet in beam and built of fiberglass, but she had so much fine wood in her that you would hardly know it. As soon as I looked around onboard, it was obvious that Alex had spared no expense in building a fine, comfortable, hardy ocean vessel. She made *Cresswell* look like a Suez Canal bumboat. Down below was an extensive stainless-steel galley with a sink and an oven and even bins for wine bottles in the bilge, molded into the hull. She had five berths: two forward in the foc'sle and two in the main cabin, with another, the quarter-berth, projecting aft from the main cabin below the starboard cockpit seat. There was a huge navigation table, four feet by four feet, and piles of pilot books and tide tables and charts by the dozen.

What a contrast to *Cresswell*, I thought, where my navigation is done on the top of a biscuit-tin lid!

Rose had a great 60-horsepower six-cylinder Couach diesel, with an electric generator supplying lights throughout the boat. An echo sounder and a speed log were fitted under the hull. She had a wind-direction and speed indicator and enough fancy gadgets to deck out a Christmas tree.

Aloft, the same standards of expensive excellence and strength showed. Stainless-steel rigging, aluminum masts, six hand winches, cotton-braided sheets, dacron halyards—you name it, she had it. I stowed away the few clothes I had brought with me: three T-shirts, two pairs of socks, my oil-skin jacket and pants, two pairs of jeans, a sailing jacket, and a pair of shoreside shoes, together with my sextant, my Shakespeare, and my Oxford Book of English Verse. Then I made a cup of tea from the supply I had toted along.

Jean-Pierre arrived late in the afternoon, as Alex and I were going diligently through the sailing inventory, inspecting every seam, every grommet, every cringle.

"*M'sieur Fougeron?*" We looked up to see a stocky fellow about 27 years old, with the light-copper curly hair and green-blue eyes of a true Breton, smiling at us. He was about six feet in height, around 160 pounds, dressed in a blue Breton sailing jacket and red canvas trousers, with a sea bag, which he clutched with a hard, strong, sunburned hand.

"Jean-Pierre . . . you must be Jean-Pierre!" Alex grasped his hand and introduced himself, then me. "This is Tristan Jones, *un Gallois*."

"*Oui, M'sieur* Tristan," said Jean-Pierre, smiling. "I have heard of you. I delivered a boat from Brest to Plymouth last October and we were forced by bad weather into Alderney, and there the people told me about you. And how is your dog?"

"Great, just great, Jean-Pierre." I laughed. "Small world, isn't it?"

"*Bien sûr*. Now, Captain, what do you want me to do?"

"Stow your gear; you can use the portside forward locker in the main cabin. Then just look around the boat for a while, so you know what's what and where it is. Then, if you've a mind to, you can help Alex and me stow these sails away."

"*Bon*, Tristan." He turned to go below.

"Oh, Jean-Pierre!"

"*Oui?*"

"There's a pot of tea on the stove, if you want a cup."

"*Merde!*" murmured Alex. "*Le thé, le thé, toujours le thé!*"

Jacques turned up late that night from Paris. He was a school teacher by profession, 26 years old, slight and stooped, with tawny blond hair and green eyes and a glum look on his face. All this was deceptive, however, for whenever any heavy exertion was demanded he became a human dynamo, with the strength of a fanatic.

"*M'sieur* Tristan," he apologized, "I am sorry I am late. I missed the train."

"That's all right, Jacques; you're here, and that's what counts."

"But I wanted to cook the dinner tonight. Look, I brought some fresh lobster from Paris." He pulled a lobster from a plastic bag.

Jean-Pierre burst out laughing; then, catching the point, so did I. Jacques had brought lobster from inland Paris to the biggest lobster-landing port in Europe!

"*Putain!*" mumbled Jacques, abashed, as he threw his Parisian lobster to one side.

Jean-Pierre was still laughing when we turned in. I went to sleep knowing that I would get on with my crew.

We spent the next day going over the boat's gear and stores and getting *Rose* ready for sea trials the following day. It was tiring work, but with Jacques feeding us we had surplus energy. The trial went well, except for getting a rope wrapped around the propellor. Here Jean-Pierre showed his mettle, for he was over the side in a flash, knife between his teeth, and had the rope hacked off the shaft in no time at all.

"Well done, Jean-Pierre!" said I, slapping him on his shoulder.

"I'll go to work for Cousteau one day," he cracked. (He did, in fact, several years later.)

Alex brought the charts to the boat the day before we were due to sail and I brought them up to date from the latest information issued by the French Navy. Meanwhile Jacques stowed the last of the fresh food and took the labels off all the canned food, marking them with a waterproof laundry marker to avoid the puzzle of not knowing what's in a can if sea water seeps into the stowages and the labels get soggy and fall off. Jean-Pierre checked all the spare sailing gear, lines, anchor chain, sail repair gear, and engine tools and spares. We turned in that night, ready for departure with the outgoing tide at 4:30 in the morning. Alex had left for Paris that evening, after wishing us *bon voyage* and pressing 5,000 francs into my hand "in case of emergencies."

The departure from St. Nazaire was straightforward and by daybreak we were out of the River Loire, headed into the Bay of Biscay with a fresh southwesterly wind on our port bow. "*Au revoir, la France. Merde à de Gaulle!*" shouted Jacques at the receding coast.

The beat to the west for 150 miles took two days, but the wind was steady, and after a day and a half we were able to come about and head southwest by south. Jacques suffered from sea sickness at first; so the going for him was rough. To relieve this, I put a chip of ice in his ears at intervals during the first two days, until the ice ran out; then made him eat raw sugar every hour, two or three tablespoons at a time, which also gave him some relief. By the end of the third day he found his sea legs and had no more of that problem the whole voyage, except for the first few hours out of a port. Jean-Pierre, a hardened yacht-delivery hand, had no problem.

We sighted Cabo Ortegal in northwest Spain on the fifth day out, just as the wind dropped. This is very unusual in those waters, and we motored under engine in a steep swell, up and down, up and down, for 24 hours, until we had Cape Finisterre on the port beam. Then the wind picked up again and we were soon bowling along south on the Portuguese Current with a fine beam wind. I had decided not to go into Vigo but to head for Lisbon, where we would have two days in harbor instead of the one day originally planned.

Rose entered the River Tagus on the eighth day out of St. Nazaire, after a fine, fast beat of almost 1,000 miles. She had shown herself to be an excellent sea boat, fast off the wind and dry off it, and compared to sailing in *Cresswell* it was like being on an ocean liner. Jean-Pierre was a cheerful, willing, hard-working soul, while Jacques was a fabulous chef, always coming up with a three-course meal, excellently prepared, no matter how much buffeting and pounding the boat suffered. In port, his *Coquille St. Jacques* and *Poulet Frit* and, at sea, his *Cassoulet Carcassonne* were culinary miracles.

In Lisbon I moored the boat in Belém, near the immense statue of Prince Henry the Navigator, who, although it seems he never went to sea, gathered together ancient navigational knowledge of the Persians, Phoenicians, Greeks, and Arabs in the fourteenth century. He gave impetus to the great Portuguese voyages of discovery around the Cape of Good Hope and across the Indian Ocean. He impelled Columbus's navigators. He conceived the modern world we know today.

In Lisbon we took on fresh water and cleaned up *Rose*. The yacht basin at Belém had all the reasonable facilties; however, it was a few miles from the city center. Jacques, Jean-

Pierre and I, leaving *Rose* in the care of the watchman, headed for town on one of the frequent trams which passed right by the yacht club.

Lisbon is one of the "sailor's cities" of this world. Its restaurants were cheap, and for $4 or so we all three had a slap-up meal, several drinks, and watched the floor shows: gypsy dancers and singers of the plaintive *fados*, sad and beautiful love songs. Then we headed for the Arizona Bar and inspected (and were inspected by) numerous lasses. We arrived back onboard tired and satiated.

The next day we worked in the morning, preparing for the run down to Tenerife, for we had decided to forgo the call at Tangier and Lanzarote, now we knew what the boat was capable of. In the afternoon Jean-Pierre and I rested in the sun, while the indefatigable Jacques went to the huge, crowded marketplace at the tram terminal in town, where the fresh food was good and very cheap. He prodded the live hens, squeezed melons, tasted grapes, and haggled handily with harrying harridans.

Several people at the Belém yacht basin spoke English, and it was a real pleasure for me to speak it again after several weeks of nothing but French.

The sail to Tenerife was without incident. We had good winds, mainly northerlies, and crashed along at between five and six knots in brilliant sunshine, glad to see flying fish and porpoises once again. At last, after eight days out of Lisbon, the great volcano of Tenerife hove into view, a hundred miles or so away on the southwest horizon, and the next day we were in the small, crowded port of Santa Cruz.

On the way south we had sighted several whales, but they kept well clear of us and seemed intent on making their own way, usually in a northerly direction. We had sighted quite a few ships, especially when *Rose* was on the same latitude as the Straits of Gibraltar. They were mainly headed in an easterly or westerly direction, and obviously this was the trade from the Americas to the Mediterranean and vice-versa.

Santa Cruz de Tenerife is not a very good place for a sailing yacht. The harbor is crowded and dirty, reeking of oil and fish, and when the wind is fresh a strong swell finds its way through the harbor entrance and makes life onboard miserable, with the boat rocking in a sickening fashion. After two days and nights of this we had enough and decided to head across the ocean for Martinique, following almost the same route as Columbus's voyage of discovery.

The passage to Martinique (which sailors call "the Lady's Passage"), a matter of 3,000 miles, took 28 days. The winds were steady in strength and direction. Mainly they were from the east, directly astern of us, and we spent days at a time with the twin genoas slung out on long running poles, bowling along at six to seven knots. It was heavy work on the wheel, for we had no automatic self-steering gear, so it meant four hours on, four off, with Jean-Pierre and I taking the cook's post when Jacques was on deck watch. Jean-Pierre was a fair cook. I made burgoo, which the Frenchmen grimaced at but accepted.

Sometimes in the evening watches, as the sun sank below the horizon ahead of us and I waited to take the dusk star sights, I conversed in low tones with Jacques. To talk loudly while someone is sleeping in a small boat (or indeed anywhere) is, to the sailor, the nadir of bad manners. Jacques was a romantic and he dreamed of the day when he would own his own boat and sail in the South Pacific.

"And, Tristan, I will have a big boat, *une goélette* . . . a schooner . . . and trade between the islands."

"But a schooner, *merde!* That's a great wooden boat, takes a hell of a lot of maintenance, and she'll need a crew big enough to build the Pyramids, *mon ami!*"

"Ah, then I shall have a crew of beautiful Polynesian girls."

"Come off it, Jacques. Have you ever seen the sheet-ropes on a trading schooner? Christ, you need to be King Kong just to haul 'em in!"

"*Bien*, then I shall look for just one big, strong man—a eunuch, you understand."

And so he went on, dreaming of a life among the palm-bedecked islands of the Southern Ocean, the escape world of a *petit-bourgeois* Parisian school teacher. But I thought none the less of him for it, for what is life without the dreaming?

While Jean-Pierre peeled the potatoes and I served a rope's end or repaired a sail, Jacques let his imagination run away with him, dreaming of the Tuamotus and the New Herbrides, the wind ruffling his thinning hair as he strained against the wheel, squinting into the sun descending into the western horizon.

"Strange chap," said Jean-Pierre to me one day, while Jacques was asleep. "Here he is, on his first ocean crossing of the Atlantic, and he can think of nothing but the Pacific!"

"It must be a terrific change for him, from what he's used to: teaching school in some crummy Paris suburb."

On the whole of this run we were becalmed once, for approximately 18 hours. We just sat there wallowing, waiting for a wind. I could have motored but decided not to: I might need the fuel later if we were further becalmed. Our average speed for the whole ocean crossing was therefore just under four and a half knots. This was without pushing *Rose* unduly. If she had been my boat I might have pushed her much harder, but sailing someone else's craft is always an inducement to prudence, at least to me.

With three men onboard, watch-and-watch (mainly heavy steering), we did not see much of each other. One was on watch, one sleeping, and the other either preparing or cooking meals or doing maintenance jobs. In these circumstances, day after day, it is not difficult to keep distance between oneself and the others in a crew, and in a small vessel that is important. The few times a day when we were all together, as at meals, the atmosphere was very friendly.

On fetching Fort de France 49 days out of St. Nazaire, we were soon cleared by customs and we berthed *Rose* in the yacht basin in the harbor. Then Jean-Pierre and I went with Jacques to the airport, where he was returning to Paris, via New York.

"*Au 'voir*, Tristan! Jean-Pierre! Next time you need a cook you know where I am. But next time make it the South Pacific. I want to go to Tahiti. Those girls out there . . . "He gestured with his hands, making downward curves.

"*Au 'voir*, Jacques. See you in Paris about September."

We watched the plane take off.

"When do we go to Cayenne, Tristan?" Jean-Pierre asked as we emerged from the airport to wave down a taxi.

"What's the hurry? We'll have a look around Martinique for a day or two, then take off. We've still got a good margin of time before the hurricanes start in late July. It's only the first of June."

"O.K., *mon capitaine*; you're the boss." We headed for an *estaminet* close to the yacht basin to sip Pernod through the swiftly falling tropical dusk.

Jacques' plane crashed outside Nantes, killing him and many other passengers. Fortunately, neither Jean-Pierre nor I knew about it until we reached France, after one of the worst trans-Atlantic voyages I ever made in a small craft, in *Quiberon*.

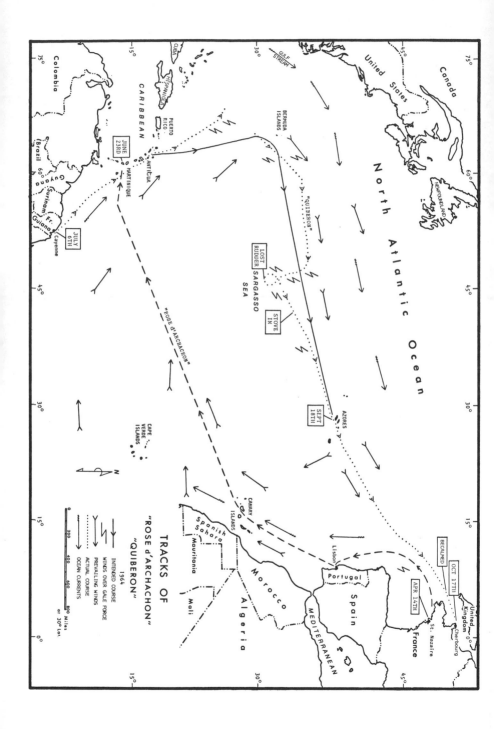

TRACKS OF
"ROSE d'ARCHACHON"
"QUIBERON"

1964

INTENDED COURSE
WINDS OVER GALE FORCE
PREVAILING WINDS
ACTUAL COURSE
OCEAN CURRENTS

0   200   400   600   800 Miles,
or 30° Lat.

N

North Atlantic Ocean

CARIBBEAN

SARGASSO SEA

MEDITERRANEAN

United States

Canada

Newfoundland

Colombia

Guyana

Surinam

Fr. Guiana   Cayenne

Brazil

Cuba

HISPANIOLA

PUERTO RICO

ANTIGUA

MARTINIQUE

BERMUDA ISLANDS

GULF STREAM

AZORES

CAPE VERDE ISLANDS

CANARY ISLANDS

Mauritania

Spanish Sahara

Mali

Algeria

Morocco

Portugal   Lisbon

Spain

France   St. Nazaire

United Kingdom   Cherbourg

"QUIBERON"

"ROSE d'ARCHACHON"

JUNE 23RD

JULY 6TH

LOST RUDDER

STOVE IN

SEPT 18TH

BECALMED

OCT 17TH

APR 14TH

June—too soon.
July—stand by!
August—if you must!
September—remember!
October—all over!

West Indies saying about hurricanes

9

En Passant!

Jean-Pierre and I tackled the fleshpots of Fort de France with gusto for three days, until a plane was due to leave for Cayenne, French Guiana. We slept onboard *Rose d'Archachon* to save hotel bills and during the day wandered around, seeing the sights, drinking *cassis* and Pernod, eating well, taking in all the movement of the colorful port, and listening to the calypso music.

Jean-Pierre, a good storyteller, gave me accounts of his previous voyages. His father had been a fisherman out of Brest, and Jean-Pierre had followed his father to sea at a very early age. By the time he was 18 he decided he would like to see more of the world than the rough gray seas of the Bay of Biscay; so he shipped in a French sailing yacht, a schooner, bound for Madagascar in the Indian Ocean. The two owners of the schooner had fallen out with each other in Rio de Janeiro and one of them had decamped back to France, leaving the other with no funds. Jean-Pierre had been summarily dismissed from the boat—stranded.

For a month, he grubbed around in the streets of Rio before finding the job of delivering a small sailing boat from Rio to Buenos Aires. This paid enough for him to make his way by air to Guadeloupe in the West Indies. From there he had delivered another small craft to New York, but the American owner of this boat had swindled him, saying he had paid for the delivery in advance. Once more Jean-Pierre was stranded. He worked as a dishwasher in Manhattan at a French restaurant on Forty-seventh Street for ten months, before he found a berth in a British yacht bound from Boston to Plymouth, England. In that way he finally got back home to Brittany. After that he worked as mate and skipper in several sailing craft, sometimes on a delivery, sometimes with the owner onboard, mainly around northwest Europe and in the Mediterranean.

His English was very basic but reasonable enough to understand. However, it was strange to hear a Breton speak with a broad New York accent, talking about "the goils" as his eyes followed the shapely lasses of Martinique.

After paying our fares to Cayenne, I still had 2,000 of Alex's francs left, and on arrival in that steaming-hot town we checked into a hotel for the night. A cheap hotel, necessarily so, with no air conditioning and millions of bugs. As we wended our way through the oldest part of the city, with its rotting wooden storefronts and creepers threatening to weigh down the telegraph poles, we noted the strange mixture of races. Prosperous-looking blacks and Chinese and desperately-poor-looking whites, mostly old men—shoeless, with only a shirt, ragged and torn, and pants, and usually with a tattered straw hat, sitting in the gutters: some drunk, some just staring hopelessly into space. Dozens of them, lining the streets down to the river.

"*Alors,* Tristan, *ils sont les 'vieux blancs.'* "

"Old whites?"

"Yes, they are the last of the convicts from the days when French Guiana was a penal settlement. Those with more than eight years to serve had to stay in the colony, after they had finished their time, for the same amount of time as their sentence. So if a man got 20 years' conviction, it meant he was out here for life. They got so accustomed to it that when the French government offered to repatriate them after the Second World War, many turned the offer down. They couldn't face returning to France. So they just hang around in

Cayenne, waiting to die."

Down on the river were a couple of hundred small wooden sailing boats, many of them Brazilian smugglers. Cattle smugglers. I learned that thousands of cattle run wild on the islands in the mouth of the Amazon. These sailors landed on the islands, defying the hazards of the world's mightiest tides and river bore, to rustle Brahman cows. They lashed them down in the holds of their 50-foot boats and sailed all the way up to Cayenne, a run of 600 or 700 miles. Here they exchanged the cattle for Scotch whisky, which they smuggled into Brazil at a tremendous profit, which they earned every penny of the hard way.

Jean-Pierre and I spent hours talking with these smugglers, trying to find out if they knew much about the Amazon farther inland; but they knew only the mouth and the islands which clutter its 280 miles of delta. I made up my mind that one day I would tackle the Amazon.

We sat in the moonlit nights by the stinking river in Cayenne, sipping *cassasa* and whisky and swatting mosquitoes as the Brazilian crewboys played their rhythmic, sexy music in between the sudden, slashing rainstorms, when they dashed under their rough canvas shelters, laughing and chattering.

"There must be many treasures up the Amazon," ruminated Jean-Pierre as we made our way back to the shabby Chinese hotel, with thousands of moths flittering around the entrance light, a bare bulb. "Gold, silver, Indian ornaments, and rare, unknown flowers."

"Yes, and good boat-building timber by the *hectare, mon ami!*"

"Ah, Tristan, always you think about wood for building a boat."

"Well, what's the good of all the treasure if you don't have a good boat to enjoy it in?"

"*Ah, merde. Bonne nuit, mon Capitaine.*"

"*Bonne nuit*, Jean-Pierre. But first, here's an old trick for fooling the cockroaches. Get some canned butter in the Chinese shop and smear some around the pisspot; then the greasy half-melted butter leads the little *cochons* away from you, they fall into the pot, and *voilà!* They can't climb out again through the butter."

"Good idea. *Merci, mon Capitaine!*"

Wakened by the sticky heat at seven the next morning, Jean-Pierre and I fled from the bug-infested hotel down the road to a clean French cafe for our coffee and *croissants*; then, hefting our seabags, we made our way to the steamy river, where we negotiated with a *vieil blanc* to paddle out to *Quiberon* in a dugout canoe. We knew she was out at anchor but we were not quite sure where, as we had arrived too late the previous night to make inquiries at the harbor master's office. But the *vieil blanc* knew where she was.

The sight that met our eyes when we finally carved our way through the thick river mist was enough to make Atilla cry. *Quiberon* had obviously not been moved for several years. The barnacles and other growth (for this is a tidal river) were two feet thick on her bottom. All the paintwork on her cedar sides was blistered off and her canvas cover (over the topsides) was rotted away to a few tattered fragments. There was slimy moss on the cockpit seats, and here and there dry-rot had set in.

"Blimey," I murmered, wiping the sweat from my eyes.

"*Putain,*" said Jean-Pierre.

The *vieil blanc* said nothing, sitting in his dugout and staring vacantly into space with dead, pale-blue eyes.

When I opened the companionway hatch and went below, the smell of rot and dankness would have made a Bastille dungeon seem like Helena Rubenstein's *boudoir*. Everything was moldy. There was a sheen of slimy green moss over the galley stove, the berths, the navigation books, the roof, the floor, everything. The cabin was crawling with huge cockroaches, up to two inches long, thousands of them. The stink from the stagnant water in the bilge was overpowering.

"What do you think, Tristan?"

"I think we'd better get to work cleaning this lot up, *mon ami*. There's $2,000 waiting for us in France once we get this cranky hulk there!"

"But it will take us a month to get her ready, and it's almost June, and the hurricane season starts at the end of July."

"Well, then, *mon ami*, we'd better get moving, hadn't we?"

The rubber dinghy belonging to *Quiberon* was the first thing I inspected. In harbor, at anchor, a boat's dinghy is like a crutch to a cripple; it is often the only way to get ashore. Of course, it had rotted completely. I arranged with the *vieil blanc* that he would purchase a dugout for me for 40 francs, and I would pay him 50. As he paddled away, Jean-Pierre and I set to cleaning the boat inside and out with river water.

It took us three days to get the boat in a fit state for us to move onboard. Then, paddling our dugout, we made dozens of trips ashore to carry the necessary stores for the long passage ahead. The engine was rusted up solid, so it was discounted. I removed the fuel tanks from under the cockpit seat and replaced them with jerry cans for extra water. The sails, being canvas, were in a pitiful state, rotted in many places, but Jean-Pierre was an expert sailmaker. He bought some canvas from a Chinese dealer, hired his sewing machine at a very cheap rate, and we soon had a fine set of working sails and storm sails. But the first thing Jean-Pierre made was an awning, as the sun beat down cruelly. Once it was rigged in place we could work a little more comfortably, but not much.

The masts and spars of *Quiberon* were not in desperate shape, and I soon had them scraped and five coats of varnish on them, topped with two coats of gray paint. The canvas deck covering over the teak boarding was frayed in many places and I spent a couple of days patching it.

We hauled the boat out of the river with one of the dockyard cranes and scraped her bottom off. One of the French harbor pilots gave me some big-ship antifouling compound in exchange for Jean-Pierre's making a sail for his racing dinghy. There was no charge for the crane and the dock berth.

Once the boat was back in the water, we were in business. It was July 2. If we were going to beat the hurricane risk, we must get out and hare to the north as fast as we could.

In Cayenne, we were too far south for hurricanes Their tracks sweep westward across the Atlantic in the area north of the latitude of Grenada. Then they change direction, mainly in a northwesterly way, toward the southeastern United States. But some of them turn due north, up toward Bermuda, when they again turn northeast and lose their force in the vast wastes of the central North Atlantic.

These latter hurricanes were the ones we were mostly concerned about, for they follow the general wind system of the Atlantic. We must follow the track they would follow, but we must get well to the east of Bermuda before the beginning of August. Otherwise we would have to hole up in some West Indies port until the beginning of October, and this would mean arriving on the European side of the Atlantic in the stormy winter season—a daunting prospect. We decided to get the hell out of Cayenne and make a run for it.

"What about another hand?" asked Jean-Pierre.

"We don't have enough money to pay anyone, and who are we going to ask to take this voyage? A *vieil blanc*, probably here for murder? Some green *fonctionnaire*'s kid? No, my friend, our best bet is to get up to Antigua, *tout de suite*, and see if there are any spare hands there that want a lift back to Europe."

On the sixth of July, after a hurried but thorough check of *Quiberon*, we cleared the port and scooted to the northwest on a broad reach, watching carefully, as the boat pounded over the heavy trade-wind seas, for any sign of weakness in the hull or rigging. She seemed to be holding together well, but we were back to rough sailing again after the pleasant, easy voyage in *Rose d'Archachon*. We had no wind steering gear, so it was watch on, watch off on the tiller for Jean-Pierre and me, with the one off watch cooking the meals on the ancient kerosene stove and doing the eternal chores: splicing lines, repairing frayed sails, pumping out the bilge (she leaked steadily).

Quiberon was a yawl, 36 feet long and eight feet six inches in the beam. She had a long, straight keel, drawing five feet six inches, and this eased the strain of steering as she held her course quite well while the wind was on the beam. She was cedar on oak frames, counter stern, and built in Nantes in 1936; so by this time she was showing her age. She had been sailed from France in 1940 by three Frenchmen anxious to escape the German invasion. On arrival in Cayenne, they had split up. Two of them had joined the Free French Navy in the West Indies while the other had stayed in Guiana, going into business. The latter had sailed the boat now and again during the war years and for a few years afterward, but since 1957 she had not moved. In less than a month Jean-Pierre and I had tried, by tremendous effort, to correct the ravages in a wooden vessel that had sat seven years with no maintenance in a humid tropical climate.

The reach for Antigua from Cayenne is about a thousand miles, and we had good steady winds, about 20 to 25 knots, most of the way. It was hard going, until we figured out how to make her self-steer her course by easing out the mizzen, handing (dropping) the main, and backing the big genoa. This kept her on a fairly steady course, though in an erratic manner, but it slowed her down to two and a half knots. However, in the hot afternoons it enabled Jean-Pierre and me to get some sleep.

On the ninth day out of Cayenne we sighted Barbados, away to the west. But tempted though we were to call at Bridgetown and get some rest, we pressed on at an average of three knots. Jean-Pierre on his off-watch cooked his specialties, which were mainly rice dishes: rice and curried fish, rice and corned beef, rice and sardines; while I made burgoo, to his utter disgust. However, he eventually resigned himself to it, coming to the conclusion that this must be Wales' unique contribution to the culinary arts.

Two days later, on the seventeenth of July, we passed the mighty volcanic peak of Mont Pelée, and, piling on sail, pressing her hard, we reached English Harbour, in Antigua, that night. Wearily we went to anchor, glad of the respite from the eternal hammering as she plunged across the tracks of the seas rolling in from the Atlantic deeps, scoffed a basinful of hot burgoo, and turned in.

In the morning, after our first night's rest since Cayenne, Jean-Pierre and I set to to prepare the boat for a fast passage to the area southeast of Bermuda, 800 miles to the north of

Antigua. We would again be on a broad reach—that is, cutting across the track of the prevailing southeast winds. Once we reached the turning point southeast of Bermuda, we could turn east and hightail it out of the hurricane area as fast as we could.

"Do you think we can get an extra crew member here, Tristan?" asked Jean-Pierre. "It would enable us to press on all day and all night. We could make 110 miles a day, instead of 75. That would give us a much better chance of being out of the hurricane area much quicker."

"I'll go to the Admiral Nelson pub and have a look round; look, why don't you come with me? I'll teach you to play darts."

"*Non, merci!* The British drink too much beer. It swells my stomach." He patted his stomach with one palm. "And then I feel like a pig: *pouf!*" He exploded his lips, as Frenchmen do, for an expletive.

"O.K., I'll tell you what: You stand onboard and make a fancy supper, and if I find someone I'll bring him back for supper and we'll tempt him with the grub. Make him eager, see?"

"*Bonne idée, mon Capitaine.*"

In those days English Harbour, on the south coast of Antigua, was slowly developing into what it is now the major rendezvous for trans-Atlantic small craft eastward and westward bound from and to Europe and the West Indies. Captain Nicholson was doing an extraordinary job of converting Admiral Nelson's old dockyard, built to maintain the wooden ships of the late 1700s, into a first-class base for modern sailing craft. The ancient cobblestone jetties, with great capstans and beautiful rose-pink warehouses, all constructed with a Georgian eye to form and style, were being slowly but surely restored to their original condition, and the locals were friendly.

After so many months drinking small drafts of wine with finicky Frenchmen, I was looking forward to quaffing foaming pints of ale from England, and I headed for the pub with pleasure. Moreover, I had received a telegram from M. Pinet, in Paris, saying that *Quiberon*'s destination in France had been

changed to Cherbourg; so I could celebrate the possibility of
nipping over the Channel to England for a few days before
returning to *Cresswell* in Toulouse.

Entering the Admiral Nelson pub in English Harbour, cool
and dim after the tropical glare outside, I found myself in
company with an English crew of four in blazers, ties and
gold badges, gray flannels, and very posh deck shoes.

"I say! You're the chappie just up from French Guiana,
aren't you? Have a good trip, old bean?" The voice that lost
the British Empire skewered my ears. His yachting magazine
fell into a pool of pink gin.

"Up and down, up and down." I slugged at a pint.

"Weah going to Americah, you know, in the ketch *Dolly
Daydream.*"

"You should do well up there. They'll welcome you blokes
with open arms!" I took another deep gulp.

"Yes, old chap, and Hamilton heah . . . " The big, sunburned, fair-haired skipper pointed the stem of his stubby
pipe at a smaller replica of himself. " . . . Hamilton's orf to
Celifawniah, having a go at the old *teevee* and *films,* and all that
jolly rot, you know."

"Should do well. He seems to be the kind of chap they're
lookin' for."

"I say!" The skipper pointed at my solar plexus with his
pipestem. "We had a simply spiffing time coming over from
the Canaries, and Neville theah sort of fell in the drink during
the night. But we were becalmed, so we didn't move, don't
you see, and he climbed back onboard."

He turned to Neville, a long, gawky-looking chap with a
permanent bend in his shoulders which made him look as if
the berth he slept in was too short. "Weahs Sissie, old boy?"
he shouted, holding his gin-and-it in a fist as big as a double-
decker bus.

"She's on her way, Skippah! Just popping some shepherd's
pie in the old oven, you know." Neville chortled.

"Sissie's our cook, Tristan. You'll meet her. Simply
spiffing!"

Even as he said it, the doors opened and a short, dumpy

figure moved toward us and eventually turned out to be a female. Not one of your everyday, graceful, smiling, charming *feminine* females. No, this was a genuwyne, beduwyne, huntin'-shootin'-fishin'-sailin'-skiin'-tenissin'-hockeyin'-beer'-drinkin' *English* female. Terribly, *terribly* English, with an accent that would have quelled the Indian Mutiny with her first tortured vowel.

"I say, Skippah old boy, it's *awfly* hot onboard," she screeched. "Wouldn't it be rahther fun to eat lunch out on the jolly old jetty?"

She had a round face, cheeks like little red crabapples, and ginger, frizzy hair which made her look as if she were in a permanent state of shock, and barbed-wire blue eyes which seemed piercing enough to freeze the hovering flies. She was wearing a blue gym slip, exactly like those worn by school-girls who exercise daily and shout "Oh jolly hockey sticks!" She was about five feet two inches, with arms like a dock worker and little thick legs. The very antithesis of sexuality. Her years—at a wild guess—the mid-forties.

"*Hullo*, who's your friend?" she shouted at Neville in a Cheltenham accent as she stared at me and through me.

I introduced myself.

"Pleased to meetcha, old chap! Weah are you bound?"

"Eastward passage. For . . . " I didn't finish saying "France."

"Nowhere near England, is it? I *say*, I *could* do with a lift, you know." She rocked back and forth on her feet.

"No, actually it's Tangier, Morocco."

"I say! What a bore! Well, it would have been naice to sail back. What are you doin' when you get back?" She was finishing pints faster than I.

I nervously replied: "Well, I'm only delivering this one, you see. Then I go back to my boat."

Skippah chimed in here. "Yes, dahling, this is the chappie from *Cresswell*, you know."

"Oh reahlly!" shouted Sissie. "Weah's your boat?" (The word was out now.)

"Toulouse, but . . . "

"Oh, my *deah!* What *fun;* I *do* so love Frawnce!"

"Well, I'm headin' for Spain when I get back."

"How terribly, simply *divine!*" Sissie crushed my arm. "My deah, I simply *adore* Spain, except for those *awful* bullfights. The poor beast simply hasn't an *earthly* . . . "

"I think bullfights are great," I said. (I didn't; but there was no harm in putting her off, I thought.)

"You simply *must* let me sail with you. You know in Southchester we're not on the coast, and my brother Willy—he's the bishop, you know—gets simply *furious* when I buzz orf in the jolly old flivver to Chichester or Bosham or wherevah. And the whole thing's such an awful *bore,* darling! When will you sail for Spain?"

"When I get back."

"Oh, gosh, *won't* it be simply *adorable fun!*" She sighed loudly.

"Yes," said I, thinking in my mind's eye of poor old Nelson and the burgoo. Then I invited Sissie, the bishop of Southchester's sister, to a game of darts. (My ale-fuzzed mind boggled at calling her by her full, tongue-twisting title.) Of course, she beat me all ends up and I had to leave the pub an hour later, before I went broke buying her pints of ale. As I wended my way back to supper onboard, I repeated over and over to myself: *Sissie St. John, the bishop of Southchester's sister.*

Through the window of the pub, as I crept back along the gravel path, with the cicadas chirping in the undergrowth and a great tropical moon hanging in the blue-black sky, I heard her high-pitched awfly, terribly up-guards-and-at-'em voice ripping asunder the calm, quiet air of Admiral Nelson's dockyard, loud enough to make the little one-armed, one-eyed devil-darling of British sailors turn in his grave, all the way over in London.

As I went onboard into the steaming aroma of rice and corned beef, I thought to myself: *Thank God Almighty and all the angels in heaven, I managed to put her off sailing with us!*

Aft the more honour—
Forward the better man!

Admiral Lord Nelson
(castigating his officers for tardiness in
leading his seamen into action when
boarding enemy ships. In the days of
sailing warships the officers lived aft, the
men forward).

10

Check!

"Did you find anyone?" Jean-Pierre asked as I went below into the humid, hot cabin, the oil lamp flickering fitfully.

I shook my head. "There's no one around who wants to go back east, except an old English biddy."

"*Quoi?*"

"*Une grande dame Anglaise.* Trouble, my friend: bloody chatter about Wimbledon day and night, brassiers in the sail locker, stockings in the porridge. Jesus Christ!" I threw my cap onto its hook.

"Then we must go on—just the pair of us, *hein?*" He set out the supper plates.

"Yep. But look, Jean-Pierre, once we get to the turning point, 65 degrees west, 30 degrees north, we won't be on a close reach anymore. We can turn her off the wind and belt off to the east on a run. Once we get past 50 degrees west, we should be fairly safe. Out of range of anything really dangerous."

"You're sure, Tristan?"

"Oh, come on, Jean-Pierre; you know as well as I do that in a small craft you can never be absolutely sure of anything, especially weather. And you should know, too, there are four kinds of seafarers under sail."

"What are they, Tristan?'

"Dead, retired, novices, and pessimists!"

Jean-Pierre grinned.

I went on. "The thing for us to do is load the dice, and the only way we can do that is to get out of here as soon as possible. Tomorrow night, after we've got fresh water and stores onboard. And shoot off north, as close to the wind as we can manage and still keep us a good speed." I tapped the salt cellar on the table.

"How long do you think it will take us to reach 65-30? What do you call it, the 'turning point'?"

"Well, if the winds are as steady getting us away from here as they were fetching us here, I'd say . . . let's see . . . If we can keep a speed average of four knots . . . say 1,100 miles . . . Say 12 to 13 days. Two weeks . . . " I reached for my fork.

"And it's now the eighteenth of July. That takes us to the thirty-first of July."

"Yes, that means we can just slide out of harm's way by the skin of our teeth, and be well clear of the hurricane tracks by the time the really serious stuff is due to start, say the second week in August."

Jean-Pierre looked serious as he leaned to his dinner. "Then we have a margin of seven days?"

"Now you know damned well, Jean-Pierre, nature doesn't run to a fixed timetable. There's always a chance that the first hurricane of the season might come a week—even two weeks, even a month—before it's expected. We can only go on the averages over the years since records were kept, which indicate that the first blow can reasonably be expected about the middle of the second week in August. Anyway, we've found that *Quiberon*, although she leaks and is cranky as the devil, will stand up to a reasonable blow. There's a thousand dollars each for us waiting in France—and hell, after all, we *did* contact to bring her back. And we *are* a delivery crew, are we not?"

"*Oui, mais* . . . "

"*Oui mais* nothing! *Mon ami*, Pinet wants her delivered to Cherbourg for a winter refit. If we wait until after the hurricane season, it means we'll hit bad weather on the European side in November. If we wait for spring, for February, it means we'll get to Europe in April, and Pinet will miss his sailing next year. And you and I, Jean-Pierre, will lose our reputations as deliverers. We'd be lucky if we could find a job scraping and painting, once that happens. You know the yachting world—how small it is, and especially in France. And how the word gets around."

"O.K., Tristan. You're the skipper. If you think we can do it—just the pair of us—then I'm willing to try. Now, what fresh food will we need?"

"Two days' fresh beef—but check the fishing tackle—20 days' apples, 60 days' onions, two weeks' cabbages, three months' potatoes . . . " I started reeling off a list, which he scribbled on his pad. "And three months' kerosene. And better buy another storm lantern; the one we have is very rusty. It's the only lamp we've got, so better make sure."

So on July 19 we weighed anchor, secured a tow from a friendly English yachtsman with his outboard dinghy, and, after he slipped our line outside the narrow harbor entrance, made course for the northeast. The routine was much as it had been on the way from Cayenne to Antiqua: four hours on the tiller, four hours off, with the boat again on the reach but a bit closer to the wind. I did not want to lose ground to the west. The aim was to stay in as easterly a position as we could. This meant that the boat was pounding down off the seas continually—close hauled, as we say.

On the twenty-fifth of July, about 600 miles north of Antigua, the wind began to rise. The sky in the southeast darkened, until by midafternoon, a full gale was blowing and we reefed the main down four hands and shortened the headsail down to No. 3 working jib (the second smallest). By midnight the seas were in a frenzy, with ghostly white horses sending lashing spray over *Quiberon* as she heaved and groaned from one huge sea to the next. Jean-Pierre hung on to the tiller, despite the regular crashing of seas into the cockpit (which, thank God, had been converted to self-draining).

By dawn—a gray dawn, full of black scudding storm clouds

and heaving, crashing, monstrous gray seas 20 feet from trough to crest— the banshee wind was screaming at storm force. I reckoned it was blowing at least 50 knots. I had handed the mainsail entirely, and we were down to storm jib and mizzen only, wallowing and weaving, twisting and squirming like a stuck pig. With all the working, *Quiberon* started to take water into her hull at an alarming rate, and whoever was not on the tiller was on the bilge pump, when he was not tending sail or trying to heat something to drink or eat.

By midday on the twenty-sixth the storm was up to hurricane force. We were forced to bring down the storm jib and let her ride bows on to the storm, with the mizzensail weather-cocking her. The movement now was much easier, but she was still leaking, not only through the hull but through the sides, where her planking had opened with too much exposure to the sun in the tropics. The decks, with the seas crashing over them, were also leaking, and everything below—everything except what was canned or tightly wrapped in plastic bags and sheeting—was soon wet through. Hove to, at least we were free of the tiller, and after making sure everything on deck and below was snugged down, we went below, to continue pumping and to wait out the storm.

By the night of the twenty-sixth, all hell was let loose on the world. It was as if the devil himself were having a fit. The seas were so huge and steep that their size alone, even without the sheets of spume whistling off the crests, was frightening. Not merely from the threat of death—immediate, absolute, contained in each one as it loomed, black and gleaming out of a dark, noisy nothingness—but from the realization of the mighty forces at violent play, forces which make anything that man can muster look like the feeble waving of a baby's fist.

"*Merde!*" said Jean-Pierre, patiently pumping. "How long do you think this will last?"

"Don't know, but we seem to be riding out well enough. It's just a matter of patience," I said, balancing myself in the plunging cabin. "Here, have some biscuits." I handed him a soggy packet of damp cheese crackers.

For three days, until the twenty-ninth, we were hove to, bouncing and crashing in the hurricane, until early on the thirtieth of July the sky to the southeast brightened and the wind dropped to gale force, around 35 knots. Struggling, I hoisted the storm jib. By midday I knew our position by sun sights, the clouds now being scrappy, allowing the sun to peep through fitfully.

We had lost 120 miles to the west! Our position was now approximately 400 miles due south of Bermuda.

"What do we do now, Tristan? Make for Bermuda?" Jean-Pierre asked as we pored over our small-scale chart of the Atlantic.

"No. If we do, we'll be stuck until October. We clean up for an hour, then set the main, reefed, and claw our way northeast. We'll still try for 65-30, or as damn near as we can get to it. If the winds are still southeast when we get there, we'll carry on northeast, until we meet up with the west wind, then run for the Azores."

Jean-Pierre balanced himself in the cockpit, holding onto the wheel, sunburned, his eyes squinting against the glare from the glistening sea, the salt shining on his hair and cheeks.

"What about food, Tristan? Do you think we have enough?"

"Sure." I leaned down into the galley and grabbed the food-account notebook from its shelf. This was where we kept track of all food consumed. Just as a housewife pays for food in the shops, we entered details of the food we used into the notebook. In this way, by comparing what we had used with what we had originally taken onboard, we could tell at a glance what stocks we had remaining. I leafed through the dog-eared pages.

"Sure, Jean-Pierre, enough for at least another two months. Anyway, if we *do* go into Bermuda, the chances of finding anyone to go with us without pay are slender. All the posh yachts will have sailed weeks ago and anyone with any brains will have gone with them. Only an inexperienced amateur would want to trust his life to a bloody old tub like this!"

Jean-Pierre nodded. "The last thing we need is a passenger."

"And if we took on a paid hand, it's going to bite into our delivery dues. Let's see—say two months; he's going to need at least 80 bucks a week, if he's any good to us. That's $640 off our dues. Only leaves 680 bucks apiece for us when we get to France."

"Yes, it makes sense. It would mean we'd be working— June to September—for 160 a month, 40 a week. *Nom de Dieu!* Six dollars a day!"

"Right. And that, *mon ami*, is exactly 50 cents an hour! If we take it that we each work 12 hours a day. Obviously we're not. We're working about 18 hours a day each, and often more. No, Jean-Pierre, to go into Bermuda would be a waste of time, and the chances are if we did go in we'd be stuck there until October, with no pay for the waiting weeks. The only thing is to push on."

All that day, the thirtieth of July, the wind gradually lessened though the seas carried on, one after the other, heaving bulges of gray-green water out of the southeast. As the wind diminished we eased out the mainsail, until by midnight we were back to full working rig. The night was clear, with millions of stars shining benignly at us from a black, velvet sky, sending reflections from thousands of wave crests on the tired, sighing ocean.

In the morning, the seas had smoothed enough for us to set the sails for self-steering, and Jean-Pierre and I were able to sleep the whole forenoon, until it was time for me to shoot the equal altitudes of the sun over the noon period. With starsights the previous dusk and at dawn, this gave me a very accurate fix. We were doing well: an average of three knots, northeast.

For the next 10 days the wind was down to about 25 knots and we steadily pounded our way northeast, until on the ninth of August we were at longitude 60 degrees west, 35 degrees north—farther east and farther north than the intended turning point.

Here, at last, we met the west wind. It came in the form of a full storm, suddenly screeching out of the evening twilight—with a weak, anemic-looking sun, pale and watery, sliding down behind coal-black hammerheads to the west. From the semitropical 70 or so, the temperature dropped to less than 50 degrees in an hour, while our barometer, the old-fashioned long-stemmed glass-tube variety, which miraculously still worked, plunged.

Our radio, a small transistor receiver, was playing music from Radio ZBM in Bermuda. If there had been a storm warning we had missed it among all the commercials for soft drinks and king-size beds. We had listened carefully as the wind whistled overhead and the seas roared by, but we were 250 miles east of Bermuda and the radio emissions were fading at regular intervals to a very weak signal. We donned our woolen jerseys.

By dawn on the tenth of August, we were again hove to, under mizzen only, slowly drifting west, with the wind, up to storm-plus force, raging over a flaying sea. We had tried to run before the storm with a spitfire jib hoisted, a tiny pocket handkerchief of a sail, but the sea movement was so violent, and I was so concerned that the mast would carry away and that the twisting, wrenching movement of the hull would cause her to open up even more, that we dared not. Instead we hove to. To this day I am sure I was right to do this, for already the hull was weakening seriously.

The rate of drift to the east I reckoned to be about two knots, around 50 miles a day; and this went on for *11 days!* For 11 days the sea rushed and battered and crashed against the fragile hull of *Quiberon*. For 11 days and nights the wind roared and screeched and tore at the rigging, while Jean-Pierre and I, taking six-hour spells, worked away at the bilge pump—steadily, like a human heart pumping the blood of life.

By the time the wind eased off we were on longitude 51 degrees west. We had drifted 540 miles, but this time the right way—east. We were about 800 miles east of Bermuda, with clearing skies and a rapidly diminishing wind.

Jean-Pierre unlashed the tiller while I prepared to hoist the working jib on the wildly plunging foredeck, holding onto the shrouds like I was welded to them. I dared not trust the guardrails, for *Quiberon's* gunnels (where the deck joins the sides) were rotten. Already, three guard-rail stanchions had collapsed under the weight of seas crashing onboard. I hanked the working jib onto the forestay, all the time with the wind blowing hard around my ears, and half the time up to my knees in cold sea water, whenever the bow plunged into the head seas. Suddenly, through the roar of the wind, I heard Jean-Pierre calling me.

I looked around. He was braced in the cockpit, feet apart, holding his arms out wide with wide-open palms and horror on his face. I lashed the jib to the foot of the forestay, clambered aft, and fell into the cockpit, wet through.

"The rudder, Tristan. The rudder. It's gone!"

"Gone? What the hell are you talking about?" I seized the tiller. It was true. There was no resistance to the movement of the tiller. The violent movement of the hull in the tremendous seas over the past 10 days had worked the rudder loose of its shaft, and it had dropped off.

There we were, in mid-Atlantic, 800 miles from the nearest land, with the wind blowing us away from it, and no rudder!

"*Merde . . . merde!*" wailed Jean-Pierre.

Oh, suffering Christ! said I, quietly, to myself.

No matter though our decks be swept
And mast and timber crack—
We can make good all loss except
The loss of turning back.
So 'twixt these Devils and our deep
Let courteous trumpets sound,
To welcome fate's discourtesy
Whereby it will be found.
How in all time of our distress
And our deliverance too,
The game is more than the player of the game,
And the ship is more than the crew!

Rudyard Kipling, "A Song in Storm"

11

Mate!

Quiberon's rudder was the inboard type; that is, it did not hang over the stern. The rudder shaft went through the bottom of the hull through a gland about four feet forward of the stern and the rudder hung down below the hull. I had never liked this type of rudder because of this very reason: if anything goes wrong with it at sea, it is almost impossible to get at it to effect repairs. I have always, *always* preferred the outboard-hung rudder; that is, one which is connected directly to the stern of the boat. It can be removed, repaired, and replaced at will, and you can always see the state of the rudder and its fittings.

At any rate, a sudden lurch of the boat had sent me flying onto the starboard cockpit seat with a rib-jolting thump.

"*Qu'est-ce que nous faisons maintenant?*" Jean-Pierre shouted over the soughing of the wind and the crash of the seas, the whine of the shrouds and the groans of the tortured hull.

"We *make* a bloody rudder, *mon ami!* We're reasonably safe from the full strength of any maverick hurricanes going east."

"*Comment? Nom de Dieu!*" Jean-Pierre threw his hands out in wild despair. "*Comment nous faisons une nouvelle barre?*"

"There's plenty of wood in the boat. We've got tools, even though they're rusty, and there's enough screws and bolts to

117

build a blasted sports arena. We'll dismantle the berths forward; there's some good mahogany there and plenty of screws. I'll do that while you take the engine to bits and get as many long bolts out of it as you can. Once we've got the berths and the engine in bits we'll see what we can build from that. We can expect a few days of steady weather, so we'll leave her hove to, bows to seas, and just plug away steadily."

"But suppose a strong storm comes up? How will we hold her head to the wind? Is the mizzen enough?"

"If a blow rises we'll put out a sea anchor. Knock out the bottom of that bucket, string it out on all the mooring lines we have, tied together, and that should do the trick. But we won't do that until the blow comes. The mizzen will hold her up to the wind in any reasonable weather."

We set to, working like navvies to dismantle the forward berths and the engine. We were fortunate, for all the while we were doing this the weather was moderating. We worked all that night and until noon the following day, when I found that we had drifted yet another 40 miles to the east. At least we were heading in the direction of Europe, even if it was stern first.

The main cabin was a shambles, with bits of wood and oily engine parts jammed onto the sole (floor) of the compartment. Soon I had two big pieces of fine mahogany, each six feet by two and a half by one inch thick, together with sufficient battens to bolt them together, while Jean-Pierre had several four-inch bolts and the inboard part of the propellor shaft, together with its bearings.

"*Bon*, Jean-Pierre; we'll use the propellor shaft as a rudder post. We'll use the shaft bearings to fix it onto the stern."

Jean-Pierre grabbed the midships stanchion as the boat lurched yet again. "But how do we fix the rudder to the shaft?"

"We'll have to drill right through the shaft, four holes; then bolt two metal plates to it and bolt the metal plates to the wooden jury rudder."

"Plates? What plates?"

"The sides of one of the steel jetty cans will do. Come on, I'll rig the shaft; you saw up the jerry can. We need two plates, eight inches by six."

For two more days, with the boat rocking and yawing, we sawed and drilled, until at last we had the semblance of a rudder hanging from the stern, with the propellor shaft bearings bolted through the transom, the shaft's upper end projecting above the transom just far enough so we could seize it with a large pipe wrench, to use as a tiller. Because the mizzenmast was in the way, it was impossible to lengthen the "tiller" so we could steer from the cockpit. Intead we rigged a system of pulleys on the stern, through which I rove lines each side from the pipe wrench, and by this means, by pulling on the lines, the tiller could be worked from the comparative safety of the cockpit.

As we finished the building of our jury rudder the weather was fine and sunny, with a fresh breeze out of the northwest. I tested the rudder all that afternoon, gradually increasing sail, while Jean-Pierre cleared up the mess below as best he could. We could spare no fresh water for cleaning, and sea water is useless against grease.

Soon we had all working sail up and were going well at four knots on a broad reach. The new rudder, roughly built though it was, steered the boat better than the original. There was now less weather helm; that is, the boat did not continually try to turn her head into the wind. I soon found that she steered herself better with the helm lashed and the main reefed down a touch. We plodded on, resting and eating, trying to recover the strength we had expended in the past few days.

Three good days of moderate, sunny weather followed, and by August 26 I found that we were at 44 degrees west, 35 degrees north. The Azores were almost exactly 1,000 miles due east of us. All we had to do was keep pressing eastward, hopefully afloat.

On the twenty-eighth of August the sky in the northwest darkened; thunderheads swelled in the ever blackening sky, and soon lightning and the roar of thunder accompanied our curses as we reefed down for yet another gale. This one came out of the north. Due north! A very rare occurrence in mid-Atlantic, if the Maury weather charts, calculated since the 1830s, are anything to go by. A 110 to 1 chance. But down it came: sheet rain, lightning, fierce wind, steepening seas lashing themselves into lunatic rage—and poor old *Quiberon*, again surrendering herself to the gods of the weather, hove to, this time under a *reefed* mizzen, in the brutish wind.

For four days we were bashed and belted, the wind and seas ever increasing in their fury. We were pushed, jolted, pelted, and pummeled *south*. This was of grave concern to me. We were drifting into an area affected by the Azores High: an area where generally there is little wind. The area the square riggers in the old days avoided like the plague—the Sargasso Sea.

Legend had it ships were seized by the clinging fronds of Sargasso weed, miles long, and—with the crews thirsting and starving to death—rotted away, until they finally sank, dragged to the depths by monsters unimaginable.

But these legends were not the cause for my concern. When this unusual northerly wind dropped, we were liable to be stuck in an area with very slight or no wind at all; and already our food and water stocks were depleted by half. I decided to go onto short rations. The fresh water would be consumed at half a pint each per 12 hours. All cooking was to be done with sea water, not as before: half fresh and half salt.

Dawn of the first of August revealed a sea of slashing white-fanged mad frenzy, with the wind howling down from the north, tearing at the rigging, plucking at every frap of canvas. Jean-Pierre and I, wet through, crawled on all fours over the crazily heaving deck, wrapping extra lines around the sails, clutching onto the guardrails and handholds, the wind seizing us, trying to push us over the side, lifelines tied around our shoulders, each working with one hand, one elbow, and our teeth.

It took us about two hours to wrap a line around the mainsail and lower the boom to reduce top hamper. All the while *Quiberon* writhed and tossed, bucked and bounced, laid over and sprang back before the ever advancing, unnumbered, immeasurable, glowering mighty seas, with the hurricane blasting the gray spume off the crests. A watery blizzard—with cannonades of windspit battering our oilskins, stabbing our squinting eyes, and richocheting off the throbbing drum-tight mizzensail—now reefed down to a mere rag. With our feet braced hard against the lee toerail and our bodies splayed low over the coachroof, hanging onto any firm hand-hold as if we were begging for mercy, we threw the line to each other time and again, gradually wrapping it aft along the boom to safeguard the mainsail against the mighty wind's tearing and clutching.

After what seemed forever, we slithered into the drunken cabin and, with the stove rocking on its gimbels like a crazed devil dog, shut the hatch and collapsed, half onto the berths, half on the sole, still clutching onto the midship stanchion, the least frenetic place in the boat.

Jean-Pierre grinned grimly. *"Et maintenant?"* he panted. "What now?"

"Rien, mon ami. Maintenant nous sommes dans les mains du Bon Dieu!" I gasped. "Nothing, my friend; now we're in the hands of God!"

Jean-Pierre grunted. He was a good son of the French Republic, a spiritual descendant of Marat and Robespierre, a confirmed atheist. Somehow he hauled himself onto his feet in that violence and hand-hauled himself to the wildly swinging stove. *"Bon. Donc, moi je vais faire du thé!"* "Good, then I'll make some tea!"

I had to smile to myself at this.

Even as he managed to light the stove, after a seeming hour of struggle with damp matches and flaring alcohol primer, suddenly, with a lurch that seemed to stop the world, *Quiberon* lifted up in the air and was thrown sideways with a teeth-jarring crash. Jean-Pierre was slammed across the boat, landing in a heap on the quarter berth. For a few seconds, which seemed to my numbed senses like a century, there was a deathly stillness after the boat lurched upright, a quiet pause, a ghastly lull.

Jean-Pierre and I stared into each other's eyes. We both

knew what was happening. We both felt like condemned criminals the moment before the switch is pulled, the second before the trapdoor is opened, the breath-stopping eternity before the triggers are squeezed. *Quiberon* had broached!

With a mighty roar, sounding to our paralyzed ears and frozen minds as if all the wild animals on earth were about to spring on us, *our* sea, the one that had waited for us all these years, after all these thousands of miles, was upon us! I remember thinking to myself, lying spread-eagled on the cabin deck: *This is it. What a pity I can't see it!* Then, it seemed, the boat tore asunder.

There was a rumble under the roar, a hiss under the rumble, a screech under the hiss, a scream under the screech, and overall an explosion of the wrath of all the forces in the universe. It was like being in the vortex of an implosion. It was as if all the energy in the world was concentrated on *Quiberon* and, through her, passed into my spine, my heart, my soul and mind. It was the essence of destruction shooting into my very being. Here was death, naked and pure. Then came the shock of bare-fanged pandemonium.

With a roar the boat drove downward, downward, *downward*—slowed, juddered, jolted, shivered, halted—rose, was *rising*. Then the coachroof side gave way before the ever ranting roar of monstrous power and I was staring up at the Atlantic Ocean as it gushed through a gap between the sidedeck and the edge of the coachroof, a gap fully a foot wide! The next few eons of time were utter chaos, as the boat filled with cold seawater.

I remember hauling myself onto my knees in that swirling vat of wet, rushing turmoil, then forcing myself upright, to find that Jean-Pierre also had stumbled toward the midship stanchion. In the deafening blasts and blares, the thunder of hell, he grabbed my shoulder.

"Ça va?" His voice was rock, steady.

"O.K.," I sputtered.

The water was up to our waists. Then we both came to our sailor-senses. At the same moment, we dove toward the bilge pump. Jean-Pierre made it first. It was underwater, but he fumbled for it and started pumping. I made for the hatch and scrabbled it open. Then I slid back into the freezing water and groped in the galley for a bucket.

There followed an effort, a wild reach for the right to *live*, of which the memory is blurred. I know that Jean-Pierre stuck to the pump while I baled water out of the cabin through the hatch like a madman for several minutes, until I realized that I would have to deal with the hole in the deck.

I staggered through the cabin and, after heaving a ton of jumbled gear out of the way, dragged the mattresses out of the forward cabin, one at a time—hauling them out, tying a lifeline around me as I clambered up the ladder, hefting a mattress with me out onto the pounding deck, the wind screeching. Somehow, I rammed the two mattresses into the gap, beating at them like a maniac until they were jammed in. Then, as best I could, I surveyed the scene on deck.

Quiberon was a shambles but, thank God, the rigging had held, except that the starboard mainmast spreader had collapsed. The deckhouse, doghouse, or coachroof (call it what you will) had been smashed in on the port side, but the starboard side had held. The hurricane was still raging, but now it was of secondary importance. What mattered now was to survive!

The first thing was to secure the top half of the mast, which was whipping around like a crazed conductor's baton. Somehow I hauled myself against the ramming wind to the mainmast and, hardly able to command my shaking finger, untied the main halyard. This I hastily yet carefully led to the starboard chainplates, where the rigging wires were fixed to the deck. This was dangerous, for the loose uppershroud was flogging around like the flaying hind hoof of a dying steer, but I managed to get to windward of it, then secured the main halyard as taut as I could to the forward-shroud deckfitting. I captured the loose shroud with a short length of line and, with a struggle, secured it.

Next I scrambled to the after end of the boom, which had been lowered onto the coachroof before the disaster, and with a herculean effort unshackled the topping lift, all the while clinging to the handrail, with the wind and spray slashing like a million rapiers. I crawled forward to the starboard chain plates and secured the topping lift, again as taut as I could. Thus the masthead was reasonably anchored on the starboard side. I squinted aloft against the flogging, flailing spreader. Time to deal with that when the weather eases off, I thought.

Through some miracle, the mizzen had survived the battering and was still holding the boat up to the wind.

Satisfied that I had given God as much help as I could aloft, I crawled back down below. Jean-Pierre was keeping a steady, agonizing, panting pace at the bilge pump, and the level had dropped about six inches. In the violence below I set to with the bucket again, steadily throwing oily seawater into the cockpit, where it would drain away.

Later, I reckoned that the stove-in happened at 9 a.m. By the time we got the boat reasonably clear of water it was 4 p.m., and obvious that the storm had done its worst. The wind was easing off, though the seas were still like restless mountains.

Jean-Pierre had kept a steady stroke at the pump for seven hours solid when I relieved him at 4 o'clock. Then I stayed at the pump for four hours, and so it continued for the two of us all that night: four hours pumping, four hours repairing damage. The following morning, exhausted, with the wind at a comparatively mild 40 knots and the boat riding safely though violently, we both collapsed for three hours, to sleep.

"What about the spreader?" asked Jean-Pierre, before closing his drooping eyelids. "When are we going to fix it?"

"Later," I mumbled. "Our first need is sleep, then some grub when we wake. Then we'll tackle the spreader, O.K.?"

"You're the boss," he murmured, half asleep.

By the evening of the second, when we woke, the weather was moderating even more, and by the morning of the third, after another night of pumping, sleeping, pumping, sleeping, it was down to 20 knots and the seas had flattened out enough so we could tackle the spreader.

"Who's going up?" asked Jean-Pierre, staring at the wildly weaving mast.

"We'll toss a coin; that's the only fair way."

I flicked a coin, retrieved from the odds and sods box in the navigation locker, and, hoping it would turn up tails (heads is always the skipper's side), watched it bounce onto the hatch coaming. Tails!

"Your privilege, Jean-Pierre."

"*Phut!*"

He tied the safety harness around the mast, secured the canvas pouch for tools around his waist, and started to clamber up the weaving mast with a new spreader, which we had cut and shaped the previous day, tied around his neck. It took him six hours to fix the new spreader in place, but by late afternoon the mast was safe again and we gingerly hoisted the mainsail to try it out.

While this was going on, I had nailed down six yards of heavy canvas over the mattress-filled gap in the deck and shored up the mattresses from below with a plank of wood cut from the cabin shelves and most of the cabin floorboards. Then I bolted three floorboards across the deckhouse coamings to add rigidity to the hull, normally afforded by the deckhouse.

Topsides and below, *Quiberon* was a devastated ruin. In any yacht basin or marina in the world she would have been beached and burned out for her metal fittings. But we were in mid-Atlantic and, wreck or no, must get her to her destination. She was our lives!

Jean-Pierre put the last bolt in place on the spreader and tightened the last rigging screw on the starboard shrouds. His face flushed with effort and pride in a difficult, arduous, dangerous job well done, he announced as I handed him a mug of soup: "*Moi, je ne crois pas ce miracle!*"

He sat in the cockpit, with a wan sun at long last shining in the west, and stared around at the floating, patched-up shipwreck of the crippled *Quiberon*, then squinted up at the sails which were pulling her at long last toward the east again.

"Don't believe what?" I asked as I spooned the hot soup.

"I don't believe we are still alive." He trailed off, dipping a hardtack biscuit into the steaming ox-tail bouillon.

"Jean-Pierre, the gods love those who die young. You'll be all right; you've got the Devil on your side."

He laughed, gripped his cup between his knees, and gave the jibsheet another few inches of easing.

Quiberon lurched on. East.

Alors, les Anglais sont arrivés!
[Oh, the English have arrived!]
Les sanglais sont arrivés!
[The bloody ones have arrived!]

Old French pun
(Alludes to menstruation and means the
blood is flowing. Originates from
frequent English invasions of France in
medieval times.)

12

An English Arrival

Quiberon was at 43 degrees west, 30 degrees north. Steadily she pounded over the moderating ocean seas, east-northeast for five days, with either Jean-Pierre or me pumping away for 30 minutes out of the hour right around the clock. Then, on the eleventh of September, the wind shifted around to the west, its normal direction, and we made good time due east for another five days.

On the fifteenth of September, to our utter surprise, we got a blow out of the *south*. In the area of the Azores this is about as rare as a snowstorm in San Diego. I was thankful, for it put the damaged deck away from the weather. This gale, however, was short lived and soon the wind veered again to the west, so that on the eighteenth of September, exactly two months after we left Antigua, we clawed our way into the narrow entrance of the tiny harbor of Fayal, on the island of Horta in the Azores.

It was midnight when we tied up at the broken-down jetty, weary to the bone but thanking all the gods for our safe arrival. After the police had entered the boat into Portuguese territory, we collapsed and slept the sleep of honest toil and utter relief, though the boat bumped the stone jetty all night.

Next day, bright and early, I went around the small harbor, called on my old friend, Don Enrique, at the Bar Sport, and explained our plight. Don Enrique was happy to see me and gave me all the news of the boats which had passed through during the previous five years. (The numbers were increasing steadily year by year, as trans-Atlantic sailing became more and more popular among a growing number of ocean sailors.)

Soon, arrangements were made to careen *Quiberon* (that is, take her out of the water) by dragging her up the ramp at the Horta whale-fletching station. We handled her just like they handled a whale, which hand-harpooners hunt in those waters. The fletching crew shackled a cable around *Quiberon*, then I dangled both her anchors and all her chain from the masthead to heel her over to starboard, an angle of 50 degrees from the vertical. The steam winch whirred, the cable tautened, and within five minutes she was high and dry on her side on the whale-fletching ramp, which was reeking with the blood and guts of the last great sperm, caught three days previously. The whole area stank to high heaven.

All day we toiled, strengthening the makeshift rudder, recaulking the garboard seam (where the keel joins the hull). All day and most of the night I caulked, while Jean-Pierre scraped off our two-month collection of barnacles and other marine life from the bottom planking.

On the morning of the twentieth we lowered *Quiberon* back down the ramp. A dead whale, a monster well over 100 feet long, was moored offshore, waiting to be hauled up the ramp as we slid down.

The next day we spent repairing the side of the cabin coachroof with the aid of two whalers. It was a rough job, but strong. Jean-Pierre made a quick tour of the local shops for a week's supply of fresh food. A hurried topping of the water tanks, two beers apiece in the Bar Sport, and we were off again, headed direct for Ushant, an island off the northwest corner of France.

On the eastern side of the Azores we got mainly fine weather all the way, with no winds over 30 knots and very few below 20. The distance direct from Horta to Ushant is 1,500 miles. *Quiberon* logged only 1,650, which shows how steady the wind direction was. We made the distance in 18 days, picking up the mighty, welcome flash of the Ushant light (one of the most powerful lighthouses in the world) on the evening of October 8.

With the wind still blowing steadily from the southwest, I decided to make straight for Cherbourg. We had good stocks of food and a third of our water supply still in the tanks. I headed east-northeast. Within sight of Guernsey, in the Channel Islands, the wind dropped to a flat calm! The gods still played with *Quiberon*.

For eight days we sat there, drifting back and forth on the strong Channel tides, as much as 25 miles east and west, as the tide flowed and ebbed into and out of the English Channel. At last, 10 miles north of Alderney, we found ourselves within hailing distance of a French trawler out of Cherbourg.

"*Bonjour, M'sieurs!*" shouted the skipper, leaning out of the wheelhouse, as his crew of four (two young boys and two old men) stared at us, bemused. I left the talking to Jean-Pierre.

"*Bonjour, Capitaine!* Where are you going? Can you give us a tow toward Cherbourg?"

"Where have you come from?" the skipper shouted through his cupped hands, as he gazed at the ravaged hull of *Quiberon*.

"Cayenne, Guiana, by way of the Azores!" Jean-Pierre hollered.

I heard it plainly over the calm, mirrorlike water from all five fishermen: "*Alors!*"

They threw a line over but it fell into the sea. "*Putain!*" they cursed in unison.

Jean-Pierre fell on deck to grab it over the side, out of the water.

"*Leave* it, Jean-Pierre." I called. "Leave his line; don't touch it! I want no claims for salvage. Throw him our line, but first fix a price with him."

"How much will you charge to haul us into Cherbourg, M'sieur?" shouted Jean-Pierre.

"Ah, nothing. I'll tell you what, *mes amis*—do you have any whisky on board?"

"I have two bottles of rum," I said (the only two unbroken bottles onboard).

"O.K., I'll tow you in at five knots for one bottle. It's only 18 miles." (French sailors use the *mile*, not the *kilometer*, which goes to show how unnatural the metric system is.)

"Done!" I gave him the thumbs-up sign. "Jean-Pierre, cast him the line!"

"*Bien sûr!*" he called as he heaved the line away.

And so we were pulled into Cherbourg on October 17, 1964—104 days after setting out from Cayenne. We had spent 99 days at sea, in a craft hardly fit for an afternoon's sail, with no engine and more than three weeks of wind over gale force. Our rate of pay, including the refit time in Cayenne, was $7 a day! With food, say $10 a day.

The name of the fishing boat which towed us in was *La Vie C'est Dure* (Life Is Hard). Very fitting, I thought.

We were met at the yacht club jetty by my old friend Marcel Bardiaux. Then, I telegraphed M. Pinet, the owner of *Quiberon*, news of our arrival, made arrangements for the yacht-club attendants to pump his boat out every day, and accompanied Jean-Pierre to the railway station to see him off for Brest.

"You'll get your money in the mail this week, Jean-Pierre. If you don't, telegraph me at the yacht club and I'll make sure you do. If that bastard Pinet doesn't cough up, I'll come back to Cherbourg and personally sink that bloody floating death trap!"

Jean-Pierre laughed. "Tristan, you are absolutely crazy, but . . . " He didn't finish, just grinned.

"So long, Jean-Pierre; I couldn't have done it without you. I'd sail with you anywhere, anytime, but as sure as hell not in bloody *Quiberon!*"

The train left, headed for Brittany, and I returned to the yacht club, where Marcel had arranged a small room for me to sleep in while I waited for the local boatyard to take charge of *Quiberon*. M. Pinet made arrangements to pay me in Spanish pesetas on my arrival in Barcelona. It seemed to be, after all, only a currency "fiddle."

Marcel Bardiaux, about 13 years before, had made a west-about circumnavigation of the world in a home-built 31-footer, the famous *Les 4 Vents*, by way of the Horn—the "wrong way" around the Horn, against winds and currents. His sloop capsized twice when approaching that lonely, wild cape-island. His adventures are described in his excellent book, *4 Winds of Adventure*, which he had published four years earlier, in '61. Marcel was a dark, broody-looking man, with a hungry stare but a great sense of humor.

Next day, as we sat in the Cherbourg Yacht Club, gazing through the wide windows at the rain whistling in a high wind across the gray, cold harbor, he described how he had smashed into an uncharted reef 65 miles out to sea from Nouméa, New Caledonia, in the South Pacific, and how he had kedged *Les 4 Vents* off the cruel, jagged reef by walking out with his anchor over the smashing surf for days on end. When he finally got her off, by the strength of his arms, he had sailed the boat to Nouméa, passing 27 wrecked craft on the way in! When he arrived in the tiny, hot, tropical port, it was with his decks awash and the boat almost sunk.

I stayed with Marcel for a week or so, exchanging yarns and looking over the new ketch he was building, a large, comfortable 60-footer, and meeting his friends. I was so anxious to get back to *Cresswell* and Nelson that I decided against a quick trip to England. I bade *adieu* to Marcel and made my way back to Toulouse.

As I got out of the taxi on the bridge of the boat basin, Nelson saw me and, throwing his head in the air, whoofing, hobbled slowly up to me. I dropped my seabag and fondled his neck while he wagged his tail like a young puppy. I took Nelson into an *estaminet* for some bock beer, which he loved, but I could see by the way he was bumping into things that his one good eye was not so good anymore.

The barman, a cocky sod, said to me: "That dog's a nuisance. I don't want him in here."

"*À ton face, crapaud!* Up your arse, Jack!"

We turned round and walked out, slamming the door.

Nelson looked up at me, his black ears twitching, and I could see that his good eye was much duller than it had been. He wagged his tail as we walked back onboard in the rain.

"Don't you take any notice, old son. We'll soon be in the sun and sailing the sea again." I tickled his ear. "Want some burgoo, boy?"

As soon as he heard the word "burgoo," he brightened up. I unlocked the companionway hatch and in a few minutes had a good pot of the gooey mess steaming away. All the while his tail waved and wagged, bumping the ladder and the stove, and I cursed the barman, thinking of the time Nelson had saved my life on the trip to Iceland, and how he had stuck by me through thick and thin, and guarded *Cresswell* so faithfully while I was away.

"Well, my old mooch," I said to him, as he scoffed the burgoo eagerly, "it looks like you haven't got long to go." I tickled his ear again. There was a scab on the back of his head and he was drooling. "But by Christ we'll have another sail before you pack off—and get some of the Mediterranean sunshine." Again, his tail wagged.

That evening I went to M. DuPont's house. Dod was ill and in the hospital in England; Joe had completed the repairs to DuPont's boat and had returned home to the Isle of Man; and *Cresswell* was the only non-French boat in Toulouse. During November I delivered M. DuPont's boat, now more ship-shape than ever, to Marseilles, along with Nelson, then returned to *Cresswell*.

After Christmas I started the slow voyage down the rest of the Canal du Midi, so as to arrive on the Mediterranean coast in the spring of '65. From there I would sail to Barcelona and pick up the money due for the *Quiberon* delivery. There was no rush, so I took my time getting *Cresswell* ready.

The first stage of the tedious canal trip was to Villefranche, a small town about 25 miles south of the city. It was tedious because, after the first novelty of chugging along the narrow, poplar tree-lined waterway, as straight as an arrow, it became monotonous. However, even in February the weather was fine and sunny, and I looked over the fields and low, vine-planted hills to the east and saw the snow-covered Pyrenees in the far distance.

On the second day, after an evening at the canalside *estaminet* at Villefranche, I headed for Castelnaudary, a town on the main road route from Paris to Spain. Just outside the town is a wide basin in the canal and set in the middle of the basin is a little green island. As *Cresswell* chugged into this basin, with wild ducks flitting across the water and the Pyrenees shining to the southwest, in sunshine and warmth, I made up my mind to stay for a week or so.

I walked into town, met some of the people in the bars, and found the place crowded with lasses from all over Europe, studying French at the local college. What with the friendly, hospitable people, their good sense of humor, their superlative cooking, their fine wines, and the peculiarities of the sex ratio, I decided to stay moored up to the island and let the canal world pass me by (at the rate of one or two barges per day). I heard the song of the sirens and *loved* it.

One good thing about being in paradise: you don't see, or even think of, snags until they crop up. So it was with me, and for two whole months I worked desultorily onboard during the day, making good the ravages of twelve months' neglect. In the evening I wallowed in the fleshpots of a fair-sized French provincial town. It was one of the happiest, most carefree periods I have known. There was no indication at all that doomsday was near.

The only *navigateur* I met at Castelnaudary was an English naturalist who was canoeing through the canal system of France. Except for some imported nuts, he was actually living off the land—collecting different kinds of grasses and leaves and making very good salads. The diet seemed to have done a good job because this gentleman was one of the toughest, fittest men I ever clapped eyes on. He was an excellent raconteur and hated Freud and Hegel, so we're birds of a feather.

During the day I worked on the boat, the sails, or the engine, taking Nelson with me for a sedate walk to the pub at the main crossroads in the evening. There I chatted with the locals for an hour or two over Pernod, then went to the restaurant for a fine meal, rendered with the simple elegance found only in that part of the world. On Saturdays and Sundays some local acquaintances came out to visit us. There were a couple of lads who sailed small dinghies on the canal basin, and I helped them repair their boats and tried to improve their sailing. Twice I took trips on the fast train to Paris, to look up friends, but always I longed to be back in Castelnaudary, amid the peace and quiet, with the fish leaping in the evening and the ducks' dawn flapping the tall trees rustling overhead in the gentle breezes, the church bell tolling on the quiet evenings, and the massive Pyrenees gleaming—silver in the dawn, gold in the evening—across the clear-air vineyards of the Aude. So the quiet spring passed.

Suddenly and irrevocably, this crystal-pure Nirvana, this sailor's dream, this hard-earned oasis of peace was shattered into a thousand fragments.

It was early, early. Outside the fields and the grassy canalside walk were soggy with dew like tiny diamonds, scattered over green baize, and rain clouds broke now and then to let the sun touch the Pyrenees. *Cresswell* rocked gently as a slow barge pushed through the calm waters of the basin, toting her cargo of Algerian wine from the bustling jetties of Marseilles.

Down below, all was quiet. Nelson was sleeping in his usual place, just forward of the saloon table. I was embraced with a cozy little friend, in hot sweet breath and blankets, while on the cabin table the bottom inch of the wine in last night's bottle shimmered in the pale-dawn light.

"I say there! *Cresswell!* Ahoy! Come along, Tristan, shake a leg. Shake a jolly old leg there!"

I stirred heavily.

"Come *along*, theah!" A loud bang on the doghouse roof. "Wakey-wakey!" Thump! Thump!

I opened one eye. Nelson was balanced with his forefoot against the companionway ladder, growling.

"Come along, my jolly hearty!" The voice was piercing.

"*Qu'est-ce qu'il y a?*" I asked my friend.

"*C'est rien, mon petit chou, c'est rien. Dors-tu!*" I nestled close.

"Hullo theah, h'loo theah! Tristan! Tristaaaaaan!" Another bang on the doghouse.

I woke and shouted: "*Qu'est-ce qu'il y a?*"

"Tristan, old bean, it's *me*. Cecilia St. John. You know . . . I met you in Antigua, back in July lawst yeah!"

"*Nom de Dieu!*" whispered the little cabbage.

"Oh shit!" said I, clambering out of bed and donning my trousers. "Bloody, flaming, satanic, bleeding, goddam, fucking *hell!*"

"*Quoi?*" my little rose asked.

"*C'est rien du tout. Attends!* It's nothing. Wait!"

I clambered up the ladder, opened the hatch door, and peered out, eyes full of sleep, into the gray drizzle of the morning, with the trees of France weeping at my fate. Standing there with brogued feet thrust apart, a dirty gray raincoat over a herringbone tweed skirt well down to her calves, her ginger hair drooping and dripping under a soggy English district nurse's brimmed hat, complete with bedraggled partridge feather at halfmast, her crabapple cheeks shining with the threat of rosy health, was Sissie, the bishop of Southchester's sister. In one hand she was holding a great leather explorer's traveling bag and in the other, streaming with rain, a tennis racket, a folded umbrella, and a hockey stick.

"Hello, Sissie. *Comment ça va?*" My surprise was so complete that I could not think of the English greeting.

"What-o, old chap, lovely day *what?* Had a *ghastly* ride down. Got a lift with a little Frenchman, *terribly* boring. He couldn't speak a *blawsted* word of English and he couldn't understand my French. But then I'm not surprised, neither can I—what, old chap? But Tristan, my *deah*, how *are* you?"

She was coming onboard! Those great brown brogue boots were actually on *Cresswell's* deck. She was dripping her way down the ladder. I fell or staggered back, into the cabin, as her beige-stockinged legs clomped into the cabin, like a medieval baron descending dank stone stairs to visit deep dungeons. Sissie slammed her great leather bag on the cabin deck, where it subsided like a tired, wet rhinoceros, then slung her racket and hockey stick down on my berth.

Ma petite choute jumped up with a cry of astonishment at the violence of Sissie's throw. Her fragile, doll-like, silky-smooth arms, her golden hair, her canto shoulders, her dove-feather throat, her kitten-cuddling breasts, her Dresden tummy, the winking eye of her delicious, delicate navel—all revealed as she threw her hands in the air and grabbed at me, shouting "*Au secours, mon amour!*" Then she turned around, terrified, to stare at Sissie, the British country woman compleat, looking like Florence Nightingale at the storming of the Alma Redoubt, like Mrs. Gladstone receiving one of the Grand Old Man's Piccadilly stragglers, like Britannia, the terrible Queen of the Sea herself, awful in the majesty of wrath, the revenge of Boadicea in her dagger-steel blue eyes—to see Sissie gazing at her as Queen Victoria would have gazed at a loose toilet roll in the Windsor Castle music room.

I cringed in the tiny space between the kerosene stove and the potato locker, upsetting the pan of bacon-burgoo, which slithered down the bulkhead. Nelson, petrified, stared dimly through his good eye, while the underwear of *ma petite choute*, like the drooping shirts of the defeated, abject Burghers of Calais, dangled in disgrace from the top of the navigation table. In the awful silence, even *Cresswell* seemed to tremble with shame before the accusing eye of the Dragon of Devon.

Sissie broke the silence, her bayonet-sharp tones cutting the calm morning of the Aude clear to the Pyrenees.

"Tristan, I think this little expedition needs some *moral support*, so I'm joining you." Her teeth looked as strong and white as the Cliffs of Dover gleaming through a Channel fog.

"Awfter awl!" she continued, eyeing my companion, who stood shivering naked, "Awfter awl, you *did* invaite me, you know!" She plonked herself on the berth, heavily, her umbrella at shoulder arms.

The honeymoon was over. Paradise was lost. Irretrievably, immutably, irrevocably. The English had arrived all right and with a vengeance!

Nelson whimpered.

Sur le pont, d'Avignon,
L'on y danse, l'on y danse.
Sur le pont, d'Avignon,
L'on y danse, tout en ronde!

[On the bridge of Avignon
   everyone dances all around!]

Old French Provençal song

13

Une Vignette Française

In a flash *ma petite choute*, half dressed, was off the boat and scampering across the fields back to Castelnaudary. The British lioness, in complete command of the galley, was making tea, frying eggs and bacon, delving into her monstrous leather bag for Keiller's marmalade (in the *correct* Scottish stone jars), throwing out the wicked penis-shaped scrunchy loaves of French bread, and smearing her New Zealand dominion butter over dry, gray, flat, Scottish breakfast biscuits —all the while looking as if Hanging Judge Jeffreys had sent her personally to negate the rights of man. Nelson and I waited, quiescent and trembling, for the coming storm.

"Friend of yours?" asked Sissie, trying to sound nonchalant.

"Er . . . yes. She was stuck . . . Gave her a bed for the night . . . teaching her English. Nice lass, in the local Girl Scouts, sort of . . . you know."

"One egg or two?" she demanded sharply.

"Two, please."

"Mmm . . . Tea? How many lumps?"

"Two, please."

"Known her long?"

"Well, she's the daughter of the canal supervisor, and . . . well, he went off for the weekend with his missus to Paris and, well . . . like . . . I said I'd keep an eye on her for them."

"Oh, Tristan, how *sweet* of you. I'm sure they *do* appreciate your concern for theah little gel!"

"Oh, I'm sure that Pierre does; he's a good bloke." I patted Nelson.

"Mmm, yes. Well, we must get this perfectly *filthy* galley gear cleaned up, and *then* I'll sort out these *ghastly* shelves. Look, you've curry and mustard, and . . . Oh, dear! What *is* this doing heah?" She dragged out a grease-begrimed French porno book from behind the recipe clippings.

"That should be in the navigation locker," I mumbled.

"Yes, I should *jolly well* think it *should* be."

She slapped my plate down in front of me—a tin plate I had never used to date, having (in my happy solitude) always eaten out of the pan. Just as I picked up my fork there was a knock on the doghouse roof.

"Hello!" I shouted. "Come on down. *Entrez-vous!*"

Pierre, the canal supervisor, a heavy, jolly bachelor of 40, clattered down the ladder, then raised his eyebrows in the Gallic way at the sight of Sissie standing there, an egg in her talon. But Sissie was all smiles as she gazed at the newcomer: a roused panther observing an unwary water buffalo.

"*Bonjour, M'sieur* Tristan!"

" '*Jour,* Pierre" I waved my fork. "This is Sissie. She's . . . English."

Pierre frowned across the bridge of his nose, a fleeting expression which spoke volumes.

"Er . . . she's the sister of . . . a . . . a bishop." I screwed up one eye, then raised the eyebrow.

In a twinkling Pierre recovered from the blow and, in the charming Midi way, took her hand gently and bowed. Momentarily, Sissie looked like the *Titanic*, about to sink. Then quickly she rallied.

"Pierre?"

"*Oui, Madame,* zat iz me," he announced in English.

"Then you must be the canal supervisah?" Sissie brayed, smiling at him.

"Oh yes, I 'ave ze verry important work for ze canal."
Pierre drew himself up, as full of piss and importance as only
a French *fonctionnaire* can be.

"How does your waife laike Castelnaudary, *M'sieur?*" asked
Sissie, sweetly.

He turned on a Dreyfus-look of injured innocence.

"Oh, but *Mam'selle*, I am not mareed. I 'ave ze girl friend, *oui,
mais* one understands it ees nozzing serious, *pas encore* . . . "

"Really? *Tea?*" bellowed Sissie, glaring at me, while I tried to
hide behind the mountain of burned bacon on my plate.
Pierre took the opportunity to escape up the ladder.

"Really?" she repeated, quietly to herself, as she refilled my
cup. "And what about that *ghawstly* hound, Tristan? What *do*
you feed it?"

"He'll take a bit of bread and bacon, if there's some left," I
said, looking her right in the eye.

She put some bacon on another tin plate, tore up bits of
bread and leaned down to offer it to Nelson, who shrank
from her, snarling.

"Come on, there's a *good* doggie," she cooed.

Nelson growled and snapped at her hand, and she jumped
back, spilling the bacon and bread all over the galley floor.
Nelson stood up, shook himself, then slowly, insolently,
turned his back and crept up the ladder.

"He's got your card marked!" I chortled, grinning at her.

She banged the frying pan, skillet, and kettle, all purposely
kept grimy with the patina of a thousand cooked breakfasts
(to preserve the flavor) into the wash bucket and scrubbed
away at them.

"You know, Siss, it's a bit off, you turning up like this out of
the blue. How did you know I was here?" I lit a Gauloise.

"Oh, I met this little cheppie at an ex-service club in London—*ghawstly* place, full of the most *dreadful* types. It was their
annual Eighth Army dinnah, you see, dahling. Awl sorts of
odd bods swanning around, you see. Awl these sort of ex-
sergeant majahs, in the most *awful* ready-made suits, and
their wives. My *deah*, it was like a kind of *bingo* parlor, and they
awl had these perfectly *primitive* flowery frocks and plastic

hair-dos and looked like Mrs. Khrushchev. I mean to say, dahling, *reahlly!* Of course the majah—he reahlly is a perfect *dahling*. You know, been in that sort of glorified caretaker's job evah since he fell orf the roof of Kensington Barracks, pretending to be an *aeroplane*. Of course he was *dreadfully* kind to me, but I must say I did feel rather like a sort of *countess* languishing in the *Bastille*. And then I met this *funny* little man, *dreadfully* sweet—works as a bargee on the docks or something—and *he* knew your friend Dod Orsborne."

"He would."

"Yes, my deah. Anyway, the majah and I had a glawss or two of bubbly, you see, whilst we tried to avoid awl these sort of *suburbanites* from stepping on our toes and spilling that perfectly *awful* beer over us, and of course as soon as he told me he knew where *Dod* was, well, my deah, I just *flew* by cab to St. George's hospital, and found the old boy."

"How was he?"

"What a *fantastic* cheppie, ebsolutely *supah!* He was sort of holding *court* around his bed, with hundreds of nurses and people absolutely *milling* around, listening to his adventures."

"That sounds like Dod, all right."

"Oh yes, dahling, and everyone was simply *dying* to heah more, of course. But my good friend Millicent, who's the matron in charge . . . Oh, my pet, what a perfect *bitch* she is. Well, she soon had awl these sort of little Irish and Jamaican hussies absolutely *flying* around emptying bedpans and dusting the bandages, or whatever it is they do in those *dreadful* places."

"So Dod told you I was here, did he?"

"Ectuahly no, dahling. When I awsked him about you he sort of felt my stocking (oh, my deah, how *sweet*, at that age; almost on his lawst gawsp) and told me you were sort of moored against a wine warehouse in Toulouse. So of course I mustered up the jolly old kit-bag, *flew* down to Fortnum and Mason's, talked them into putting this jolly lot"—she nodded her frizz toward the elephantine explorer's bag, bulging with all kinds of food—"these bally *vittels*, on deah Willy's account, then orf I trotted to Victorloo Station. What a *horrifying* place that is, my deah. And then I absolutely *tripped* over the shoe-shine, almost *fell* into that *dreadful* green-painted station mawstah's office and, *reahlly,* dahling, simply *rushed* over to Toby's desk. What an ebsolute *pet* he is."

"Toby?"

"Oh, my deah, of course you don't know him; he was in the Guards with *dahling* Willy, simply chasing those *awful* Germans awl over the jolly old desert, you know, Victorlah Cross and awl that. Anyway, he's assistant station mawstah now, or at least that's where he recovers from his late nights at Boodles. Some sort of *dreadful* chorus girl. Oh, *poor deah* Toby . . . But Tristan dahling, I mustn't gossip, must I?"

"No." I rose to give Nelson some of the scraped-up burgoo. "So how did you find me?"

"Well, of course I caught the Golden Arrow train, which simply *whizzed* to Paris . . . And those *awful* taxi drivers, such dreadful *peasants,* my deah. And a simply *awful* row at the Gare Austerlitz with this *beastly* fellow, waving his arms about and simply *screaming* at me . . ."

"So what did you do?"

"Well, my deah, what on earth *could* I do? I sloshed him with the jolly old hockey stick, and my pet, you should have seen the *gendarmes* blowing whistles, with their capes, *képis,* and simply *huge* batons. It was *supah,* until this charming little inspector tootled along and sort of frog-marched me to the train. And you see, dahling, I didn't have a *cent* in my bag, only poor dahling *sweet* Toby's train ticket, and I met this perfectly *supah first-class* French motor-car salesman, with his *ghastly* sistah, and he treated me to an ebsolutely *febulous* dinnah. But of course he was playing the old game, you know."

"Sissie! You didn't . . ."

"Oh, of course not, you *funny* old thing. I mean I'm a big girl now, after awl, and he *had* seen my hockey stick." She picked it up and swiped at the clean towel she had hung in the galley. The crack was violent enough to rock the boat.

"*Then* what?"

"Oh, he was practicing his English and awl thet jolly rot."

"So what did you do?"

"Well, naturally dahling, I pretended to be Finnish, and this simply *low* bitch of a sistah actually knew a few words in that dreadfully *obscure* lingo, you see. Awfully embarrassing."

She grabbed the towel and started wiping the pots.

"And then?"

"Well, thank Gawd, they alighted at some ebsolutely *hovel-ridden* spot and thet was the lawst I saw of them, but I had a perfectly *delightful* grimace at his sistah. What a *bore!* Dahling, you've reahlly no *ideah!*"

"And?"

"I arrived at Toulouse at 2 o'clock in the morning. It was simply *pouring* down and this perfect *angel* of a portah put me up in a sort of dosshouse, and when I saw myself in the looking glawss . . . Well, my pet, I was a downright *fright*, and all these perfectly *sweet* little cheppies were making cawfee and those *dreadful* sort of sticky buns."

"*Croissants.*"

"Whatevah. And dahling, they were *practically* at my feet."

"Really?" said I, staring at her great brown brogues. "Well, now you're here, what are you going to do?"

"Oh Tristan, *dahling*, I do *so*—reahlly, honestly—want to sail to Spain! I means it's so dashed *interesting*. And you know, with my brother Willy a bishop, an *Anglican* bishop, it's ticklish you see. Cetholic countries and awl thet jolly rot. And I'm perfectly *ambitious* to sail the Mediterranean."

"But Sissie, how are you going to support yourself? I mean it all costs money: food, fuel. All the rest of it."

"Yes, I know; what an awful *bore*. But you see, my pet, I get my quarterly allowance in June, and then I can pay you back every penny. Say a guinea a day?"

"A guinea a day? Make it 22 shillings, lass, and you're on."

"*Dahling!*" She grabbed my hand and almost shook my arm out of its socket.

"But where are you going to sleep?" I asked, recovering.

"Oh, anywhere, old top. You know, I'm simply *used* to roughing it. Why, when I was on the trans-Sahara expedition, with awl those simply *peasanty* people mooching around in the night . . ."

I didn't let her finish. "Well, I'll tell you what I'll do. I'll give you the forward dodger. It's almost empty, except for some rope and tackle, spare sails, and all that. It's completely separated from the rest of the boat. You can doss in there. Do the shopping, look after the galley, and keep out of my way, for Christ's sake, when I'm working. And . . ."

Her freezing blue eyes were shining. "Oh Tristan, *dahling!* And *what?*"

"Don't feed Nelson."

"Of course not, pet."

"And Sissy, don't ever let me hear you call him a 'hound' again!"

She seized my thin shoulders in a grip which would have killed Ghengis Khan, gave me a dry, vinegary kiss under my left ear, and danced off clumsily, singing to herself: "Oh, a laife on the ocean wave, a home on the rolling deep!" Her hair, now dried out, looked like caulking spunyarn.

Nelson padded down the ladder, staring at her. "Jesus Christ!" I said to him softly. "What *have* we let ourselves in for?" Nelson seemed to raise the brow over his good eye and sigh.

So Sissie, the bishop of Southchester's sister, moved her great leather-kit bag, umbrella, tennis racket, and hockey stick into the forward dodger—a minute, triangular space no longer than four and a half feet, three and a half in width, with a height of about two feet eight inches.

In order not to seem inhospitable, I gave her the old seal-oil lamp, which could burn French cooking oil, so that she could delve into her Bible when she was not diving into her gin bottles, six of which clinked away as she unloaded the sinister leather bag forward of the bulkhead.

The following day, Pierre, the canal supervisor, came onboard early for the trip to Carcassonne. He had promised to help me on this leg, but when he stepped onboard and saw Sissie, it was clear that he was not sure that he did not regret his promise. He brought cheese and sausage with him, which we ate between Sissie's severe Scots biscuits. Pierre and I shared a bottle of wine and Sissie was as faithful as ever to her Booth's Dry London Gin.

It was a beautiful sunny day, with the air clear and fresh as only the air of the Aude can be. The trip was a steady chug—when we were not laboring at opening and shutting the lock gates. Eventually, rounding a bend, we saw before us, stretched out on a long rolling green hill, the fairytale fortress of Carcassonne, built during the Arab invasion of France in the Middle Ages. It was a staggering sight: great long rosy-pink curtain walls, with delicate-looking turrets strung along the ramparts, and flags and pennants flying from the main keep.

"When we get to Carcassonne," said Pierre, "my cousin iz coming down to ze jetty to take uz for ze ride into town. 'E 'as a restaurant zere. We 'ave ze *Cassoulet Carcassonnais, hein?*"

"Right, *mon ami*, you're on."

Sissie, standing on the foredeck, muscles heaving, fuzzy ginger hair frightening all the peaceful cows on the canal bank, looked like the games mistress from one of those English finishing schools where the windows are always open. Porridge, Cicero, kippers and cold tea for breakfast; "Fight the Good Fight" querulously sung in the drafty assembly hall; Plotinus, beef stew and dumplings for lunch, hockey in the rain, sticky buns and tea at 5 o'clock; a cold-water bath; cold lamb cutlets in the freezing dining room; "Jerusalem" belted out, shivering; then off to bed, girls, and quick about it!

As we emerged from a moss-lined, ancient, wine-colored brick tunnel into the meadows again, the bright sun shining behind the dark, sturdy shadow of the games mistress, Pierre squinted up at her. He seemed baffled in the presence of this representative of the *fourth* sex. Why, he wondered, had an empire been flung for them from the snowy heights of Everest to the burning sands of the Kalahari; why, for them, had men smashed their way through the bitter strength of watery wastes and defied the turn of the world itself? Pierre was confused, mystified. French *savoir-faire* and *sang-froid*, Gallic courtesy, charm, the *bon mot* and the *mot juste*—the veneer of a civilization imposed, absorbed, acted upon and reflected for more than a thousand years was utterly vanquished in the presence of this daughter of perfidious Albion.

She stood there, feet apart, electric ginger hair subduing the wind itself, North Sea eyes glinting, a figurehead which would have made the dragon bows of King Harald Fairhair's longships turn and run back to the icy fjords of the northland in panic and shattered defeat. As for the Arab foragers of Carcassonne, they would surely have pleaded to kiss the cross at one slight flutter of Sissie's jibsail.

We tied up at the jetty and piled into Pierre's cousin's *deux chevaux* Renault, a most peculiar kind of auto with a corrugated aluminum body. It seemed to be continually moving on its knees, as indeed it did whenever we attempted to ascend any gradient greater than one inch in a mile.

Pierre's cousin, Antoine, was a lively man of about 30 with five interests in life: his kids, food, sex, rugby, and politics. He talked very fast in his Midi accent, mainly about the inequities of the French tax system since de Gaulle had taken power. Antoine was a *pied noir*, a "black foot," as the ex-colonials who had been thrown out of Algeria after independence were called. His family, which had lived in that country for 130 years, had been displaced by the abject (to them) surrender of the country to the Algerians by General de Gaulle. Antoine hated him. I have never known a head of state who was hated as much as de Gaulle was hated in the Midi at that time—not even in South America, where the worst types of tyrants are sometimes in ruthless power. If Antoine had met de Gaulle's car on that road, he told me, he would ram it at full speed.

I changed the subject to rugby, for Antoine's loud, rough language was too much even for Sissie's bull-like ears, though she must have had a job to pick up his Midi *patois*.

We entered the town, a jumble of medieval houses and twisting, cobbled lanes. It was a startling contrast to see people in modern, twentieth-century clothes and cars in a stage setting for a medieval romance play.

Antoine's restaurant was spotless and well run. The meal was enormous and delicious: a great steaming *cassoulet* as the centerpiece and crispy, juicy, tender hanks of venison strung on a rail to one side. We made short work of the whole table, wine and all, while Sissie contented herself with a green salad bowl, so overflowing it looked like the hanging gardens of Babylon smothered in French dressing. We toasted *la République.* The French drank a health to Her Majesty *la Reine d'Angleterre.*

After dinner, with everyone merry as spring sparrows, the children were ushered in, all soaped, combed, brushed and shipshape, to greet *les Anglais.* It was immediately obvious that all five of Antoine's interests in life had been seriously indulged. The food was splendid, the children were robust, well clothed, intelligent-looking, pretty; and there were *seven* of them. Their ages seemed to be from about 13, a lad, to a tiny boy tot of three or so. Like all French children of the middle class, they were delightful to others, if not among themselves. The four boys shook hands. The three lasses curtseyed and smiled daintily.

I sang to them, in literally translated French, *It's a Long Way to Tipperary,* and everyone, kids and adults, demanded an encore. Sissie took a shine to Martin, three years old, a bonny little chap who with his golden blond hair, blue-blue innocent eyes, and cherubic face looked like Gainsborough's boy in the painting "Boy in Blue."

Sissie, for once in her life actually changing into a female-female, hoisted little Martin onto her thick, brown-beige-stockinged knee, so that the spiky hairs of her tweed skirt scratched the little lad's bottom, making him squiggle. After several minutes of cooing and cuddling, he longed to get away. Sissie said to him in her English-finishing-school French: "If you are a *good* boy you will become the president of France. Imagine that, the president of France, just like General de Gaulle!"

Martin, struggling to get away, kicked her shin "unintentionally." Then he said in his sweet, piping, lisping voice, but loudly: *"Moi, je n'aime pas ce générale* (I don't like that general)."

"Oh dear, why not?"

Martin turned his curly head, looked straight at her with his innocent blue eyes, and chirped, *"Si les cons peuvent voler, il est le capitaine d'escadrille!* (If cunts could fly, he'd be the squadron leader!)"

There was a momentary hush in the crowded restaurant. The air was still; forks halted, frozen midway 'twixt plates and mouths. Sissie gawped, horrified, eyes bulging like the Medusa of the Midi. Then suddenly the whole restaurant burst into raucous laughter and loud cheers.

I treated little Martin to a big, big sherbet.

As I walked out one evening, all on a summer's day,
I spied a little frigate-ship a-passing by my way,
I hoisted up my signal, which she so quickly knew,
And when she saw my bunting she immediately hove to-oo-oo.

Chorus: *She had a dark and roaming eye,*
         And her hair hung down in ringlets,
         She was a nice girl, a proper girl, but,
         One of the roving kind!

Sailor's song (early nineteenth century)

14

Messing About in Boats

It was well into the evening when we left *Chez Antoine*—Sissie, Pierre, Antoine, and I. As we pulled out of the parking lot, Antoine suddenly stopped the ancient Renault—with the bow projecting halfway across the busy road, and extricated himself. In a flash he was back, wheeling a rusty bicycle with cobwebs on the wheel spokes and straw sticking out from inside the saddle.

"*Regarde*, Tristan, he geev you zees," explained Pierre, puffing at the Caporal stuck between his teeth. "Eet come very good for you. You steer ze boat; *Mam'selle* Seesy, she get on ze bicycle and go ahead fast to open *l'écluse* (the lock), and *poof!* When ze boat arrive, ze lock she is open, *non?*"

"I say, what an ebsolutely *smashing* ideah!" wheezed Sissy, crunched in the minute back seat and surrounded by parcels of food moulded by *Madame* Antoine, dog hairs from Nelson (who was moulting), and a distinct aroma of Booth's Dry London gin. She was busily rubbing her shin, where darling *sweet* little Martin had struck home. She reached over and patted Pierre's shoulder. "Well *done*, old chep. Ebsolutely *splendid* ideah," she said.

Pierre winced with the blow, which shook his cigarette from his lips, sending him, with a muttered *Merde!* groveling for it in the toy- and lollipop-stick-littered lower reaches of

151

the Renault relic.

When Pierre recovered his *sang-froid*, he aked me: "Ow you like zees, Tristan?"

"Great! All I need now, Pierre, is a wheelbarrow and a walking stick with a wheel on it."

We all got out and helped Antoine to secure the cycle to the car roof, using my belt and Antoine's suspenders. Sissie squealed and pranced around, to the curiosity of half the population of Carcassonne, who had gathered around making remarks. *"Putain!" "Sacré bleu!" "Ma foi!"* The men stared at Sissie's thick, beige-stockinged legs; their wives peered, bemused, at her great brown brogues and unkempt hair, the color of sunlit whisky.

With a cry from our English games mistress, "Home, James, and don't spare the horses!" a muttered *"Merde!"* from Antoine and Pierre, and subdued "Jesus Christ!" from me, we were off, rattling our way along the cobbled streets of the medieval town, me thinking about Childe Harold coming to the dark tower and Charlemagne triumphantly clopping along on his giant white charger, surrounded by paladins and pomp, palatines and palaver. Suddenly the dystrophic Renault rumbled into a pothole with a bone-shaking jerk and jolted me back into the twentieth century. Inside the car, the air was so thick with the smoke of Gauloise and Caporal cigarettes (together with the whiff of Sissie's favorite perfume, Booth's London Dry gin), you could have cut it in blocks, wrapped it up, and sent it to your old grannie in Donegal.

Back at the boat, with Nelson observing the proceedings from under one raised eyebrow, Sissie quickly laid out tea, biscuits, and beer in the cockpit, for it was a fine April evening. Then she disappeared to her lair forward, from whence came the distinctive clinking tones of her mystic alchemy. When she came back aft, her hair, unbelievably, was even more frizzy, her eyes even more like a gale-whipped Spithead Channel on a boisterous winter morning.

While we were unlashing the bicycle, the two Frenchmen and I had been loquacious. Now, as Sissie made her way back along the deck under the dim waterfront lights, shoulders hunched forward, the Frenchmen were struck dumb and stared at her shadow in trepidation. But Sissie was in fine fettle, and grasping the mizzen shrouds with one hand, as if she were strangling a peacock, and gin glass in the other hand, she gave forth, swaying like a bo'sun's mate off Cape Hatteras.

"Ceptain Tristan, dahling, an' *vooz, Messieurs, notre* . . . er . . . gallant allies. I wanna shing you a shong . . . for awl your kindness a *shplendid* evenin' end en ebsolutely *topping* dinnah . . . I'm going to shing . . . *Allons enfants de la patria, le jour de gloire est* . . . "

Her tuneless anthem got no further. Nelson, guarding the gangway just in front of her, suddenly roused on his forefoot, thrust his black head at her, and snarled. Sissie lost her balance and over she went, with a great splash.

We all peered outboard. She had grabbed the rubbing strake and was trying to haul herself back onboard. We reached down and, clutching her tweed jacket, rescued her. Then, grinning all over and smothered in blankets, she traipsed to her tiny compartment, gin glass still in hand.

When Pierre left with Antoine, who was driving him back to Castelnaudary, I went forward to see if Sissie was all right. I clambered halfway down the forward ladder and knocked on her bulkhead.

"Come!" she cooed.

I stepped down and, crouching low, peered inside the forepeak. I had not, until this minute, seen how she had nested in, and I was amazed. She had tied all the spare lines and sails shipshape on one side of her tiny space, leaving herself enough room to stuff her sleeping bag into a tiny tunnel about as big as a dog kennel. The Eskimo seal-oil lamp shimmered fitfully on the ship's side, above a religious calendar. She had hung a tatty bit of lace over the tiny porthole, and her leather bag lay against the great balk of the bowstem like a fat pasha leering in the gloom.

Her ginger hair quelled, her cheeks still rosy red (though by now I knew it wasn't only good health), Sissie was sitting and reading the Bible, her thick legs drawn up under her chin and dry blankets wrapped around her shoulders. She looked like Quasimodo, the Hunchback of Notre Dame, in his cubbyhole above the vaults and rafters of the cathedral. All the scene needed was a vampire bat and a black cat.

"How are you, lass?" I tried to sound nonchalant.

"Oh, *splendiferous*, Tristan my *deah!* Oh *bless* you. So jolly *thoughtful* and kaind!"

"Yes . . . er . . . Well, good night, Sissie."

"Good night, deah, *sweet* Tristan!" She waved one hand like a hunting hawk about to grab a fieldmouse.

"Good night, then."

"Quite. And what would you laike for brekky?"

"French bread and tomatoes."

"Oh . . ."

She was thinking about her miserable Scottish biscuits, as gray, flat, and cheerful looking as the stone flags outside the Presbyterian kirk in Gallowgate on a wet Sunday night in December.

"Very good, Skippah," she said quietly, in a tiny little girl's voice.

All was calm again in *Cresswell.* The ship's dog had made his point; the skipper had made his. Now the whole company knew their stations. God was in his heaven; all was right, again, with the world. Law, priorities, and the preordained order of velvet-gloved, iron-fisted command was reestablished. The voyage could proceed in good order. The sword scratch of Francis Drake, across the distant, windblown, lonely, cold sands of Tierra del Fuego, now reached into the nethermost backwater of the European canal system.

"You old bastard," I whispered to Nelson as I turned over and closed my eyes. He woofed softly, returning the sentiment.

From Carcassonne south, the Canal du Midi is a series of short stretches of poplar-lined straight ditches. The scenery is like something out of a fairytale, with green meadows reaching back to the blue distance of the foothills of the Pyrenees and little farm cottages, with red-tiled roofs, nestling among the olive trees. Every 30 yards or so was a rod fisherman, for in those days the canal was alive with trout and perch, and the country Frenchman is a great fisherman and hunter.

Sissie, to my relief, was off the boat and on the bicycle. She peddled furiously along the towpath, ginger hair flying, thick legs moving like piston rods, from one lock gate to the next. By the time *Cresswell* chugged up, the heavy gates would be open. The boat would glide into the ancient, hewn-stone basins as Nelson and I sat at the wheel in the sunshine, me lazily smoking as I steered with one foot, Nelson chewing a bone. Then, as we slid alongside, I would dawdle up to the mooring lines and chuck them to Sissie, who stood on the lockside at the ready, like an enthusiastic soccer goalkeeper, straining at the leash.

Catching the lines (she never missed), she looped the bow-line around the bollards. Then, at the double in the hot sun, she ran back to the entry gates, her sturdy, musclebound limbs flashing like an Olympic half-miler's, scaring all the piglets, chickens, and the octogenarian lockkeepers. She would grab the great, 60-pound lock key (a sort of spanner), shove it into the mechanism, and wind away like she was extracting all the worldwide Shell Oil deposits. In 30 seconds the massive lockgates swung shut, as if of their own cowardly volition, under the icy blue eyes of the English games mistress. Sissie then took off for the forward lock, with a regular one-two, one-two thumping step, conjuring visions of the Light Brigade making their dash to the relief of Talavera or the Spartans running to staunch the Persian flood at Thermopylae.

The lockkeepers, usually dressed in baggy blue jackets and jeans and smoking hand-made cigarettes, were mostly retired barge skippers. They had viewed the world along the canals with a cynical eye from Dresden to Marseille. Until now, they had imagined they'd seen everything, but they were flabbergasted at this performance. Sissie flashed by as if the honor of England were at stake. They stared as only a Frenchman can stare: mouth open and one eyebrow arched, as they followed her progress in the steaming noonday heat.

Arriving at the forward gate, Sissie would grab the key, then stand panting for a minute, until the *éclusier* had recovered and made his way to the water-inlet valves, shaking his head. Then he'd look at me and gaze again at the apparition, who by now was waving and cooing.

"Awl ready, Tristan dahling! I say, what cracking *fun!*"

She'd grin all over her face and kick one leg up, like a practicing ballet dancer, her short blue gym slip wet with sweat. When the lockkeeper would look again at me, I'd wink at him—a great, long, worldly wise wink. He'd shake his head and probably mutter to himslf: "*Merde alors! Les Anglais! Les Anglais!*"

For a couple of weeks we shoved on steadily, pausing only for lunch. Each morning I heard her heavy brogues clomping aft along the deck through the predawn mist. Rubbing her red, blistered hands against the early morning cold, she'd whisper to Nelson, keeping guard at the companionway: "I say, Nelson, old chappie, good morning! Good doggie!" Cozy and warm in my blankets, I'd hear Nelson softly growl, reluctantly shifting out of her way. They I'd turn over and sleep again, while Sissie crept around the galley like a poisoner preparing a stiff dose of strychnine, careful not to make the slightest noise lest the captain wake.

Each morning I rose to a sizzling hot breakfast, set out on the clean, blue-checkered tablecloth. (Blimey, I thought, when I saw Sissie take it out of her bag, what would Tansy say?) Then a shining knife, fork, and spoon and a steaming mug of tea, made in her china pot. Then she'd jump up the ladder, giving a last look to check on whether I'd let the breakfast go cold, and off she'd go, traipsing through the vineyards, damp with the early morning dew, to the village, six or seven miles away, to buy fresh supplies for the rest of the day.

Even at her galloping lope, the village was often far enough away to keep her off the boat for an hour or two. I tried to make sure of that when I chose the nightly resting halts. This gave me time to have my breakfast in peace and do a lot of work: chores on the engine, splicing broken lines, touching up scuffed paint, and a host of other maintenance jobs. I did this so she wouldn't see me working. Then I could maintain my pose of idling, lounging—a gentleman at leisure. That's the only thing that keeps Sissie's kind of person content, it appeared to me then.

. . . The further you get from England
The nearer you come to France . . .
So will you, won't you,
Will you, won't you,
Won't you join the dance?

From "The Lobster's Song"
(Lewis Carroll's *Alice in Wonderland*)

15

Dismasted Yet Again

One day Sissie came back wet through, caught in a shower. It was 7 o'clock and we were due to shove off at 7:30. Puffing, she unloaded 50 pounds of tomatoes, potatoes, grapes, flour, and other odds and sods into the food locker. She had lugged it all at a swift trot over a muddy field and through several thorny hedges.

"You're late," said I lighting a Gauloise. "What happened?"

"Oh Tristan dahling, it's such a terrific *bore*. I hobble along as fawst as evah I can, and sort of grab all the stuff I can lay my grubby hands on, and stuff them right under the shop-lady's nose, and simply *scream* at her that you're waiting and in an awf'ly terrible *rage*. But you know, my pet, they just stand and stare at me, and, well, when it comes to counting up the bill, well dahling, it's an *outrage*. It reahlly, simply is! It takes these dreadful, *ancient* peasants about an hour to count up to five, my deah. I've seen nothing like it since deah Daddy was in Baluchistan! It simply is—just a sec, dahling, tea coming up. Fresh milk or that *ghawstly* condensed stuff?—simply *awful*. Reminds we of that mucky, gooey glue we used to use in prep school."

"What happened?" I demanded.

"Well, actually nothing, except that I was waiting for this simply *shocking harridan* to count her miserable centimes and

159

sous and God knows what. Why is it, Tristan dahling, that these blawsted Continentals are so awf'ly slow at *counting?*"

"It's the metric system that does it, love. It stultifies part of their brains. They start thinking in 10s. The next thing they know, by the time they're eight years old, all they can do is count to 10, and that's it." I stirred my tea

"*Reahlly?*" She was hurriedly scrubbing the pots, pans, plates and cutlery, while the tablecloth was soaking in the new *plastic* bucket, waiting for her to rush-wash it before hanging it up to dry and dashing for her bicycle to start the grinding day at the nearest lockgate. "How very interesting!"

"Yes, Sissie, and what's more, the metric system—at least as far as linear measurements go—is based on an error."

"How so?"

"Well, you see, when the French revolutionaries figured out this load of codswallop, they based the meter on the idea that there were 10,000 kilometers between the Equator and the North Pole. That's 10 million meters, see?" I took a sip of tea.

"Mmm?"

"But the silly sods were mistaken, 'cause there ain't 10 million meters from the Line to the Pole. You see, Sissie, the world ain't like an orange. She ain't a round sphere, she's an oblate spheroid."

"Deah me," said Sissie, finishing the last plate and rushing for the tablecloth. "I *do* hope it's not catching!"

"Sort of round, sort of spherical, but flattened out top and bottom, see, and fattish at the Equator. That's because of the continual spin of the world, causing a centrifugal outward thrust of the molten-liquid rock core." I lit a cigarette.

"Reahlly?"

"Yes. So when the French figured out the meter, basing it on distance on the earth's surface, they were wrong. So the meter isn't really a meter. It's a bit shorter, in fact."

"Marvelous. That'll teach those dreadful upstarts—what, old chep?" She was busy rubbing away at the sudsy table-cloth, and Nelson glared at her as a fleck of soapy foam landed on his black, glossy back. "But what about our simply marvelous little *yard?* I mean to say, what's thet based on?"

"The bloody *truth*, girl! It's based on the distance between King Edward the Second's nose and the end of his forefinger. And it's been proved right, 'cause they exhumed the old bastard's skeleton a hundred years ago and checked it!" I took another swig of tea.

"But why *three* feet?"

"Because it's divisible into 12, and so is two, and four, and six. But what's divisible into 10?"

She thought for a minute. "Mm . . . two . . . and five . . ."

"And that's all, right?"

"Ebsolutely, my pet."

"Right. So which is the more *flexible* number?"

"Twelve."

"How many weeks in the month?"

"Four . . . which . . . Oh dahling, how terribly *clever* of me: it goes into 12!"

"How many degrees in a circle?" I asked flicking my cigarette ash.

"I've simply no ideah."

"Three hundred and sixty, again divisible by 12! How many minutes in a degree, in one hour of the sun's passage around the world? Sixty! How many seconds to a minute, or miles to a degree? Sixty!

"When it comes to distance and navigation, we don't use the metric system at sea, though of course some overclever sod will be sure to wangle it in for depths. Nature doesn't go in 10s, except for the number of fingers on an ape's paw, so he won't strain his brain trying to figure out a complicated concept like 12!

"The friggin' metric system chills the minds of children and puzzles peasants simply because it isn't *natural*, Sissie. The country folk still use the *douzaine*. Anything that isn't locked into nature and the process of the universe is *bad*. It cuts against the grain. Bureaucrats love the metric system: it breeds a race of morons who are incapable of dreaming up the question: Yes, but why?

"You see those tricky little twos and threes lurking there . . . and 16. What a beauty *that* one is!" I lit another Gauloise.

"But come on, gal, we've got work to do."

She dashed up the ladder, scrambled over the guardrail, rushed for the bike, and was off peddling, while Nelson and I sauntered up to the helm and into the early morning sunshine, me with my can of ready-made tea and Nelson with a bone. After I started the engine, we settled ourselves comfortably and were off for another 20-mile joyride, while the Dragon of Devon drove her panzer corps through another 10 of Cardinal Richelieu's heavy lock gates.

I allowed Sissie one short breathing spell in Narbonne, where, with her antique box camera slung around her neck and her Rhodesian infantryman's hat perched on her hair, she marched ashore—to the amazement and consternation of a dozen dockside loafers—to photograph the cathedral. She wanted to send deah Willy *pictyahs*. I waited, at a safe distance, to see her clomp away over the cobbles; then, leaving Nelson in charge, I struck out for a nearby pavement-bar to sip Pernod and watch the local talent pass by on its way to work—a constellation of stars.

We arrived at the Mediterranean end of the canal at Sète, a dreary place, consisting of a soulless town and two walls sticking into the sea. The wind on that coast in the month of May is hard; so we settled down to wait for a calm before raising the mast. It took four days, and when it came, Sissie was on one of her shopping expeditions. I decided to get the mast raised anyway, for I was anxious to reach Spain and the waiting pesetas. I had very little cash: just enough for supplies for the voyage to Barcelona, which Sissie was obtaining.

As soon as the wind dropped, I took a line ashore, to a far bollard. Then, with the aid of blocks stropped to the bollard, I slowly raised the mainmast. It was heavy work, but eventually I had the mast teetering in place, supported only by the fulcrum pin in the tabernacle at its foot and the long line ashore.

With the sea running into the harbor quite lively, I did not want to tie the long line from the masthead to the bollard, and so, as there was a gentleman observing me, I asked him to hold the line. This he could do easily for there was little strain on it, as it was passed around the bollard five times. He could hold it quite comfortably with one hand. He was an elderly, kind-faced gentleman, wearing a black beret and a raincoat against the cold.

"*M'sieur*," said I, holding out the line to him and pleading civilly, "will you please hold this line for me for two minutes?"

That was just long enough for me to step onboard, catlike, so as not to shake the mast, and drive the second pin into the tabernacle and the stout wooden wedges (with a copper British penny sandwiched between for luck) under the heel of the mast. Then it would be reasonably seized, until I could get the wire forestay rigged to the knighthead on the bow, and I could take my time rigging the shrouds. I was gloating over the prospect of getting the heavy job completed before Sissie got back. Otherwise, she might begin to think her presence was necessary.

The gentleman smiled and nodded. "*Mais certainement, M'sieur.*" He reached out a withered, ancient claw and took the line.

"Now," I said, still hanging onto the line, "Whatever you do, *M'sieur*, don't let go of the line until I call out to you. O.K.?"

"*Mais oui, M'sieur, bien sûr.*"

I relinquished my grip on the rope and made for the boat. Carefully stepping over the guardrail and creeping over the deck, I picked up the tabernacle pin. Just as I did, I saw a flash of movement out of one corner of my eye. It was Sissie, peddling back as fast as she could, about half a mile away. I determined to rush the job so she wouldn't have to help me. Nelson was near the gentleman, watching the line.

In went the pin with great hammer strokes. Then down I swung into the forward dodger hatchway to knock the wedges in, fishing around in my pocket for the penny. Hell! I murmured to myself (I couldn't find it) . . . "Blast it!" I started to knock the first wedge in; then, as I jerked myself out of the extremely dangerous way, the mast heel started to move forward. There was a groan, and a noise of slowly splintering wood. As I crouched to one side, horrified, there was a tremendous crash as the mainmast slammed down with all its weight on the doghouse roof.

Covered in wood dust and chips and gibbering to myself, I clambered shakily ondeck. The scene was chaotic. The mast lay with its head hanging over one side of the stern, its heel, foot, and stem split open like an egg whisk for one-third of its height.

Dazed, with bulging eyes, I turned to the jetty. The silly old bastard had let go of the rope to give Nelson a bleedin' biscuit!

I stood for a second or two, not believing my eyes, then sat down with a plonk on the shattered grabrail of the doghouse. Right at that moment Sissie clattered to a halt, cooing to the dog lover, "*Bonjour, M'sieur*, what an ebsolutely *spiffing* day!" I groaned.

She looked at me, then at the mast. "Oh deah, I say; what *awf'ly* rotten luck, old chep."

"Arr, pipe down!"

Brokenhearted, I make my way below, hardly able to see, and collapsed on the berth. But by the time the Dragon clomped onboard I had recovered enough to realize that I could not possibly rant and rave at a kindly old man. I couldn't blame Nelson: he was almost blind by this time; and one thing was sure: it was no fault of Sissie's. If anyone was to blame it was me; the fault was mine, fair and square.

I'd been a bastard with Sissie. I'd been too proud to let her help me, when she was not only willing but able to, and now I'd got my just desserts. Served me right! I wiped away the bitter mental tears and, as she unloaded herself of a hundredweight of supplies and sadly looked at me, grinned, elbows on the table, fists at my forehead.

"You're late," said I, "what happened?"

She dropped her bag as her district nurse's hat fell off, rushed to the table, grabbed a forearm, murmered "Oh, Tristan, *dahling* . . . !" and burst into great sobs.

"Now come on, Siss, there's work to do. So stick the kettle on—we'll 'ave a cuppa tea, then get started."

I forced her hand off my arm, but it took all the effort I could muster to do that and to get the words out.

Silence. Utter and complete, except for the low hiss of the stove under the kettle, as Sissie crept forward into her cubbyhole; but my brain was seething. No mainmast, no money, no mastmaker south of Brest. Jesus Christ, what a pickle!

Sissie crept back. I guessed she'd had a quick swig at the Booth's for she was toting her Bible. As I sipped miserably at the Burma Blend (from Fortnum and Mason's—no *common* tea for Sissie), she leafed through the pages, mumbling. As it got louder, I realized she was reading a psalm: "The Lord is my shepherd; I shall not want . . . he maketh . . . "

I stopped her in her tracks. "Oh, hell, Sissie Sinjohn, if you're going to start Bible punchin', for Crissake go forward." Then I felt cruel, but only to myself. I'd no more words.

She looked hurt. Great tears sprang to her eyes as she closed the book and turned to stare out the hatchway. Then, slowly, she smiled. Reluctantly, I turned my head to see what she was beaming at. On the jetty, all wired and bundled up, was a heap of telegraph poles.

"Tristan, dahling," she said, softly and quietly, "do you see what I see?" She wiggled her chins at the timber, smiling sweetly, then turned to look at me as I stared at the poles, then into her red eyes.

I grinned, reached over, grabbed her shoulder as she laughed, and shook her. "See it . . . *see* it? Holy smoke, Sissie, I can *taste* it! Come on, let's get the tools ready!"

She burst into bloom like a full rose, face flushed, then jumped up the ladder, gym slip swinging, and shouted: "Oh jolly, *jolly* dee! Hey ho, hey ho, it's orf to work we gooo!"

I couldn't move for a minute. My heart was piecing itself together again while my sides were splitting with laughter and my spirits were soaring with villainous joy.

After nightfall, with Sissie engaging the enchanted and astonished night-watch *gendarme* in whispered high school-French subterfuge, I crept ashore with the wire cutters, carefully snapped the binding wire over a choice selection of poles, silently dragged one over the jetty to a dark corner, sawed a 12-foot (none of your bloody meters here!) length of beautifully straight-grained pitch pine off it, and quietly wangled and waggled it into the cabin.

Soon, Sissie was back, breathlessly telling me about the *gendarme*'s ambitions on her Anglican virtue ("Oh dahling, orl these froggies are interested in, reahlly, is simply *sex*, my deah. Oh *what* a *bore!*").

We set to with the plane and the rasping iron, the radio turned up loud to drown the noise of our working (and Sissie's talking). By midnight, a brand new plug for the mast was ready, shining white in the one electric bulb's glare; by 3 o'clock the plug was shoved into the shattered splints of the mainmast; and by 4 o'clock, the whole thing was served and tarred, tight as a drum, with my best codline and small stuff. To make a good job of it, and for luck, I put two lines of fancy braiding around the footend of the serving. Her Majesty's Dockyard at Portsmouth couldn't have made a better job, I prided myself, probably unjustly.

By 5 o'clock—with the *gendarme*'s machine pistol resting on the jetty so he could give these two, generous, friendly British lunatics a hand to get their mast up—the job was done.

I rigged the sail on the mainmast, leaving the mizzen lashed ondeck (time for that later, in the safety of Spain). Sissie rigged the headsails, and after a cheery *adieu* to the *gendarme* we were off, into the Mediterranean.

The weather in the Gulf of Genoa was windy but the sea was kindly. As I stared at the frontier marker between France and Spain, sliding by in the early morning sunlight, Sissie said to me: "I say, Tristan, old bean, I simply don't understand why you even *attempted* to get that *awf'ly* heavy mast up on your own. Why didn't you wait for me to get back from those dreary shops?"

I decided not to tell her one truth, but to tell her another.

"Sissie, when I arrived in Alderney from the Arctic and the

Baltic, I met an old friend, Aussie Bill. He and I made two smuggling runs to France back in 1959."

"I say! How terribly exciting. What was it, perfumes and awl thet jolly rot?"

"No, it was whisky. Six hundred cases of the stuff."

"How perfectly *splendid!*" She handed me another mug of hot Burma and a jam-smeared "bikky."

"Anyway, Aussie told me that the French government had a warrant out for my arrest. Then, as they couldn't lay their hands on me, they tried me *in absentia* on a charge of *contrabande*. They couldn't find me guilty, because they had nothing more than hearsay evidence, but they banned me from entering France—from stepping on French soil—for the next eight years. The trial was in Paris, at the Palais de Justice, in 1960. In November of 1960."

"And now it's only May 1965. That means . . ."

"Yes, it means that since September 1963, ever since I arrived in Bordeaux, I've been banned from *being* in France. If I was detected, the boat would have been seized and I would have got an automatic five-year sentence." I pulled on my Gauloise and sipped my tea. "And there I was in Bordeaux, broke, dismasted, with the boat in ruins . . ."

"Why didn't they catch you?"

"Too busy figuring out the bloody metric system, I s'pose." I gave the wheel a jerk to "bite" the helm. "Trying to find the end of that friggin' recurring decimal."

"And you've brought the boat right through the jolly old middle of Frawnce?"

"Yeah, and not only that, Sissie, we hobnobbed with the high and mighty, too."

"Oh jolly *dee!*"

"And that's not all."

She hovered, expectantly.

"We sailed out of the country with one of General-bloody-Charlie-de-Gaulle's flamin' telegraph poles!"

"And a rusty bicycle. Whoopee!"

She gave the jib sheet an extra heave as Nelson panted at my feet.

PART III

¡Vamonos!
May 1965-April 1969

Ulysses speaks:

I put forth on the deep and open sea
With but one ship and that small company
Which until then had not forsaken me . . .

Both I and they were growing old and slow
When we were come unto that narrow strait
Where Hercules once set his landmarks

To warn men not to venture farther . . .

We kept our poop straight turned toward the morning.
And in our oars had wings for our mad flight.

Dante, "Inferno"

I had a love I thought was true,
Her hair was gold, her eyes were blue,
She said that she would wait for me
On the coast of Barcelona.

She swore by all the stars above
I was her one and only love—
That she'd be mine and marry me
On the coast of Barcelona.

I gave her silk, I gave her gold—
With chains she did my heart enfold—
Another's taken her from me
On the coast of Barcelona.

Her heart was ice, her love was cool—
We're bound away for Liverpool—
And never more—I'll go a-roving—
On the coast of Barcelona!

Sailor's ballad, late 1800s.
(This is a terrible, sloppy verse, but the
melody is haunting. Typical
Victorian seaman's ditty—probably
bowdlerised. I heard it first from
Dod Orsborne.)

16

Ups and Downs

I was a bit concerned at the prospect of sliding past stormy Cabo Creus, the first great prominence on the coast of Spain. The going was slow, for *Cresswell* was beating into a southwest wind. Our jury mainmast had not been tested before we departed Sète, through circumstances beyond my control—or *force majeure*, as the French and seaman say. In other words we'd had to get out . . . fast.

As it was, the mainmast stood up very well to the hard movement of the sea off cruel Cabo Creus. A few alarming squeaks and groans to begin with, when the boat hit the short, nasty seas off the cape, but everything held together well, and I suppose the same can be said for Sissie. As the night wore on, she kept up a continuous supply of hot tea, soup, cocoa, and "bikkys" smeared with butter and jam (Keiller's Scotch marmalade), and French sausage.

This was indeed luxurious sailing for me. Alone, I would have gone all night with a mere handful of burgoo, steering hard and jerky. It was like comparing the Waldorf-Astoria to the forepeak of H.M.S. *Bounty*.

The mizzenmast and its gear—the boom, the gaff, the shrouds and backstays, bottle screws and parrels—were all lashed down along the starboard sidedeck, and the ancient French bicycle was secured on the port side. Now that Sissie was foredeckhand, as well as cook, Nelson sulked aft on the poopdeck, as far away from her route of march as he could get. He was enjoying the sail immensely, as if he knew it might be his last, but the only time he showed much activity was when dolphins flashed out of the sea, though he couldn't see them until they were close to the boat. Then he would lift his head off his forepaw, eye gleaming, tongue hanging out, and watch them, almost grinning. Nelson loved the dolphins, and his tail wagged lazily and thumped against the after mooring sponson every time they showed up.

The rest of the time he guarded the two fishing lines that were trailing aft, waiting for one to judder and stiffen, its victim jerking and twisting. When a catch was made, Nelson banged his tail hard on the deck and yelped, with his good leg tapping at the nylon fishing line. Sissie nipped out of the galley like greased lightning, gutting knife in hand, and before I'd drained my mug of tea the fish would be split open, cleaned, and soaking, and Nelson would have its head.

All the while this was going on, Sissie made cooing noises to the fish. "Now come along theah. My, what a perfectly *hendsome* fellow! Good swimmah; strong, too. Just the ticket for Sissie and Trissie, what? It's orl right, Nelson shall heve his sheah of the loot. Whoops! Mustn't drop you over the side, must we?"

With shortened mainsail and working jib, it took three days to reach Barcelona. It was misty—foggy even—when we chugged up the long port entry, with a thousand small fishing craft heading this way and that and hundreds of mussel floats lining the passage. These are great bargelike rafts, moored permanently to the seabed, and from the decks long poles stick out to either side, as many as 200 to a raft. From them lines are weighted down to the seabed and on these lines the mussels make their clinging home, until they are ready to be picked for the restaurants of Barcelona and Madrid.

Passing them in the fog was like sailing through a Chinese parchment, through a pearl-misty painting, with an almost complete loss of the senses of dimension and direction.

It was about six in the morning when we slid into the inner basin of the harbor. I took one look at the Royal Barcelona Yacht Club, tucked away in one corner of the great port, with a few hundred million-dollar sail and motor "gin palaces" sitting there, all trying to outdo each other in their white enamel paint and gleaming silver-chromium-plated metal, varnished like an undertaker's dream. On each floating mansion was a short, stocky, swarthy deckhand, scrubbing away like mad. I tried to imagine the chaos which would be caused by Sissie's arrival at the club, and decided not to go there.

Instead I headed for the town's fish-landing dock, hard by the bows of the "replica" of Columbus's *Santa Maria* (which really isn't because the lines of the original *Santa Maria* are not known. But it keeps the tourists happy and the dollars rolling in. So who cares?).

In Franco's Spain, while repression by the Nationalists was hard, the immigration laws were probably the slackest in the world. Any foreigner of any kind, no matter if he was a rapist on the run or a multimillion-dollar art forger, so long as he had money, was—if not welcomed with open arms—at least allowed into the country and to stay there as long as his money held out. The immigration laws, heavy and restrictive until the late fifties, had been completely liberalized so that the 15-odd million tourists from the industrial nations of northern Europe could flock to the beaches of the Costa Brava. Another million or so footloose exiles of every conceivable kind had taken advantage of the easing off to settle their restless wings in Franco's shaky roost.

Besides, Spain was cheap. For example, the cost of living there was less than a third of that in France. Living was inexpensive; the natives were ground down by the most insidious secret-police organization ever; labor, with no rights whatsoever except the right to starve, was dirt cheap; and the sky was nearly always blue.

Thus when *Cresswell* gently nudged into the fishdock of Barcelona, there was no palavar from the police. It took the aging *guardia civil*, gun-husbanding the dock in case a fisherman might express discontent with his hard-earned pittance, about an hour to realize we had arrived. He lumbered over, as heavy and cumbersome as a furniture van. He wore the fog-gray uniform, the heavy pistol, the Sam Browne belt over one shoulder, the tight, round, clerical, snowy white collar showing below the tight, round, gray, hangman's collar of his jacket. On top of his red-faced, white-haired head was perched the shiny black leather helmet, with the brim turned up fore and aft so he could sleep leaning with his back to a shady wall. He came over with measured tread, thumb stuck in shoulder belt. Reaching the edge of the jetty, he stood for a moment or two, gazing at Sissie.

Still in her English-finishing-school blue gym slip, she was perched on the bowsprit, holding onto the forestay with one gnarled, blistered claw and gesticulating in sign language to a congregation of about 50 sunburned fishermen of all shapes, sizes, ages, and conditions. The fishermen, Catalan Catholics to a man, from a culture where there are strictly two kinds of women (the Virgin Mary's reflection and whores), stood numbstruck, hypnotized by this *señora inglesa*, with her red hair, red face, red eyes (from a sleepless night), red arms, and (*Dios mío*) red legs (the skirt of this strange apparel came only to her *thighs*). They all, from 92 to 13, followed with their eyes the sweaty gym slip over her almost flat chest, bulging Michelin-tired waist, and the fat-dimpled nether folds of her haunches, down to her knees (*two* of them, looking like Tweedledum and Tweedledee), thrust apart. Down, down went their gaze, lascivious and longing, to the wrinkled British Army khaki wool socks collapsing over the pontoon-like Irish-ditch-digger brown brogues. Not a word was said, except by Sissie.

"Oh Tristan, what *charming* little cheppies; they seem so jolly friendly and absolutely *sweet*. What an awful shame they cawn't speak one teeny-weeny word of English. What a dreadful *bore*. I think I shall give thet deah, sweet little cheppie . . . " She gestured at a nefarious-looking sprucer of about 15, with oily hair and wily eyes (he looked as if he'd been whelped in a dockside whorehouse). "I think I shall give him some *bikkys*, he looks so sort of *wan* and, oh deahry *deahry* me, so hungry and *lost*. I'm sure these *dreadful* brutes must work him into a *frazzle* out there on those *awful* scungy old boats."

The *guardia civil* stared, unbelieving. So did I, for a few seconds.

Then, recovering, I said quietly: "Sissie, for Christ's sake get down and shut up. Here I am, trying to come in as peaceful and unnoticed as I can, and there's you, readin' 'em the riot act. For God's sake, try to be inconspicuous!"

The lechery in the air from the crowd of fishermen and dock workers was tangible. You could have cut it up and sold it on Forty-second Street.

"But dahling, I was only trying to be *friendly* to the poor little cheppies." She pouted. "And you know, my pet, that I always *try* to be inconspicuous, or whatevah."

"*Dios mío*," muttered the *guardia civil*.

I was getting angry with embarrassment. "You're stood up there like a spare prick at a wedding! Stow yourself below and get some decent Christian clothes on. They're all drooling."

Sissie, with flirty-flighty waves for the gawping crowd and a petulant stare for me, clomped aft to go below. The *Guardia* absent-mindedly groping for his pencil, accidentally dropped his notepad in a puddle of fish slime. "*Mierde!*" he muttered. Then, seeing that the notebook was irretrievably sunk in gook, he looked at me again and shook his head, making his shiny black hat wobble. "*Mierde!*" he muttered again. He took a last look at Sissie's ginger hair, disappearing down the companionway, and again shook his head. "*Dios mío!*" he exclaimed.

That was our official entry into Spain.

Sissie made a cup of tea and a corned beef sandwich which she handed up into the cockpit, where I was busy raising the mizzenmast. She had secured a pale blue ribbon around her frizz and tied it with a round turn and two half-hitches. She looked meek and submissive again; so I knew she was after something.

"Well done, lass," I said as she handed me the tea.

"Tristan, dahling," she said in a small voice.

"What now?"

"Do you need me this awfternoon, my pet?"

"No."

"Goody-goody gumdrops!"

"What?"

"I did so want to see Gaudi's cathedral and take some snaps for deah, deah Willy!"

"Right-o, love. Now don't get into trouble. And watch these Spanish blokes; they're all dick and devilry, you know."

"Oh Tristan, *dahling*, it's so good and kind and sweet of you to worry over tiny little me. You *are* a sweety pie!"

I glanced at her giant brogue boots.

"Sissie."

"Yes, my pet?"

"Promise me something?"

"Of course, my angel. What is it?"

"Be careful here."

"Of *course* I shell, dahling," she huffed, climbing out of the forward hatch. She shook her hockey stick at me. "I should just bally well laike to see anyone, just *anyone*, jolly well try any monkey tricks with me!"

She brandished the hockey stick again, sending the waiting Spanish horde of would-be marauders staggering back five yards from the side of the boat, where they were panting for another view of the first British sex object they'd ever seen.

That afternoon, after the siesta, I went to the bank to pick up my share of the loot from *Quiberon*: $1,000 in pesetas. It had been hard earned—bloody hard earned. But it had not been paid into the bank: Pinet had reneged on his debt! It was many months before he finally paid me.

I decided to sail for the Balearic Islands, where there might be a remote chance of earning money. But first I had to refit *Cresswell's* mast again; so I headed for Arenys del Mar.

PLAYBOY

SAVINGS VOUCHER

You can receive 12 issues of PLAYBOY for just $19.97. (That's $41.43 off the cover price.) **A FREE edition of PLAYBOY's 50 Hottest Nudes and PLAYBOY's Tanned and Topless** is reserved for you with your R.S.V.P. PAY $4.99 IN 4 EASY INSTALLMENTS. Cancel at any time for a full refund on all unmailed issues.

PLAYBOY'S COVER PRICE	YOUR COST	YOU SAVE
$61.40	$19.97	$41.43

☐ Bill me in 4 easy installments of $4.99 each.*

☐ Full Payment enclosed.

Name _____
(Please print)

Address _____ Apt. No. _____

City _____ State _____ Zip _____

* Total price 12 issues = $19.97. Rate applies to U.S., U.S Poss., APO-FPO address only.

TWO FREE GIFTS! with your paid subscription

R.S.V.P.
1-800-765-1155

JHN1010

BIG &
saving Gifts!
2 FREE
(See details on other side)

BUSINESS REPLY MAIL
FIRST-CLASS MAIL   PERMIT NO.47   HARLAN, IA

POSTAGE WILL BE PAID BY ADDRESSEE

PLAYBOY

P.O. BOX 2002
HARLAN IOWA   51593-2217

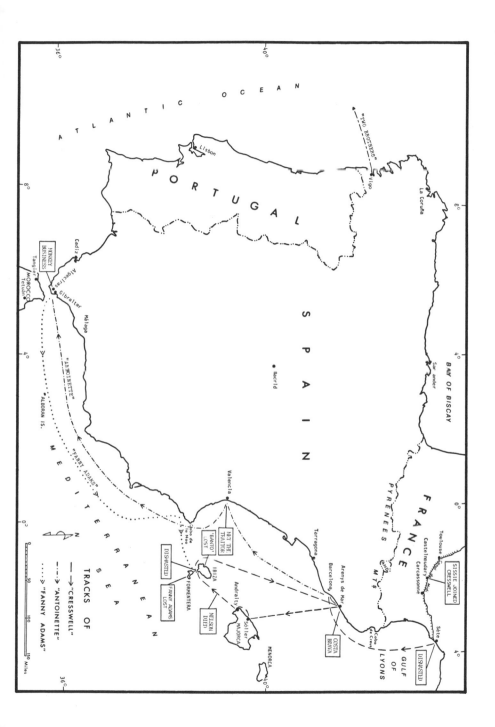

¡Abajo con la intelligencia!
[Down with intelligence!]

General Quipo de Llano
in a pro-Franco radio harangue, 1936

¡Es mejor morir en sus pies que vivir en sus rodillas!
[Better to die on your feet than live on your knees!]

Republican slogan, used by "La Pasionaria"
(Dolores Irribarra) in 1936 but coined by
Emilio Zapata in Mexico in 1910 .

17

El Caudillo

Arenys del Mar is on the Costa Brava, the Wild Coast, about 20 miles northeast of Barcelona. Nowadays, it has been "developed" far beyond the point of vulgarity, having been the first slice of the Mediterranean coast of Spain to be invaded by hordes of northern Europeans looking for cheap holidays. This invasion started in earnest about 1966. At the time *Cresswell* fetched the small fishing harbor, Arenys was still a sleepy village.

Both Barcelona and Arenys are in the province of Spain known from ancient times as Catalonia, and Barcelona is its capital. The Catalans speak their own language, a mixture of Spanish and something like medieval Provençal, the language of southern France. For centuries the Catalans have been struggling for some measure of autonomous self-rule from the autocratic, stiff-necked, myopic government of Madrid. Many bloody rebellions against the authority of Madrid have taken place since the unification of Spain after the ejection of the Moors in the late fifteenth century.

The culmination of the Catalan struggle for self-rule was the bloody three-year struggle against Franco during the Spanish Civil War of 1936-39. After decades of chaos under a weak monarchy, a republican government of Spain was declared in the early thirties with libertarian aims, including the

formation of trade unions and the division of the vast country estates among the peasants. This led to a polarization: on
the right, landed gentry, the church, and the army; on the
left, city workers, the more informed peasantry, the liberal
intellectuals, and the separatists of Catalonia in the northeast and the Basques in the north.

The middle class in Spain was small and weak; so there was
nothing to hold the center together—nothing to prevent the
natural movement of the right and left factions to the
extremes of fascism and communism. By 1936 the stage was
set for one of the cruellist, bloodiest struggles in recent
history. Cruel because brother was pitted against brother,
father against son. Bloody because generally no quarter was
given, no prisoners were taken in battle.

The 1936 Spanish rebellion started under the ostensible
leadership of General Mola (a classical frontman), but he
conveniently disappeared in an air crash as soon as the rebellion seemed to be making headway. Then the real force came
to the fore: General Francisco Franco Bahamonde, commander in chief of the Spanish Army in Morocco. A hard,
ruthless, military tyrant, who—legend has it—once had a
soldier executed because the man happened to splutter when
Franco was addressing him.

For three long, terrible years the strife continued, with the
German Nazis and Italian Fascists, on the one hand, aiding
Franco with ruthless massacres of civilians from the air
(almost unheard of in Europe before then), and the Russian
Communists, under Iron Joe Stalin, coming to the assistance
of the government forces. England and France, perforce (to
their eternal shame), adhered to a nonintervention pact,
which left the arena clear for the dictators to perfect their
blitzkrieg and terrorism of civilians.

Eventually, despite the heroic resistance of Madrid and the
Basques in the north and the Catalans in the northeast,
Franco's slaughter of his fellow countrymen prevailed and
the government collapsed. Then, with the surrender of the
last centers of resistance, the real agony of Spain commenced
—and continued for 37 years. Prisoners of war, who gave

themselves up at the cessation of fighting, were summarily sentenced, either to death or to long terms of hard labor in foul camps and prisons. Known sympathizers of the government—the legal, elected government of Spain—were rounded up also and meted out the same treatment; those who were not shot or imprisoned were deprived of their civil rights, including the right to work. The suffering brought about by these injustices can never be fully appreciated. Highly qualified doctors, scientists, writers, poets, and men of all levels of skill were reduced to shining shoes and selling lottery tickets in the cafes, while the victorious rebels lorded it over them.

I remember the scenes in Valencia back in 1950: the poverty, the ground-down humility of the people before the snarling arrogance of the Falangist party officials as they strutted in peacock magnificence, in their gray coxcomb uniforms through the suffering streets, Italian pistols worn loose at the hip, always ready for the slightest sign of defiance . . . I remember.

By 1965, on the surface at least, for the benefit of foreign visitors, Spain was becoming a more liberal country, though women in slacks or with bare arms would be turned back from entering the churches, and would be liable to arrest if they wore a bathing suit away from the strictly (though unobtrusively) surveyed tourist beaches. Still, no criticism of Franco or the government was allowed, and every bar, every restaurant, every public meeting place was eavesdropped on by Franco's all-pervasive National Security Police in civilian clothes. No one trusted anyone when it came to expressing politics.

In the smaller towns there was one advantage that foreigners had: the secret police had been mainly recruited from the criminal or stupid elements and thus were incapable of learning a foreign language. A kind of code was used among the British and Americans: Franco was "Fuck Face," the secret police were "the Busys," etc. Foreign expatriates' money was one of Spain's major sources of foreign currency (apart from the millions of dollars donated to Franco's gang of butchers by the United States government in the guise of "military" or "economic" aid).

When *Cresswell* entered Arenys harbor, the scars of the civil war showed only in a few empty plots of land in the town and in the infinitely sad faces of the majority of the inhabitants. In fact, the small harbor was abustle with activity. It was mroning, and the Spaniard rises early to get a day's work done before siesta, which begins at 2 o'clock. Women, young and old, were gutting and selling fish, while their husbands, sons, and brothers repaired nets on the jetty. Others scrubbed the decks of the fishing boats, for the Catalan is a clean sailor and keeps his boat immaculate.

Many of the older women wore black, as was true throughout Spain. The civil war had widowed approximately 2 *million* women—in a strongly Catholic country where remarriage was frowned upon.

As Sissie tied the lines on the jetty bollards, wearing her usual rig of blue gym slip, white panties, British Army socks and brogue boots, the native population turned up to gawp in amazement, while some of the young boys hared back to the town to advise and hustle their friends to see the *señora inglesa*. I tried to look unconcerned and sat in the cockpit, staring at the distant blue hills. Soon the dockside was crowded with the usual audience, staring and chattering, bemused by Sissie's antics. Nelson padded up and down the deck, growling at the mob of mongrels attracted by the crowd of onlookers.

Two of the Civil Guard eventually sauntered down and entered the boat and merely noted our names and passport numbers and the boat's name. Then off they sauntered again, amid the silence of the audience.

"Shall I do the shopping today, Tristan?" Sissie asked.

"How are we off for food?" I asked.

"Oh, there's enough for tonight. We have those *scrumptious* tinned sausages, four *ducky* little eggs, and I can make some chips. I know you ebsolutely *adore* your chippies!"

She clambered about onboard, followed by every eye for a hundred yards around—the male eyes lascivious, the female eyes threatening death.

"Yeah," I replied, wearily; "I absolutely do adore chippies."

"I know, my deah, and I shall peel oodles and *oodles* of pota-toes, and we'll jolly well *feast* on the wretched things!"

"That's right. Then you can go into town tomorrow and do your shopping, when we look a bit more like part of the furni-ture, for as sure as God made little apples, if you go into town this morning you'll have a train of kids behind you that'll make the pied piper of Hamlin look like a flamin' amateur."

"I know, dahling. Isn't it simply awful the way these poor little souls simply *cling* to one?"

"Yeah, like a dose of crabs! Now come on; let's get cracking on sandpapering this paintwork."

"Oh, goody gumdrops. 'Twas on the Aisle of Capree weah Ai found yuh . . . "

Sissie clomped down into the after dodger and was shortly out again with the sheets of wet and dry sandpaper, the scraper, and some cheesecloth. Soon she was rubbing down the coachroof, the toerail, the sides of the boat. All through the long, hot afternoon she slaved away in the sun, while the once-bustling jetty went deathly quiet as the audience mean-dered away in a body, as if to a signal at 2 o'clock, to their siestas. I went into the engine compartment, taking my time about an oil change and dozing now and then, while Sissie, humming and rubbing and clattering, woke Nelson and me at annoying intervals. With eyes half open, I thought to myself: Ah well, it's all in a good cause; and let her carry on at the hard, sweaty job without interference.

At 4:30, as if to a bugle call, the crowd of onlookers return-ed. It was as if they were the chorus in some surrealistic mel-odrama, and by 5 o'clock practically the whole town was at hand to stare at Sissie as she scraped away on her knees at the side of the boat. Trying to look weary from my labors on the engine, I emerged from below the weather deck and, sighing as if from fatigue, went down into the cabin—to lie down and doze yet again.

When Sissie woke me it was dark outside. Inside the cabin the oil lamp was glowing, and from the galley came the delicious aroma of frying sausages, eggs, and chips.

"Wakey, wakey, dahling," she cooed, shaking my shoulder with the delicate touch of a slaughterman about to fell an ox. "Wakey, wakey. Din-dins!"

"All right, for Christ's sake, Sissie. Who do you think I am, bloody Christopher Robin?" I rubbed my eyes, Nelson twitched his nose.

"I've heated up the new chinah plates Toby sent . . . they're such *dahling* Wedgwood—and I shall make you some hot chocolate for your beddy-bye-byes."

"Oh, all right. Where's the grub?"

We ate in silence, for I was still half asleep. Afterward, replete, I turned in on my berth, sipping cocoa while Sissie did the washing up and Nelson dozed, giving the merest flicker of his tail now and again as he dreamed of his randy youth and his old master, Tansy Lee. Soon—after a "Nighty-night, Tristan dahling. Tootle-oo!"—Sissie disappeared forward to her dismal den. I was lulled to sleep by the tinkle of her gin bottle and the rustle of her Bible pages as she performed her nightly meditation.

After a good, long night's rest, I was wakened by the sound of Sissie scrubbing down the topsides. I turned over and dozed off again for an hour, finally rising from my berth for breakfast. Again, sausage and eggs, but this time no chippies.

"What's happening ashore?" I asked Sissie as she washed up yet again. (A creature of habit, our Sissie.)

"Ebsolutely nothing, deah," she replied, stepping carefully over Nelson, who was in his accustomed place in harbor, at the bottom of the companionway ladder, right slap in front of the galley.

"Hmm, must be a religious holiday or something," I said. "It's a weekday, but normally the locals would have been out at the crack o' dawn. You know all about that, Sissie. What saint's day is today?"

"No one reahlly *particulah*," she replied. "Must be one of those dreadfully obscure little shepherd gels who kept seeing visions and awl sorts of odd things in those dreary, ebsolutely *peasanty* hills. Too much of that awful red wine, if you awsk me."

"You'd better get the shopping list together. And for Christ's sake, Sissie, put something *decent* on to go into town. One of these days these randy Spaniards are going to lynch you for wearin' your flamin' Bridget Bardot fantasy kit!"

She frowned and thought for a minute; then her red face brightened like a boozer's at pub-opening time.

"I know, Tristan, dahling!"

"Now what?"

"I'll weah my hiking geah!"

"Right. Anything but that damned gym slip; it makes you look like Oscar Wilde in drag."

But by this time she was twinkle-toeing forward, and after a few minutes of huffing and scuffling behind the forward bulkhead she emerged wearing the most God-awful English country woman's suit. It was beige, the same color as beer spew, and looked about as appetizing. The skirt reached down to midcalf, and, having lost the belt, she had tied it around her thick waist with a length of spun yarn. The jacket had a vent in the back and there were leather patches on the elbows. Below the skirt she wore thick woolen stockings, and the *ensemble* was completed by her Irish brogue boots and her Rhodesian infantryman's hat, worn at the usual angle of 45 degrees from the horizontal. She clomped down the companionway and made a pirouette in the narrow galley space, knocking two mugs from their hooks on the deckhead.

"Like it, Tristan deah?"

"Fan-bloody-tastic! Makes you look like you're off to Paddy McGinty's wedding."

"Who's that?"

She pirouetted again, this time avoiding the crockery but stepping on Nelson's tail. As Nelson prepared to lunge at her, she jumped back, grabbed the shopping bag, and clambered up the ladder.

"Jesus H. Christ!" I said to Nelson as I delved into the paint locker. "Bloody women!" Nelson, mollified, wagged his tail and whoofed. But minutes later, just as I was about to start painting the deckhouse, Sissie was back.

"Tristan, dahling! There's this awful little Civil Guard, sort of armed to the gills, and he simply refuses to let me go out of the dock gate. I *did* try to explain, but you know these Continentals. Cawn't understand a dratted word of English."

"Why won't he let you out?"

"I simply cawn't *fathom* why—he seemed such a *sweet* thing. But every time I show him my shopping bag and point to the village, he keeps giving me the most awful leers and sort of prods me with that dreadful little popgun of his and points at this fort of tremendous great floating gin palace in the harbor. Of course, dahling, I keep pointing back at deah, dahling *Cresswell*, but he insists on shouting *No!* at me and prodding me with his dratted little gun!"

"Oh shit," said I, laying down my pot and brush; "here we go again. Come on, let's go and have a word with this flamin' rozzer!"

As Sissie and I walked to the dock gates I noticed, just outside the harbor, at anchor in the bay, a great white pleasure craft. She must have been all of 250 feet long, with her funnel and paintwork spotless. Then I saw that the harbor was crawling with Civil Guards, but they were different from the ones we'd encountered previously. They were very big men, all immaculately uniformed, their Sam Browne belts and boots glistening in the sun, and all very heavily armed, with two pistols and a tommygun to each man. The most striking difference between these men and the usual Civil Guard was that their helmets, turned up fore and aft, were covered in gray cloth. They glared at me and leered at Sissie as we passed.

"What do you think it's all about?" Sissie asked.

"Blowed if I know. The only thing I know is that this lot looks stupid standing there," I replied as we bowled up to the guard at the gate. He was youngish, about 25, tall, and glowering.

"*Hola, amigo!*" I exclaimed, trying to be friendly. "What's happening? See, we're on a boat here and need to buy food in the village . . ." I got no further.

"*Vaya, Señor* . . . Go away. No one is allowed to pass through these gates. *El Caudillo* is in the ship there, the *Aguila.*"

"Who?"

"*El Caudillo, Generalissimo* Francisco Franco Bahamonde, the Father of Spain."

"Oh, I see. Well *la señorita*"—I nodded at Sissie in her suffragette's costume—"*la señorita* only wants to go shopping for some bread and potatoes, and maybe some eggs."

Sissie had managed to conjure up, from somewhere in her Saxon depths, two great big tears, which oozed from her steely blue eyes.

The Civil Guard, disturbed, became apologetic. "I cannot help you, *Señorita*," he told Sissie. (Nothing like a female tear to bring out the *caballero*.) "You see, I have my orders. It is absolutely forbidden—any movement between the town and this gate or this gate and the town. I am sorry, but these are my orders. Tomorrow . . ."

"But we have no food *today!*" I protested. "*No tenemos comidas hoy dia!*"

"I am sorry, *Señor*." Again he gestured with his machine pistol.

I smiled in resignation and turned to go back to the boat, taking hold of Sissie's elbow as I did. Then I looked up the hill and along the wall, away from the gate. Only 10 yards from the gate the wall was in ruins. The guard followed my eyes, then looked at Sissie (now weeping dollops) and back at me.

"*Bueno, Señor*, the orders said nothing about the wall. If your *señora amiga* wishes to go that way, well, who am I to stop her?"

"What about the other guards?" I asked him.

"A guard guards what he is told to guard, and no one has been told to guard that place." He pointed with his chin at the crumbled wall.

"*Gracias, Señor*. Come aboard for a drink later on." I smiled at him.

"*Gracias a Usted, Señor*. But we are *el Caudillo's* bodyguard and therefore incorruptible. Go with God and tell your lady to watch the change when she buys from these infernal Catalans!"

"Come on, Sissie, I'll see you safely over the wall."

I led her up the hill, she scrambled over the rubble, did her shopping, and scrambled back the same way.

Franco was in Arenys for three days. The whole town was under curfew from sunset to dawn, the harbor was patrolled day and night by at least 150 of Franco's bodyguards, and Sissie and I continued using the broken-down section of the wall, under the steady gaze of the guards, the whole time.

Which says something about Spain.

I went to an ale house I used to frequent
And I told the landlady my money was spent.
I asked her for credit. She answered me "Nay—
For a custom like yours I can get any day!"

Chorus: *And it's no, nay, never* . . . .
No, nay, never, no more—
Will I play the wild rover—
The wild rover no more!

From The Wild Rover.
A nineteenth-century seaman's ballad, it
originated in Bristol, England. It is
probably the only chorus in English which
contains seven consecutive negatives.

18

A Lucky Break

Because of the shortage of funds due to M. Pinet's nonpayment of the thousand dollars for the delivery of *Quiberon*, Sissie and I were not able to do very much toward smartening up *Cresswell*. Just a coat of gray paint topsides and a coat of blue on the rubbing strake. We could not afford to haul her out of the water and scrape and paint her bottom; and as there is no tide in that part of the Mediterranean, we could not careen her. However, we did as best we could on our small resources before taking off south to Majorca, the largest of the Balearic Islands.

Before we sailed, I trekked back to Barcelona, hitching a ride on a farm truck, and searched the yacht club and the boat-building yards for any yacht deliveries which might be in the offing. At last, through the good offices of the chief steward of the Royal Barcelona Yacht Club, I found one. Her name was *Antoinette*, a 58-foot yawl. She was being built for an Englishman, Aubrey Cord-Green, who had achieved some repute as an actor.

When I finally contacted him in Barcelona, I found that he was about 35, a slight, blond, mouselike man with a large mustache, pale blue eyes, and an effeminate manner. He wore straw sandals and an artist's smock, suitably daubed with paint, and below that a pair of pink canvas Breton fisherman's trousers.

"Oh my goodness; yes, yes *indeed!*" gushed Aubrey, when I introduced myself. "Yes I *do* need someone to deliver my dear *Antoinette* for me!"

"When and where to?" I asked.

"Anywhere outside Spain, my dear boy, preferably on the way to England. I thought of the French canals, but she's too deep with her seven-feet draught. What do you think?"

"Mmm. Well, Aubrey, I reckon your best bet . . . By the way, what's all the hurry, anyway?"

"Well, you see, they started building her 10 months ago—and it's going to be another blasted month before they get her finished. They're installing this Italian diesel, you see, and if I don't have her out of the country within one year of her keel being laid, I shall have to pay a whacking great tax on her and all her gear. Something like $30,000—two-thirds of her total cost. So you see, I simply *have* to have her out."

"Right. When's the finishing date?"

"The end of May."

"O.K. I'll be back here at the end of May with one deck-hand."

"Oh, we can take on a local sailor for that," Aubrey said, eyeing the glistening male bodies around us.

"Not if I'm taking her to Gibraltar, Aubrey. I never met a Mediterranean Spaniard yet that ever handled a sail proper-ly, and I'm damned if I'm going to start a bloody training school. If you want a good fast passage, let me pick my own crew. Anyway, it'll cost you less."

"But these Catalan sailors are such *hunky* creatures . . ."

"I don't give a monkey's tit about that. My crew or nothing. Right, Aubrey?"

"Oh, all right, then," he muttered. "But you're a spoil-sport!"

"Maybe so, but I want a crew, not a parliament!"

"All right, Tristan. I'll give you 500 pesetas as a good-will bond, and expect you at the end of May. Contact me at the yacht club."

"Right-o, Aubrey."

I shook his soft, pudgy hand—like shaking a wet haddock—
and made my way back to Arenys.

"Yoo-hoo, Tristan!" Sissie called as I trudged back along
the dusty jetty, weary with thumbing short, bumpy rides
from Barcelona. "Tea and bikkys ready!"

"O.K., cut the cackle. Here." I handed her the 500 pesetas.
"Get into town and get some grub. We're off to Majorca this
evening."

Sissie was soon back, with bread, potatoes and fish, and I
had the sails ready to hoist and the mooring lines ready to let
go.

"Why all the hurry to leave, Tristan?" She stowed the food
in the galley. Her usual convoy of admirers had gathered on
the jetty.

"That 500 pesetas is all the money we have in the world.
When that grub's gone we're in trouble, old girl. But there are
thousands of tourists in Majorca, and chances are we can
make a few dollars taking them out on day charters. We have
to exist for the rest of this month and the whole of May . . ."

"I say, Skippah, what a *splendid* ideah! Awl aboard; come for
a sail round the old lighthouse, what? And I can make awl
sorts of jolly old sandwiches." Her eyes shone brightly as she
grinned up through the hatch.

"A dollop of burgoo and a swig of rum is more like it. Come
on; let go the mooring lines. Let's get moving. We've only
three gallons of diesel oil left and there isn't much wind.
We're going to have to cosset her all the way."

So, to the infinite regret of the lascivious male eyes on the
mole, we wore out of Arenys del Mar as the sun set on the
mountains above Barcelona, a blood-red splendor of fire over
the magenta blue heights of Catalonia. Sissie soon had fish
and chips sizzling in the galley while I fiddled and fussed with
the sheets and halyards to maneuver *Cresswell* yard over tan-
talizing yard with the teasing wind, a Mediterranean early
summer wind, changing forever this way and that.

By dawn, when I dowsed the storm lantern hanging in the
mizzen shrouds, I saw that we were only eight miles or so offshore. The sea was mirrorlike, an oily-looking flat surface

without a ripple, except where the breeding basking-sharks cut their fins in weaving patterns and, now and again, a dolphin leaped in his early morning joy.

By noon it was so calm that we handed the main and rigged the awning to ease the sun's glare and heat. I sat twitching the bottom fishing lines, hoping for some nice, tender sole, while Sissie, humming her tuneless dirges, set to airing the mattresses and repairing clothes. Nelson basked in the shade in the cockpit, now and then snapping at an odd fly emerging from the cabin. All day and all night we sat there. Finally, in the dawn, I cranked up the engine and headed south over one of the flattest seas I have ever seen, to put some distance between us and the rocky shore of Catalonia.

Minutes after I capitulated to the flighty Mediterranean wind goddesses, a slight breeze picked up from the west and tiny ripples shivered the oily sea. In a trice we had the awning down, the mainsail hoisted, and were moving as a sailboat is born to move, silently, except for the creaking of the parrells on the mast and the jingle of the blocks aloft.

Kindly, the wind steadied and we soon had a fine breeze, on a broad reach, over an almost varnished sea, and at dusk the high mountains of Majorca hove into view, at first dull gray, low on the southern horizon, then blue, then dark green, and finally, as the sun set in the west, turning to beige, then gold. After dusk, only a diadem of twinkling points of light showed that the island awaited us, as I steered with one bare foot and ate more of our rapidly dwindling food.

Dawn found *Cresswell* only five miles off the small port of Sóller, and by noon we were at anchor in the harbor, just off a sandy beach packed with bodies in various shades of sunburn, idling, lounging, walking, running, splashing in the sea, and shouting German.

"Ho, Englander!" someone called out as we paddled ashore in the dinghy. "*Velkommen. Wo ist du* come from?"

"I say," chortled Sissie, "what jolly fun!"

"Yeah," I agreed. "They're still guarding the beaches—they've got the D Day trauma. Look how they're all drawn up in defensive phalanxes, all huddled together in strategic spots, like S.S. divisions."

Nelson, left onboard, was patrolling the deck, glaring at the Germans with his one eye. Sissie and I hauled the dinghy several yards up the beach, then plodded through the sand toward the tiny town nestled in the folds of the mountains.

"How much money you got, Sissie?"

"Two hundred fifty pesetas."

"Give me 25; I'm going to have a scout around. You go to the small local shops and spend that money wisely. Don't go to the tourist places, they'll skin you alive. Get dried fish and rice and beans. Nothing imported, understand?"

"Of course, you silly old thing. I shall try to get enough for two weeks. Now don't you fret, Skippah. Orf you go, and have a jolly old time among these *dreadful* peasants!"

"I'll try and rustle up some business for tomorrow."

"Tootle-pip, old bean!"

She swung her shopping bag back and forth and soon her blue gym slip and frizzy red hair disappeared behind a sun-bronzed mob of blond Volkswagen nut-tighteners and their *hausfraus*.

I made for the nearest bar, which was pulsing full of Teutonic tourists. The noise was deafening. Spanish waiters rushed to and fro with trays of San Miguel beer and *tapas* (little plates of tidbits). Music blared from a record player: "Malaguena," "Spanish Eyes," "It's Later than You Think" (the latter, sung in German, sounded like the "Horst Wessel Song"). I ordered a Terry brandy, speaking to the barman in Spanish.

"What's the crowd for?"

"*Señor*, they have come to watch the soccer finals on our television—*una grande juego de futbol*."

"Soccer finals? Who's playing?"

"England and Germany."

He rushed to serve another 50 beers, then rushed back. I could tell by his face he had me marked for a Briton.

"Who do you think will win, *Señor?*" he asked me.

"England, of course."

"*Seguro*. Sure." He winked at me, then nodded at the crowd

of Germans. "But don't tell *them* that!"

He poured me another brandy, saying "*¡Salud, amigo!*" and I put my hand in my pocket to pay; but he restrained me. "That's on me, *Señor Ingles.*"

A blond giant next to me, about seven feet tall, with shoulders like a barn door, hearing us converse, turned around. He spoke to me just as the television was turned on and the match began. From his patronizing attitude, it was obvious that he took me—dressed in scuffy corduroy pants rolled up to the knees, a patched blue shirt, and a straw hat—as a Majorcan fisherman.

"*Hola, amigo.* My name is Franz." He clapped my shoulder, making me wince. "You like football, yes?" He spoke in a gutteral accent in basic Spanish.

"*Si, Señor, si. Me gusta mucho.*" I slumped my shoulders, third-world-wise.

"Germany win!" He thumped the counter, then glared at me. "*Si?*"

"No, *Señor*. England win!"

"Germany . . . *Alemania!*"

"England!" I replied. "*Inglaterra!*"

Franz slapped a huge roll of banknotes on the counter and his face turned apoplectic. "I say *Germany*, and I bet anyone, *anyone.*" He glared around him as his beer-sodden voice rose above the television commentary. "*Anyone!* Ten thousand pesetas—*zehntausand pesetas*—that Germany will win!"

"*Señor*, I accept your bet," I murmured quietly.

The barman looked aghast. I gestured toward him and said to Franz: "I don't have the money with me, but my friend, the barman here, will vouch for me. Right, Pepe?" The barman caught on, "Right, José!"

As the match, the European final, ground on, I fingered the 15 pesetas I had in my pocket as the barman slid yet another free brandy over the counter with a wink. At halftime the score was 1-0 for Germany. At the scheduled end of the match, the English had evened it 2-2. The overtime would decide the game.

As this was announced, I stood there and sweated. If Germany scored, I would have to go down to the beach and sell my rubber dinghy to the first taker. That would fetch 10,000 pesetas easily, but then I would be left with no means of getting ashore—and no means of ferrying day-trippers to the boat.

Five minutes passed as excitement mounted in the bar, the hundred or so Germans thumping tables with their beer mugs and me getting ready to fight my way out of another Dunkirk. Then, suddenly, England slid 2 goals in and the match was over. England had won! Franz collapsed, almost in tears. I ordered him a beer, as he counted the 10,000 pesetas out on the counter, and slipped the barman 100 pesetas.

"How did you know England would win?" demanded Franz.

"Because, *Herr* Franz," I said in English, "They always do in the end!"

At first he was nonplussed; then, breaking into a smile, he turned polite and meek. "I should have known, I should have known," he said in English.

I offered my hand and he shook it with his great paw. Then I turned to go, throwing 1,000 pesetas on the counter.

"A drink for everyone!"

"*Si, Señor!*" the barman shouted as he swung into action and I slid out into the afternoon sunshine. As I plodded through the powdery sand to meet Sissie by the dinghy, my shirt and pants were wet through with sweat. That German was a *big* man, a *very* big man,

"Yoo-hoo, Tristan. I say, I found some supah dried cod in this *extraordinary* sort of ebsolutely gloomy little *cave* of a shop, straight out of El Greco."

"Cod be blowed! *Here.*" I handed her 2,000 pesetas. "Go and get some meat and bacon and butter—and caviar, if you like. We're in the money!"

Sissie's face lit up, her crabapple cheeks shining in the glare of the sun.

"Tristan, dahling! Wherever did this come from? You haven't been sort of *naughty*, have you, my pet?"

I told her briefly what had happened. She threw her thick

arms around my neck and hooted, then danced a jig in the sand.

"Oh, jolly, *jolly* day!" she crowed, as the fat German *hausfraus* stared at her in astonishment. "Whoopee! *We're in the money, we're in the money, ta ta ta ta ta.*" She ran up the beach, kicking sand in all directions.

"Wait a minute!" I called after her. "There's a bloke in that bar over there, big feller, a Jerry. Name's Franz. Built like a panzer tank; you can't mistake him. He's just lost 10,000 pesetas. Got a face like a hanged spaniel. Go and tell him he's invited onboard to dinner tonight, and to bring his missus. We'll meet him on the beach at 8 o'clock. And if he likes, he can bring two friends as well. We'll really push the boat out."

"Oh Tristan, you absolute dahling! A party! Oh whack-o! I do *so* love a party."

"And Sissie."

"Yes, Skippah?"

"No singing tonight—right?"

"Oh, you silly old *deah* thing, of course not!" She disappeared into the bar. Later, Nelson wagged his tail as we clambered onboard, loaded down with good food.

We stayed at Sóller for a week, bought some paint with our new fortune, and spent the mornings sprucing up the topsides and deck. In the afternoons we lazed around, Sissie on the beach, me at the bars—in between strengthening the mainmast.

The anchorage at Sóller was well protected by a seawall, great blocks of pinkish-gray stones, and the local fishing boats were tied to it stern to. Now and again a non-Spanish pleasure yacht came in to spend the night: big, sleek schooners and ketches from the south of France, usually with the large crews the French seem to favor, waving their arms around and climbing the rigging. (The average French youngster's idea of enjoying himself is to make lots of noise.) Long, sleek, motor yachts came in (usually Italian) with uniformed crewmen, all with the name of the boat emblazoned on their T-shirts, and the usual complement of bikini'd nymphs, pyjama'd dowagers and harassed-looking owners.

The odd British wanderer wore in with weatherworn ensign and blistered paintwork. One of these, one sultry evening, caught my eye: at little 24-foot sloop. She was called *Tea
Pot*, and as soon as I sighted the baggy-wrinkle on her rigging
I gave her close attention. (Baggy-wrinkle is pads made up of
old rope fastened to the rigging wires to prevent the sails
from chafing against them. It is usually the hallmark of a
deep-water sailor. At that time it was little seen in the Mediterranean.) Setting out the anchor on the sloop's deck was a
raffish chap of about 25, just under six feet, burned by the
sun to a deep copper color, wearing only a pair of very tatty
pants.

I hailed him: "Ho, there, *Tea Pot! Tea Pot* ahoy!" The sloop
swung closer.

"Hello!" came the reply, over 15 yards of German-infested
harbor water. "That's *Cresswell*, eh? Heard all about you in
Cherbourg last year. Come on over!"

He held up a bottle of beer.

"Be right with you!" I scrambled into the dinghy and paddled over.

"Peter Kelly's the name," he said, reaching with a calloused
hand to shake mine. (I had noticed that the port of registry
under the name *Tea Pot* was Ramsey, Isle of Man.)

"Glad to meet you, Pete."

"I also heard about you from Joe, who met you in Toulouse.
He's a mate of mine. Met him in Plymouth on my way down
to the Med; he was coming up from France," said Peter as he
handed me a beer.

"What are you doing in these parts?" I asked him, when we
had settled down in his tiny cockpit.

"Oh, just roving around a bit. I'm a fisherman by trade, but
I built *Tea Pot* in my spare time. Took me two years. Then I
saved up a few hundred quid and took off for the Med. Did a
delivery from Plymouth to Spain on the way down that paid
me a bit more. But things aren't too good now. I'm living
mainly on the fish I catch."

All was shipshape and clean on the boat. The cabin was
spotless, as was the deck. All the lines were neatly coiled,

even though he had only been at anchor for a few minutes.

"Looking for some work, Pete?"

His eyes were a startling blue, the peculiar Manx blue, flecked with green (like the Irish Sea itself on a sunny spring day), set in a ruddy, sunburned, hard face with humorous line around the eyes and mouth.

"Depends what it is."

"I've to deliver a 58-footer, brand new, from Barcelona to Gibraltar at the end of this month. I'm looking for a mate. No cooking—the owner's doing that; he's coming with us. Seems a good bloke, a bit strange, and doesn't know the stern from the bow. But he's paying well—150 bucks for a short run like that's not bad."

"What about *Tea Pot?*"

"Well, accompany *Cresswell* to Andraitx. I've an English biddy with me . . ."

Pete looked at me quizzically, then smiled.

"No, nothing like that, for Christ's sake," I said. "She's old enough to be your mother and about as pretty as the ass end of a double-decker bus." He grinned as I said this and handed me another beer. "But she will look after *Cresswell*, and Andraitx is a good safe harbor, from all accounts. You put *Tea Pot* out to two anchors and she can keep an eye on her for you while you're away with me. She can pump her out . . . "He didn't let me finish.

"My boat don't leak!" he exclaimed, proudly.

"Well, anyway, she can look after her for you. And while she's in town, shopping or frigging around, my dog Nelson will be on guard." I swigged at my beer. "What d'ye say?"

"O.K., Tristan; sounds fair enough. When do we leave for Andraitx?"

"Right away."

I explained to Sissie that she could look after the boats and feed Nelson while Pete and I delivered *Antoinette* to Gibraltar. She was not too enthusiastic about the idea until we arrived in Andraitx, at the western tip of Majorca. Once she saw the port (one of the most beautiful on earth) she fell in love with it. Besides, there was a small colony of very toffee-nosed

English ex-colonials at Andraitx, all very much birds of Sissie's feather.

She could not leave the boat as she had not yet received her allowance from England and was temporarily penniless. I left her just enough money for her and Nelson to eat for two months . . . all I had, apart from the fares for Pete and me to get to Barcelona.

Has anybody here seen Kelly?—
Kaye, eee, double ell, wye—
Has anybody here seen Kelly?—
Find him if you can!
He's as bad as old Antonio—
Left me all alone-io—
Has anybody here seen Kelly—
Kelly from the Isle of Man!

Edwardian music-hall song.

19

An Actor, Bullfighter, and a Traitor

Aubrey was waiting for us at the Barcelona airport, jumping up and down excitedly in front of the waiting crowd of welcomers. He wore a red-and-white-striped collarless shirt, green corduroy pants, and an artist's straw hat.

"How are you, Tristan, my boy? She's all finished and ready for trials." He looked at Pete with an appraising eye.

"Aubrey, this is Peter Kelly. He's a Manxman and he's my mate for this trip." Pete stuck out a huge mitt and squeezed Aubrey's hand hard enough to make him wince.

"So very pleased to meet you," simpered Aubrey, eyeing Pete from eyes to knees and back again.

"Hi."

Aubrey was accompanied by a young man of about 23, dressed in a Spanish-cut suit of gray pinstripe, extra wide at the shoulders with a narrow waist. A white flower was stuck in his buttonhole. Very dark, swarthy complexioned, with two gold teeth and two gold rings on each hand, he looked like an Andalusian gypsy, which he was.

"Now, my boys, I want you to meet Manuel," said Aubrey. We shook his hand—firmer than Aubrey's but still limp.

Manuel bowed from the neck as we were introduced. At

the back of his head was the little pigtail which matadors wear.

"Manuel is an up and coming bullfighter," Aubrey gushed, "becoming more and more famous by the week. Oh, absolutely, *by the week!*"

As Aubrey spoke, several young girls and matrons crowded around Manuel, who drew himself up to his full height of five feet eight and, putting one foot in front of the other, preened himself. He studied Pete as if he were something which had dropped off a baggage cart and slowly, arrogantly, lifted his nose into the air.

"Pleased to meet you," said I in English to Manuel. We all made for the airport bar.

"Manuel is coming with us as far as Málaga," said Aubrey, as soon as we were settled down over drinks. "His family lives near Granada, so we can drop him off at Málaga and he'll go on from there. Then the three of us can carry on sailing to Gib. All right with you, Tristan?"

"O.K. with me Aubrey. Has he done any sailing?"

"No, but his friends have power boats and he's made a few trips with them."

I studied Manuel as he sat bolt upright on his stool, taking no notice of us and pulling long, stern Andalusian faces at every female in the place, young and old. Noticing his pigtail, they smiled wiltingly under the gaze of this *macho de machos.*

On the way to the taxi I murmured to Pete, "What do you reckon of this one, mate?"

"Smells like a Tangier whorehouse."

"Well, maybe he can handle a line. Looks strong enough. Maybe he's O.K."

We piled into an ancient Ford taxicab and took off for the boatyard. *Antoinette* was lying at the jetty, gleaming white and pristine in her newborn elegance.

"There she is!" squealed Aubrey as the cab turned into the gate. "My darling *debutante*, and soon she'll be skipping over the sparkling blue seas, wearing her *bee-ay-yu-ti-ful* new ball gown!" He bounced up and down on his seat.

Onboard, in the varnished interior of the cabin, very flashy and poorly carpentered, Aubrey poured four glasses of Spanish champagne. It bubbled over, onto the *varnished* cabin sole, and Aubrey dived for a wiping-up cloth as the three of us, Pete, Manuel and I, stood there stiffly. Aubrey was on his knees in a flash, mopping up the small puddle of wine. Then, bobbing back on his feet, he grasped the midship's sponson and gave a toast: "To my beautiful, darling queen of the dancing seas!"

"*Salud. Buenas viajes,*" intoned Manuel, stern and masculine.

"Cheers, Aubrey," Pete said, grinning.

"May she live long and die happy, and may the skin of her ass never cover a banjo." I gave the old Celtic sea toast, staring into space.

Aubrey tapped me on the wrist and said: "Now, now; naughty, naughty!"

"Traditional, from Liverpool," I told him. "Now Aubrey, Pete and I are going to scout around the boat and find out where everything is, O.K.? While we do that, you and Manuel nip over to the shops and get the stores in. Here, I've a list; that's the basics. Two weeks' supply for four men. Anything else you feel like getting in—well, that's your concern. We'll be out for trials tomorrow, and all being well, we'll take off for Málaga the day after."

"Can't I stay and show you around?" Aubrey asked. "I've been here all the time the boat was building; I know where everything is."

"When you get back, if there's anything we've missed or can't find we'll ask you and you can show us where it is. Also, when you get back you can give us a run around the engine installation."

"Oh well. Come on, Manuel, *vamonos a las tiendas.*" Aubrey and his bullfighter minced and strode off.

"Bright pair," said Pete.

"Live and let live, Pete."

The following day the four of us took *Antoinette* for trials in Barcelona Bay. The first thing we found was that the big Italian diesel engine had been installed at an angle to the boat's centerline, under the cabin's dining table. Instead of angled through a universal joint, the propellor shaft had been led directly through the stern gland at 25 degrees from the hull centerline! This caused the boat, when under power, to go in circles.

"Bloody typical!" said Pete. Aubrey's face dropped as I told him we could not use the engine.

"You'll have to get the engine reinstalled, Aubrey, if you want to use it on the trip down to Gibraltar."

"But that would take a couple of months!"

"Right. So if you want to be off before Spanish customs get round your neck, we'll have to do it under sail. No alternative."

"That's O.K., Tristan," said Pete. "The winds are fairly lively this time of year. Mostly northeasters, offshore."

"Oh, all right then," said Aubrey.

"We'll look over the sailing gear and take off tomorrow. No sense having a special sailing trial outside Barcelona and coming back in again. It'll cost a fortune in towing fees."

We found all the halyards and sheets to be led wrongly, so Pete and I rigged new leads with small blocks. Then we checked the bilge pumps, topped the fresh-water tanks, and were ready. We could run the engine out of gear to generate electricity, and this was relegated to Aubrey. Pete had the responsibility of caring for the sail gear and topsides; Aubrey looked after the galley, the engine, and below-decks cleanliness (he was very finicky); and I took on the navigation, responsibility for hull maintenance, pilotage, ground tackle, and overall responsibility for the voyage as skipper. Manuel was to be a spare hand, to assist the others as needed.

On June 4 we arranged a tow out of Barcelona Harbor and were off at last. The first afternoon and night the wind was slight and *Antoinette* gently rocked and bobbed her way southeast with all her sails up—the genoa, staysail, mainsail, fisherman's staysail (which hoists between the main and mizzen masts), and the mizzen. We made about 50 miles during the night, until the wind freshened with the dawn. Then we took in the genoa and hauled up the working jib and soon we were bowling along with a stiff northeast wind, southwest, off the mouth of the river Ebro.

This part of the coast of Spain is very low and the sea is shallow, with mud and sandbanks built up on the bottom from the effluvia of the Ebro. Therefore I stood out to the offing, into deep water. As we headed out the wind rose even more, and by dusk it was blowing a full gale and veering, to northwest first and then round to west. This meant that *Antoinette* was soon close hauled on the port tack and beating heavily against the rising seas and the wind. The Mediterranean is shallow and any increase in wind soon builds a very nasty, steep lob of seas.

As *Antoinette* was a newly built craft, Pete and I were wary of the construction and the rigging; so at the first sign of the wind's rising, we decided we would both stay ondeck at night. By evening the seas were hard and the boat was pounding.

Manuel was collapsed over the lee lifelines, spewing into the sea, while Aubrey manfully did his best to help us, retching all the while. But to give him his due, he *tried*.

By midnight, Pete and I had shortened the sail to storm jib and mizzen, and the boat was just barely making headway due south. With a big deckhouse, she made plenty of windage and was thrown around from one sea to the next.

Between retches over the side, Manuel slithered back into the cockpit, to bend on his knees and mutter to himself. "What's he doing?" I asked Pete, over the roar of the wind and the slash of the spray.

Pete bent over Manuel to hear him, then straightened up and staggered toward me, cupping his hand by his mouth.

"Telling his rosary, Skip: 'Ave Maria' and all that stuff!"

"Oh, well; in that case we'll be all right, eh?" I dodged another half ton of sea water as it crashed over the side.

"Yeah, we'll be all right." Pete grabbed the binnacle as another sea came onboard, out of the black-gray frenzy of the *tramontana* wind and sea.

All night Pete and I stood watch and watch, making hot cocoa and struggling with the kicking, bucking rudder. By dawn the gale was steady and I knew we'd seen the worst. The wind hauled around again to the north and soon we were under all working sail, bashing away southwest.

After Pete and I finished our breakfast of burgoo and tea, Manuel, disheveled, gray-faced and haggard-eyed, asked me: "*Señor Capitán* Tristan, for the love of God, please take me into port, any port. I will give you 10,000 pesetas to get me into harbor!" (Aubrey was supine in his berth, moaning now and again. Pete was on the wheel, in his oilskins. I was somewhat tired, and perhaps a bit jumpy after a night of anxiety.)

"Look, I can't take you into any of the ports of Castellon; they're too small and dangerous. The entrances are shallow and narrow. You'll have to stick it out until we reach Valencia. More boats get lost trying to get into harbor in a panic than were ever lost at sea. No, my friend, you'll just have to grin and bear it."

Another sea crashed onboard.

"But I am so afraid! I am so afraid!"

Manuel whimpered, gazing with hopeless eyes at the moderate seas. Then he collapsed, crying softly; his head falling onto his chest, as Pete came up through the hatchway.

"What's up, Skipper?"

"He's feeling rough . . . he's a bit scared."

"Maybe we should send for a crowd to watch him; then he can be *brave!*" said Pete, relieving me of the wheel.

We fetched Valencia the following day, still in steep seas but with a moderating wind. Until we entered the harbor, Aubrey staggered around, sick as a dog but doing his best, while Manuel cluttered up the cockpit, causing Pete and me to clamber over him to get below or at the sheet winches or forward to handle the sails. But as soon as the water flattened out inside the harbor entrance, Aubrey spruced up and patted the doghouse roof.

"My sweet girl, my beautiful debutante, was that nasty sea so awful for you? Well, never mind, you've made your very first party." Pete and I looked at each other, hardly able to keep from grinning.

As the boat crept alongside the Valencia Yacht Club jetty, Manuel stood on deck, one foot in front of the other and a hand inside his shirt, looking intrepid and *macho*. He said nothing as he stepped ashore. He did not even deign to look at Pete or me, but was off as soon as Aubrey had shaken his hand.

"Gonna miss him" said Pete.

As Aubrey gallantly clambered back onboard his boat, I said to him, "How are you, Aub? Feel like going on?"

"Certainly, old chap. I can't abandon my darling girl on her first outing, can I? Can't let a bit of the old *mal de mer* stop me, what?" As he went below, Pete said to me: "He's a funny bloke, but you have to admire him."

I nodded. Aubrey, after all was said and done, was all right; he hadn't abandoned his vessel, which many other people would have done.

"Hey, Aub!" I called as he disappeared forward to fiddle about dusting.

"Yoo-hoo?" he called out.

"Pete and I are going ashore tonight for a ramble."

"Right-o, my boy, permission granted!" Aubrey sang out.

"No, Aub, we weren't asking *permission*. What we wanted to know is if you'd like to come with us."

"Really, I say, what splendid fun, what a fabulous idea!" Aubrey stuck his head out the hatch and smiled all over his elfin face.

That evening we went ashore, with Aubrey in his golfing plus-fours and terribly English flat-peaked cap, and made for a cheap but clean restaurant in the main square, the *Café Balanza*. We ate great plates of rice and seafood with Tarragona wine and told tales of voyages past, while Aubrey explained the intricacies of the stage and dropped names as profusely as the *Valencianos* dropped the shells of the shrimps on the cafe floor.

The bar of the cafe was crowded with men drinking wine and nibbling *tapas*. Like most Spanish bars, it was very noisy, with waiters calling out orders to the barmen, dishwashers crashing plates and glasses around, and the customers all trying to outshout one another. As we sat gazing at the scene, Pete suddenly stiffened.

"Tristan!" he hissed.

"What's up, mate?"

"See that bloke, at the end of the bar, near the door? That thin-looking feller with the sport jacket and brown shoes?"

I saw a youngish chap, about 22 or 23, clean shaven with wispy, mousy hair, a weak, receding chin, a snub nose, and shifty eyes, standing quietly by himself drinking a beer, one foot on the bar rail.

"What about him?"

"I was reading the local paper earlier on, and his picture's in it. He's from Gibraltar and he's over here claiming *political asylum*. They had this article, with him saying how Gibraltar really belongs to Spain, and how the Gibraltar government is repressive and cruel, and how old Franco is the bee's knees, and how all the Gibraltarians want to become Spanish."

"That's bullshit, Pete. They held a referendum in Gib last year and only two percent wanted to join up with Spain!"

"Right, but they also had an article about this bloke—Percy something, his name is—in the *London Daily Telegram* a few weeks ago. I read it in Palma. They said he was a bloody sprucer, that he'd been in the nick several times in Gib for burglary and thieving. Seems he's living off the fat of the land here, hobnobbing with Franco's mob."

"Despicable character, rough trade, I'd say," Aubrey observed. "Ignore him!"

"Ignore him be blowed!" declared Pete, standing up.

"What're you going to do?" I asked.

"Teach him a lesson!"

"Now take it easy, Pete," I said in a low voice. "Remember, these buggers are using him, even though they know he's a lying sod. They aren't going to stand by while someone knocks him around."

"I'm not going to fight him," said Pete quietly, "I'm going to buy him a drink!" He sidled over to the bar.

Aubrey looked agitated, but I grinned at him. "Come on, Aub, let Pete look after himself; he's a big boy. Let's move on to another bar." As we went out the door I looked out of the corner of my eye as Pete, who was smiling and chatting with the Gibraltar traitor.

Aubrey and I did the rounds of the Valencia bars that night, returning onboard around 2 a.m. As we clambered down the companionway ladder, all was dark below, but it was obvious that Pete was onboard for the hatch was open. "Sshh," he hissed as we descended.

"What's up, Pete?"

He grabbed my elbow and Aubrey's shoulder. "Come on forward," he murmured.

We shuffled after him, feeling our way through the dark cabin. The door in the forward bulkhead was open, and in the gloom I could see a body lying on the port berth. Pete shone his torch on the body's face. It was Percy the Traitor, unconscious, and on his forehead, right across it, was tatooed a great big Union Jack!

"I got him pissed in the Balanza. Cost me 100 pesetas to get him tattooed down near the fishdock," Pete said, grinning in the torchlight.

I shook his hand. Aubrey made a tch-tch sound, shaking his head.

"What do you reckon, Skip?"

'There's a bit of breeze outside, Pete; let's get the hell out of here!" Pete made for the ladder.

"Aren't you going to land him?" Aubrey asked. "The police will find him and chase us."

"*Land* him? Shit, Aub, he's going with us to Gibraltar!"

As I let go of the sail tiers, Pete was already ashore, casting off the mooring lines. Half an hour later we were out to sea, with our guest bound to the forward berth. By dawn we were well out of Spanish territorial waters and bound for the Rock.

"Pete, you're in charge of Percy. Look after him." I said as we headed out.

"I will," said Pete gruffly. "I'll look after the cowson . . . "

Aubrey shook his head as he stirred the stew and flicked his snow-white dishcloth at flies in the galley.

Percy woke up during the night, but we didn't hear a peep out of him. He just lay there, tied loosely to the berth, staring into space. Then, as he realized what was happening, he started to cry softly to himself.

"Shut up, bastard!" called Pete. "You're going home. There's no charge against you—we're not at war with Spain. And if you stay indoors and hide for the next 10 years, you should be O.K. So stop *skriking*; you'll soon be home with dear old Mum."

The traitor moaned in dismay at the forthcoming reception from all his chums, his old school friends, and workmates.

"Pipe down, you bloody twicer, or I'll give you the deep six!" shouted Pete.

The next day the weather was fair, with a good stiff northerly blowing off the land, giving *Antoinette* a broad reach and a fairly calm sea; so she made very good time, with all her working rig and the genoa pulling like artillery mules. All went steadily, with Pete and me tending the steering and the sails and Aubrey rustling up the grub, with frequent mugs of tea in between times.

The evening was splendid, with the wind easing, the moon and a thousand stars hanging in the sky and the twinkling lights shining on the Spanish coast under the black clumps of the Sierra Nevada.

After supper, Aubrey, having found his sea legs, cheerfully offered to take a watch so that Pete and I could get some extra sleep. I handed over the wheel, but it was soon obvious that Aubrey had no idea of steering by compass. Some folk are like that, and it takes them ages to get the idea of keeping the lubberline, which appears to remain still, over the right spot on the compass card, which of course appears to swing from side to side.

After an hour of coaching him, I finally said: "Look, Aub, I'll tell you what. The night's all clear—no clouds about. What about if you steer on a star? Look, I'll set her on course, then you choose a star as near to dead ahead as you can, and just keep the star there. See, it's simple!"

"Good idea!" Aubrey exclaimed.

After I set the wheel on course, Aubrey picked out Sirius, the Dog Star, shining brightly to the west, about 60 degrees above the horizon. I watched him steer for a few minutes. Satisfied, I left Aubrey and went below to get some shuteye and was soon asleep—or at least in that comatose state, half awake and half asleep, which sailors call sleep. Suddenly I was sitting bolt upright, awake. The boat was going round and round in circles, with the sheet blocks clattering and banging as the sails jibed, suddenly filled, then jibed again. I clambered out of my berth and was soon up the ladder ondeck.

"What the hell's happening, Aub?" I called, as the main boom slammed across the cockpit yet again. Aubrey had the wheel almost hard over to port and the boat was describing a perfect circle through the water!

"Nothing, Tristan, I'm doing as you said," he replied, still staring ahead into space. "I'm following the star."

Again the main filled, and I grabbed the wheel. "Which bloody star?" I demanded.

"That one there. See it?" He stretched his arm out to point at a particularly bright body passing across the horizon, steadily.

"Aub, you nit, that's a bleedin' airplane!" I shouted, getting back on course. "Look, it's a patrol plane, flying round and round the horizon. Probably a customs flying boat, for Christ's sake. Can't you see his green light?"

"Oh, I say, I'm most awf'ly dreadfully sorry!"

"Never mind, Aub. Tell you what: how about you and me having a nice hot cup of cocoa?"

"Sure thing, Skipper." He bounced down below and lit the stove.

"Aub!"

"Yes?"

"Make one for Pete, too. It'll be his watch in 15 minutes."

"What about our friend up forward?" Aubrey said quietly from the hatchway.

"Sod him. Let him sleep, if his conscience will let him."

Aubrey sneaked a cup to Percy anyway, but I pretended not to notice it. He was like that.

The following morning, out of the misty west, with a good southeast wind pushing *Antoinette* onward to the Straits, we saw the mighty Rock loom out of the low clouds. By dawn we were tied up at the old submarine pens.

Percy sniffled as he was entered by a courteous, grinning, hard-eyed bobby.

Aubrey had his boat, safe and sound from Franco's customs; Pete and I had earned $150 each; Manuel was back with his worshipers, and little Percy was home again safe, almost sound, and beyond temptation's reach.

For South Australia we are bound;
Heave away! Haul away!
For to sail the Horn around;
We're bound for South Australia!
Heave away you rolling kings,
Heave away, Haul away!
Heave away you rolling kings,
We're bound for South Australia!

Halyard shanty,
mid-nineteenth century

In the orginal version, as Tansy Lee (1866-1958) sang it,
"Rolling Kings" was "rollikins" which is an old English
term for drunkards. However, the Australian,
when drunk, *is* a "rolling King."

20

Monkey Business

Gibraltar is one of the crossroads of the sailor's world. Most of the ships and boats of all sizes passing in and out of the Mediterranean call there, for stores, for repairs, and simply because it is (for the most part) an oasis in a sea of corruption, injustice, ineptness, and inefficiency. Gibraltar, a six-square-mile gray, capsized rock jutting out of the choppy Straits, with the clouds scudding over its peak betimes, foretelling strong winds, is a bastion of *habeus corpus*. The only one for a thousand miles in any direction.

Now, in June 1965, *habeus corpus* and Gibraltar were under siege again. The Franco government had closed the frontier, preventing the Spanish labor force from working in the great dockyard and stopping the supplies of food from the Andalusian mainland; even stopping the supply of water, which augments the rain caught on the great concrete catchments which cover a great area of the sun-scorched seaward side of the Rock.

The Gibraltarians had only three exits from their Rock to the outside world: by air from the airfield which ran right up to the frontier fence; by ferry to Tangier in Morocco, across the Straits; and by small craft, mainly visiting craft of British origin. Many of the latter were making a good living carting fresh vegetables and other supplies from Morocco and Portugal. The small-craft harbor was therefore busy and crowded as *Antoinette* lay alongside.

Percy the Fink was landed under the jaundiced eyes of an immigration officer and two helmeted bobbies, who were detailed to escort him up the narrow main street. After taking leave of a grateful Aubrey, Pete and I took up the rear of this party, while crowds of Maltese, Indian, and Arab shopkeepers and shoppers of all races jeered and shook their fists at the erstwhile friend of Franco. At the *Café Suisse*, a renowned sailors' resort with a long bar, fast service and dancing girls, we left the procession and entered to slake our thirst.

The place was roomy, seedy, noisy, and very packed. We forced our way to the crowded bar through the hurlyburly, and came up behind a small, rather scruffy-looking fellow, wearing an ancient greasy fedora and a broken nose.

"Excuse me, mate," said I, reaching my arm forward to get at the bar.

He turned, quickly looked me up and down, then grinned. "Yeah, right, cobber; never stop a good man from getting to his booze."

I ordered two cold beers and passed one over the crowd back to Pete, who was scanning the girls, sitting at tables around the periphery of the room. The little man spoke again, after taking a great draught of his beer.

"I heard you did a good job on that bloody drongo!"

"Teach him to shoot his mouth off, won't it?"

The little man extended his hand. "Willy Clossart's the name. From Adelaide, South Australia. They call me Closet. Why don't you and your mate come over and join my skipper? He's over there."

I gazed over the heads and through the crowd and saw, sitting in the shadows, a sad-looking elderly gentleman, wearing half-lens spectacles and reading a London *Daily Telegraph*, his thick gray hair falling in wisps over his forehead.

"Right, Willy—er—Closet." I made my way, taking Pete's elbow, toward the skipper's table. He looked up as we approached, staring short-sightedly through his specs. "That you, Closet?" he asked, gruffly.

"YES, IT'S ME, HENRY, GOT A COUPLE OF FRIENDS HERE: THE BLOKES THAT BROUGHT THAT BLOODY DRONGO BACK FROM SPAIN WITH HIS HEAD TAT-TOOED WITH THE POMMY FLAG!"

A wide grin broke over the old man's face as he stretched a hard, calloused hand to me.

"Please to meet you. Henry Willon's the name. You'll have to speak up, I'm deaf."

He cupped his hand to his ear and his mouth fell open under his straggly mustache as he waited for my reply. I introduced myself and Pete, and we sat down. While Henry talked to Pete, I caught "Closet's" attention.

"How deaf is he, Willy?"

"Deaf as a post, mate—when he wants to be." Closet said quietly. I glanced at Henry, who seemed intent on catching Pete's coversation. Henry appeared to be around 65.

"What boat are you off?" I asked Closet, who was ordering beers all round.

"*Cuatro cervezas, por favor,*" shouted Closet.

"Right, mate," the Gibraltarian waiter replied pointedly; "four beers."

Closet turned to me. "We're from *Fanny Adams*, power boat. You must have seen her when you came into harbor. She's right at the end of the berth, nearest the harbor entrance. Fifty-five footer, ex-admiralty harbor launch."

"No, can't say as I noticed her. What are you doing, cruising?"

From the looks of their clothes—Henry in a rumpled old pinstriped tropical suit, no socks, and leather sandals and Closet in an oily, once-white coverall and battered fedora, both with four days' growth on their chins—they seemed more like Bowery bums.

"Cruising? Well, you *could* say that. Henry's been in the Med almost since the end of the war. You know, doing a bit here, a bit there. Summer in Gib and Tangier, winters in Barcelona and Ibiza. I'm his engineer. Met up with him in the south of France, oh, 15 years ago. We've been together ever since, off and on. I just rebuilt Henry's engine."

"What are you going to do?"

Closet hesitated a minute. "Well, we're thinking of heading east for Formentera. Henry's got friends there."

"When?" I was all ears.

"HEY HENRY!" Closet shouted across the table. Henry, who had gone back to studying his paper, looked up sharply and cupped his ear. "WHEN ARE WE LEAVING?"

"Dunno, depends when we can get enough fuel." His gruff voice tailed off, sorrowfully. He looked like an elderly bloodhound.

"HOW MUCH FUEL DO YOU NEED?" I shouted across the table.

"We've enough to get halfway. I need another 100 gallons."

"HOW MUCH MONEY IS THAT?" Pete asked.

"About $80. But I can get it cheaper in Spain, in Algeciras. Got a mate there. I can get it for 50." Henry lifted his pint and gulped hard.

"IF ME AND PETE PAY FOR HALF THAT FUEL, TWENTY-FIVE DOLLARS, AND FOR SIX DAYS' FOOD, SAY, WILL YOU TAKE US TO IBIZA? IT'S RIGHT BY FORMENTERA . . . AND WE CAN GIVE YOU A HAND."

"O.K., mate, you're on," said Henry.

"But we'll have to see the boat FIRST. If we DO come on, when do we LEAVE?" Pete asked.

"Whenever you're ready," Closet rejoined, eagerly.

"What about now?" I asked, in a quiet voice.

"Whazzat?" Henry shouted.

"I SAID WHAT ABOUT NOW?"

"Right, mate," said Henry, standing up, his grubby shirt hanging outside his trousers, which were held up by a black suspender to port and nothing to starboard. "Right, mate, come on!" He limped toward the door of the bar.

Pete looked at me, then back to Henry.

Closet patted my shoulder and laughed. "It's all right, mate, Deaf Henry's been like that for years—infantile paralysis. Don't let it worry you; he was once a racing car champion. Only problem now, apart from his hearing and the lameness, is he can't see more than three feet in front of him. He's a good bloke, though, straight as a die!"

When we came at last to *Fanny Adams* I could hardly believe my eyes. There was not one drop of paint on her, apart from what had stuck between the wood grain years before. Besides she was *filthy*. Her capstan was just a block of rusty metal, her decks were strewn with litter, and her wheelhouse windows were gray with the grime of seasons. Inside, the wheelhouse was a shambles. Dirty shirts and socks were piled on top of cardboard cartons full of old newspapers, and a line of damp underwear, which might or might not have been washed, hung overhead. The brass compass binnacle, set in the wheelhouse forward window shelf, was green with verdigris and its small window was cracked and thick with grime. A small shelf of navigation tables, dirty and oily, completed the bridge deck, while in the middle of the wheelhouse an old deckchair, with half the canvas seat hanging in tatters, provided the only sign of comfort.

"Good old girl," mumbled Henry, patting the wheelhouse door.

Down below was a nightmare of greasy gunge and dank dirt. The galley was shoulder deep in unwashed pots and pans and alive with cockroaches. The paintwork was filthy and the place smelled like a garbage dump. We passed through the galley at Henry's urging and came to the engine compartment.

The contrast was staggering. In the midst of all this nightmare of dirt was a shining, polished, pristine, eight-cylinder diesel. I looked at Closet, whose eyes were shining with pride. This was his baby! It was amazing.

The whole boat was a midden, with years of piled-up dirt and gunge both topsides and below, and here, sitting in the middle of a sailor's nightmare, was this beautifully kept engine, all its brasswork highly polished and the bilge below painted spotless white, while all around it, greased and gleaming on the bulkhead and ship's sides, was stowed a fortune in tools and engine spares. "Jesus Holy Christ!" murmured Pete, who looked like he'd just found Aladdin's cave.

Closet opened the air bottle to start the engine, which in a few seconds was purring like a sewing machine. I looked around for the bilge pump and found it in good order. Miraculously, there did not seem to be a great deal of water in the bilge.

"When did you pump out last?" I asked Closet.

"Little bit three days ago. Henry can't understand it. By rights she should leak like a sieve, but she never has. She's double diagonal teak on oak frames, built for the Pommy Navy before the war. She was a steam launch."

"Yeah, that explains it; then, they built them like churches," I said, clambering up the ladder out of the dismal depths of *Fanny Adam's* living quarters.

"Well, shall we take off, Tristan . . . Pete?" asked Henry jovially as he limped ondeck.

"O.K., why NOT? But what will you do for STORES?" I shouted.

"Get 'em in Algeciras—much cheaper." Henry turned to Closet and roared: "Closet! Let go fore and aft!" Then he limped back into the wheelhouse to gaze intently through the windows. I stared in astonishment, for I couldn't see through the grime, except for vague shadows ahead. Closet rushed back onboard and grabbed the wheel from Henry.

"I'LL TAKE HER OUT, HENRY!"

"Right-o, Closet!"

Henry sat down on the tattered deckchair and relaxed, gazing gloomily into space, as Closet maneuvered the boat out of the yacht basin—sticking his head out the wheelhouse door for a second or two, then rushing back to the wheel to make any necessary adjustments to the course.

We were off. The engine hummed, the boat rode smoothly to the moderate sea in the Bay of Gibraltar, and 30 minutes later we were sitting alongside the fueling jetty in Algeciras. The voyage had passed easily, the only untoward occurrence being when Henry had limped below and emerged a few minutes later with a great paper bag full of grimy pornographic pictures. "These are my 'rudies,' " he said, handing them to Pete. "Bought 'em in Tangier."

We soon cleared the police, for Henry was well known and was looked upon as an eccentric madman—and therefore, in Spanish eyes, as semi-sacred. We decided to sail in the morning, and Pete cleaned the foc'sle berths for himself and me. After a supper of shepherd's pie, we all went ashore for a drink or two in the bars by the waterfront. As we sat outside a bar watching the thousands of winking lights spread over the mighty shadow of the Rock across the bay, as the moon rose over Europa Point, we fell into conversation with a wealthy-looking Spaniard, obviously an aquaintance of Henry's.

"Lads, this is Alfy," said Henry, gesturing to his friend to take a seat. The Spaniard looked at the four of us, one by one, imperiously.

"*Señor* Alphonso Rodriguez Lopez, *a sus ordenes.*"

He bowed slightly to Pete and me in turn. He was well dressed and well fed, and his perfume and hair oil balanced the ground-down poverty of everything around him—southern Spain, *Fanny Adams*, and us four *estrangeros*.

"Have a drink," said Henry.

"*Con mucho gusto*," replied *Señor* Alphonso.

"What's he say?" murmured Henry, gazing at Closet and cupping his ear.

"HE SAYS O.K., HENRY!" shouted Closet.

Settled down, *Señor* Alphonso spoke in excellent English. "I am the owner of extensive vineyards inland from here, toward Jerez, but you know, *Señors*, every evening I drive down here to watch the twinkling lights over there, on my beloved Gibraltar . . . Gibraltar *español* . . . for that wonderful rock is as much a part of Spain as my vineyard, as much a part as I am. And yet she has been in the hands of the English for so many years. So many centuries these interlopers have trod so arrogantly on the soil of sacred, holy Spain, center of the civilized world. *¡Dios mío!*"

"But the Arabs held it for centuries," I chimed in, as Closet kicked me under the table. "The Spanish never held it for more than a few years. And anyway, didn't it come to England through a royal marriage? I seem to remember . . ."

"Gibraltar is Spanish, all the same," he replied. "England has no right to the place; it is joined onto Spain." The señor's eyes flashed as he spat the words.

"But so are France and Portugal," said Pete. "Are you going to claim them too?"

Lopez, agitated, swallowed his sherry and ordered another.

"Look, *Señors*," he said, "I know that *Señor* Henry here is a good friend to Spain." Henry was gazing into the dark, over the bay, at the electric-light-spangled Rock. "Maybe you will consider a proposition I have for you."

Closet picked up his ears. Pete stretched his legs in front of his chair and folded his arms.

"There is plenty of money in it for you. In Gibraltar there are 22 apes, are there not?"

"Mmm," said Closet, nodding his head.

"And if the apes leave the rock, legend has it, the British will quit also. Right?"

"Mmm."

"And if someone were to steal those apes and bring them to Spain?"

Lopez fingered the gold tie-pin on his chest. Closet flicked his cigarette.

"You mean you want us to . . ."

"*Si. ¿Por qué no?* I will pay you 1,000 pesetas for each ape landed here in Algeciras." He rubbed his thumb and first finger together.

"But they are guarded by the British Army, in a special reserve high on the Rock," Pete said.

"There are ways around that problem," said Lopez. "Bribe the soldiers."

"Mmm," said Closet, jumping up. "Right, *Señor!* When do you want them?"

"Anytime, anytime," said the Spaniard quickly. "Just bring them here, to the outer mole. There, you see it—just up the road."

"Right, *Señor*. We will be here in two nights' time with the apes."

He shook Henry, who was snoring loudly. We then made our farewells, were off to the jetty, and boarded *Fanny Adams.*

"What a twit," said I to Closet, "thinking he could get us into a bloody stupid move like that!"

"Stupid for him, maybe, but not for us, by Crikey!"

"What's the deal, then?" asked Pete.

Closet spoke quietly. "Look, those apes on the Rock are Barbary apes, right? The same as they have in Morocco. They were probably *brought over* to Gib by the Moors. Well, if we nip over to Spanish Morocco and go to Tetuan market, we can buy a hundred apes just the same as the Rock apes. And they can be bought for 100 pesetas apiece!"

He grinned as he went below to start the engine. Pete whistled softly, I smiled, Henry snored in his wheel-house deck chair; and five minutes later we were off, on the 30-mile plod to Tangier.

From Algeciras to Ceuta, in the then Spanish Morocco, is only about 20 miles. In those 20 miles were three totally different worlds. First Spain—southern Spain—just below the superficial level of a few trucks and trains and strutting Falangist soldiers and police, still living in the past: a sometimes glorious past, of the sixteenth to eighteenth centuries. The country was redolent with evidence of the victory over the Moors, the brave overseas discoveries of Spain's ancient navigators, and the rape of half the world.

Next, Gibraltar, because of Franco's intransigence a virtual island, a moiety of modern, twentieth-century progress, with well-stocked shops, full of packaged foods and electronic equipment and well-dressed, clean inhabitants, living under the protection of the crown's justice.

Then, to the south, under the shadow of the hazy, blue Atlas Mountains, Morocco: Spanish Morocco, with flies, dirt, disease, and pestilential beggars on every corner, with muezzins wailing in the mosques, the males sauntering around in caftans and *burnouses* while their women hid themselves in *purdah* or walked the streets cocooned in *yashmaks.*

Many looks of disdain and distrust were cast at us, four "infidels" as we wandered around the dusty marketplace (the *souk* of Tetuan), inquiring after Barbary apes. But our money was good; at 120 pesetas per ape, the Berbers remembered Mohammed's axiom: "When Allah sends a fool, take his money and go on your way, praising Allah, for Allah is great!"

In the evening, when the faithful were called to prayers and the dancing boys and their sisters (the nautch girls) prepared for the night's labors, a rusty wheezing wagon trundled its dusty way to the coast with a cargo of 15 apes and four exulting infidels: a retired racing driver, an exiled Australian crocodile hunter, and two British sailors. The next morning *Fanny Adams*, scarred and paintless, wallowing in the Mediterranean sunshine with the 15 apes onboard, was plowing her way back over the Straits.

They were friendly little fellows, about two to three feet high (more like chimpanzees than apes), all grinning and chattering away. We had them tied round the deck on ropes to prevent them from clambering over the boat. The chatter was deafening; the cost of bananas to quiet them was staggering.

At Algeciras, which we entered by moonlight, we waited while Closet went ashore to send for *Señor* Lopez, who rushed to the jetty, beaming, and accompanied by the district head of Franco's Falangist party in full uniform, together with three Civil Guards. Pete, Henry, and I hustled the apes down the gangway and into the Spanish Army truck waiting on the jetty, where the lights had been turned out for the occasion. As the apes trooped down the gangway, Deaf Henry leading them, I was reminded of Noah and the ark.

"Only 15?" asked Señor Lopez, after greetings were exchanged. "But there are 22 on Gibraltar!"

Closet explained: "We're going to collect the others tomorrow night. We had to bribe the soldiers and we ran out of money. But with the 15,000 pesetas you'll pay us, there'll be no problem."

Grudgingly as the Civil Guards gravely handed the 15 chattering, grinning, scratching apes up into the truck, Lopez handed over some money and Closet counted it.

"But there's only 10,000 here, *Señor!*"

"*Si*, the rest you will get when you come back with the other apes. Make sure you get them all. We have friends there who will tell us if there are any left, any babies."

He glowered at Closet. The Civil Guards felt their pistols, and one of them spat in the harbor, just missing *Fanny Adams*. Henry glared at him.

"Never you fret," said Closet, "we'll have the lot over here in two days' time. Come on lads, let's get some fuel onboard and be off, before the Gibraltar police miss us!"

As we let go the lines and slid away into the gloom, we saw Lopez and his fat, medal-bedecked party-chief friend, together with the Civil Guards, wave to us—to the accompaniment of 15 apes screaming away in the truck.

"Closet," I murmured, as the boat picked up speed.

"Mmm?" He slid 5,000 pesetas into my trouser pocket.

"You're not going back to Morocco for more apes, are you?"

"What do you think I am, a bloody fool?" He turned from the compass and grinned. "No, mate, we're heading around the Rock and getting the hell out of here, east. We'll put as much salt water between us and *Señor*-bloody-Lopez as we can. Head straight for Ibiza.

"But won't they trace us there?"

"What, and become the laughing stock of Spain—using Falangist party funds to buy Barbary apes from Spanish Morocco? You must be joking!"

Waking suddenly from a doze in his deckchair, Deaf Henry looked sleepily at Closet, in the shadows cast by the low light of the compass binnacle. "Closet!" he shouted. "Ain't left any of those bloody monkeys aboard, have you?" Henry's bleary eyes danced.

"Christ," said Pete, standing at my elbow, counting his share of the pesetas, "and I thought I'd seen everything!"

"Yes," I replied; "no one will ever believe it."

"What, about the monkeys?"

"No, about them." I nodded at Henry and Closet.

Fanny Adams wallowed away, unconcerned, while over the

airwaves from Radio Gibraltar thumped the strains of "The March from the Bridge over the River Kwai." (What did the engine driver say when the boiler burst? . . . Bollox! And the same to you!) Pete and Closet roared out the chorus while I spun the wheel to keep the boat heading eastward. Henry grinned as he dozed.

All through the warm night *Fanny Adams* motored on, bumping and grinding from one oily sea to the next below a plethora of planets, an upturned stadium of blazing stars. Slowly Gibraltar, a beacon of light on a horizon of misty crystal, sank into the west, astern, while ahead the moon, huge and lustrous, rose out of the waters of the sea, the sea of Ulysses. Away to the north and south, on both sides of us, long black shadows thrust themselves from the eternally moving rim of the world to the edges of the universe, beyond the pulsing stars. The Pillars of Hercules, holding up the heavens!

The days are sick and cold, and the skies are gray and old,
And the twice breathed airs grow damp;
And I'd sell my tired soul for the bucking beam-sea roll
Of a black Bilbao tramp;
With her load-line over her hatch, dear lass,
And a drunken Dago crew,
And her nose held down on the old trail, our own trail, the out trail,
From Cadiz bar on the Long Trail—the trail that's always new.

There be triple ways to take, of the eagle and the snake,
Or the way of a man with a maid;
But the sweetest way to me is a ship's upon the sea
In the heel of the North East Trade.
Can you hear the crash of her bows, dear lass,
And the drum of the racing screw,
As she ships it green on the old trail, our own trail, the out trail,
As she lifts and 'scends on the Long Trail, the trail that's always new?

Rudyard Kipling, from "L'Envoi"

21

Encounters

Deaf Henry, Pete, and I stood watches on the wheel of *Fanny Adams*. During the night Pete and I snatched some sleep in the pounding focs'le, stretched out fully dressed on the bare berths. Henry's smelly blankets had been relegated to the paint locker in the bows in the hopes that their denizens, a thousand cockroaches, would seek out their accustomed habitat and leave us alone. Henry, off watch, dozed in his deckchair. While he was on the wheel either Pete or I stood by, for he could hardly see the compass and was continually wandering off course.

As the first pale-pink slivers of the dawn sneaked over the horizon, Closet emerged up the ladder from the galley, bearing a metal bucket. On top was a layer of yellow tin plates with rusty patches on them, then a layer of rubbery fried eggs, below them a sliced loaf, and fetching up the bottom three pounds of cold, crispy rashers of bacon. Beaming, he plonked it on the wheelhouse deck, then sprinted below again to bring up a kettle of steaming tea, strong and well laced with condensed milk. We polished that off in short order.

By midforenoon, as we stood braced in the wheelhouse, spinning yarns of past voyages and mutual acquaintances, the weather livened up and soon *Fanny Adams* was hard put to maintain headway against a strong easterly breeze. With her

228

engine full out in a flat calm, she could manage eight knots, but her topsides and deck structures were so high and ungainly that in a 20-knot wind against her the speed was cut to a stagger of about three knots. The bow dug into the seas, lifting two or three tons of water with each surge upward and sending streams of sea water flailing back to the scuppers and against the wheelhouse windows.

Henry snored away in his chair, Closet stayed below, and I clambered down to keep him company for a spell. He was humming softly to himself. Oil can in hand, he fiddled with the engine as the boat pitched and rolled, heaved and groaned, the bilge water slopping around his sneakers. Every now and then, as the boat gave a sudden lurch, a can or a tin plate or a cooking pot came crashing out of the galley shelves. They would roll around in the oily bilge water on the engine-room sole for a few seconds while Closet tightened a nut; then he picked them up and threw them into the huge sink, already piled high with similar debris. The stench below, from the engine fumes leaking from the patched-up exhaust, from the stinking bilge water, and from Henry's blankets in the fusty cabin, was almost overpowering. With the engine roaring, conversation was impossible, and after a few minutes even I, with my cast-iron stomach, was forced to retreat to the comparatively hygienic wheelhouse.

"Everything all right, mate?" asked Henry as I shook my head at the top of the ladder to clear the fumes.

"FINE: HENRY, FAN-BLOODY-TASTIC!" I shouted at him, as he closed his eyes again.

"Lovely old girl she is, mate!" he murmured, settling down again.

The first night out from Algeciras, and all the forenoon, no sights were taken. It was just a matter of head out, turn left, and go east. Closet had drawn a straight line from Europa Point on Gibraltar, east. The chart he drew it on was the scruffiest, dirtiest, oiliest, most dogeared, tattered and torn chart I had ever seen in my life. While he was below, engine tending, I inspected it. It had been last brought up to date in *1948!* It was a chart for the whole western half of the Mediterranean, on a scale of about one inch to 50 miles! On one side of the chart, over Spain, a shopping list had been scrawled in red ball-point: "Five pounds spuds, 2 cans beans, 5 pounds flour." On the other side, various memos and graffiti showed up over central Italy and Malta: "See Closet about fresh-water pump" and "Get passport renewed. Problem: where is it? Search bilge in after cabin." The rest of the chart, the sea areas, was covered with lines of previous courses over which *Fanny Adams* had plodded. Some of these course lines puzzled me; they wandered senselessly from side to side of the Med, willy-nilly, from Algeria to Spain and back. When Henry woke to take over the wheel just before noon, I asked him about them.

"WHAT ARE ALL THESE LINES GOING ASHORE IN AFRICA, HENRY?"

"Oh them, mate," said Henry, laying his great, blunt sprawling finger on the chart. "Well, that's where we got lost now and then. But it's not too bad in the Med. All you do is turn north or south till you come to a coast, and then you can tell where you are."

"HOW DO YOU MEAN? HOW DO YOU KNOW WHERE YOU ARE?"

"Well, if the coast is to the north, it's got to be Europe, right?" Henry rubbed the inside of his glasses with his thumb. "And if it's to the south, it's Africa. Closet gets a good enough sight at noon to give us the latitude, and now and again we can work out the longitude. And anyway, we can't really get lost, unless we wander out of the Straits of Gibraltar in a rainstorm!"

I looked at the chart again. It is the height of discourtesy to interfere in the navigation of a vessel on which you are a guest—unless you are asked or unless the vessel is standing into the gravest jeopardy and the navigator is either dead, unconscious, or drunk. Pete and I stood back and watched, quietly anxious, as the navigation routine of *Fanny Adams* was unveiled before our astonished eyes.

Noon passed with no sign of Closet, until he thrust a greasy, rusty biscuit box full of corned beef sandwiches up through the hatch onto the wheelhouse deck. But the box slid to the open wheelhouse door as the boat rolled over. At the door, before I could grab the box, a great dollop of sea water, streaming aft from the rearing bow, slopped over and drowned the sandwiches. Henry, sitting on his chair, signaled me to give him the biscuit tin. He drained out the water, started digging out a soggy sandwich, then handed the tin to me, grinning. "Nothing like a bit 'o salt with your meat."

"YOU SAID IT, HENRY!"

At 4 o'clock, after making a great pot of tea, Closet was ready to take a sight. He delved into the navigation cupboard for the sextant and tables. From a battered wooden box he took out the sextant; it was green with verdigris, white with salt, ancient as the moon. It took him about five minutes to shoot the sun, balancing himself on the sidedeck, near the wheelhouse door, and guarding his instrument against the salt spray. Then he clambered over the doorsill, staggered to the navigation table, and thumbed through the greasy volume of computed angle tabulations, all the while making notations on a piece of wrinkled brown wrapping paper and mumbling to himself as he made the calculations.

Suddenly, from below the misty haze ahead, an island appeared, a long, low, dark gray hump. Pete pointed it out to Henry. "LAND AHEAD!"

Henry hobbled unsteadily to the tatty chart and traced a grubby finger along the dead-reckoning line drawn from Gibraltar eastward. Several times his finger traced back and forth along the line. "Hmmm," he said, after a while, "shouldn't be any land here!" Closet was still crouched over his sight workings, with a wrinkled frown.

Even as Henry repudiated the existence of land thereabouts, I sighted, to starboard of *Fanny Adams*, through the open wheelhouse door, a small fishing boat quite close to us. I tapped Henry on the shoulder.

"What's up, mate?" He looked even more like a lovable, confused old bloodhound.

"BOAT ON THE STARBOARD BOW, HENRY. HE'S VERY NEAR."

"Good show!" chortled Henry, grabbing the binnacle rail. "We'll nip over and ask him where we are!" He turned to Pete. "Steer for the boat, son!" Pete changed course, peering through the splintered salt-encrusted window.

As we approached the tiny fishing craft we saw that she was manned by two figures tending the lines. Both were wearing the blue shirts, black trousers, and straw hats of Spanish fishermen. As we came closer we could see they were sunburned to a mahogany color and looked friendly enough. Closet slowed the engine down and put it out of gear, so that *Fanny Adams* sat there wallowing 50 degrees either way, a sickening motion. Henry staggered outside onto the deck, clutching the guardrail, and bellowed in English: "Hello there! I say, what's the name of that island?"

"*Buenos dias, Señor*," came the reply.

Henry cupped his hand over his ear and turned to Closet. "What's he say?"

"HE SAID *BUENOS DIAS*," Closet bawled.

"Oh! *Buenos dias!*"

Henry paused, filled his lungs, and again shouted, again in English: "What's the name of that island?"

"*¡No comprendo!*" came the reply, loud and clear.

"What's he say?" Henry shouted at Closet.

"HE SAYS HE DON'T UNDERSTAND."

"That island—what name?" Henry shouted again.

"*¿Sordo?* (Deaf?)" The fisherman pointed at Henry with his chin.

"What's he say?" Henry again asked Closet.

"*Sordo.* He says it's called *Sordo.*" Closet replied and turned to the chart.

"Sordo . . . mmm . . . Sordo . . . Can't find it here, Henry."

Henry gazed at Closet, then at Pete.

"Oh Christ, Pete, *you* have a go!"

Pete cupped his palms around his lips and hailed: "*¿Como se llama esta isla, Señors?*"

"*¡Alboran . . . Isla de Alboran!*"

"*Gracias, Señors. Buenos Tarde!*"

"What's he say?" mumbled Henry.

"ALBORAN!"

"Oh. What's that?"

Closet let go of the guardrail and staggered back into the wheelhouse to pore over the chart again. "Blimey," he said after a while, as I looked over his shoulder, "that's funny; we're much farther south than I thought. I can't understand it."

I looked at the nautical almanac tables he had been working from. "Er, Closet . . ." I nudged him.

"Wazzup, Tris?"

"You been using this page of the almanac?" I pointed at the grubby nautical almanac.

"Yeah, why?"

"Nothing, only it's open for *May*—and this is *June*."

"Oh Gawd!" He passed a sweaty, oily hand over his forehead. "No wonder I couldn't get the sight right. Look, this is where I had us."

He laid a nail-bitten finger on the chart. He had *Fanny Adams* in the *Bay of Biscay*, in the *Atlantic*, to the *north* of Spain, outside the port of Santander! He reached for the ruler and drew yet another line on the chart: northeast, direct from Alboran to Ibiza.

"Right, Pete. Change the course to oh-four-five!"

"Oh-four-five it is," answered Pete as he swung the wheel, bringing *Fanny Adams* onto a course where she no longer bashed directly against the seas but slid across them at an angle of 45 degrees, thus easing the motion as she plodded into the swift-falling dusk of the Mediterranean summer. Sure enough, after a couple of hours, as the great blood-red disc of the sun sank into the western horizon, we sighted to the north the snowy peaks of the Sierra Nevada, glowing a rosy pink above misty blue, rising out of a sea shining emerald-azure, with the dolphins leaping. Closet, in the heaving wheelhouse of *Fanny Adams*, slapped down before us yet another kettle of steaming hot tea.

Dawn found us off Cabo de Palos and dusk off Cabo de la Nao. By now it was calm, a typical western Med summer

calm, with a glassy sea and a clear sky. Closet slowed the boat
to three knots and *Fanny Adams* trundled on into the night,
picking up the light of Es Vedra (on the southwest corner of
Ibiza) at midnight, and creeping into the harbor at dawn. We
tied up stern first to the seawall, inside the port.

Henry and Closet would drop Pete and me here, as they
wanted to go to the island farther south, Formentera, where
they had many friends. They intended to say there for a day
or two before carrying on east to Malta.

"Malta, that's the place!" said Henry, leaning back in his
deckchair, closing his eyes dreamily. "Do you know, Tristan,
you can get a good bowl of nourishing soup there for next to
nothing. Sixpence, even less!"

"I can wait there until my aunt dies. I'm the only benefici-
ary in her will and she's 92, and when she croaks I can refit
Fanny and get her all painted up smart, and Closet and me can
head for the Nile! Always wanted to see the Pyramids."

He rambled on and on, a man of 68 who had never lost his
boyhood dreams—who, in fact, was living them. As Closet,
Pete, and I listened to him dreaming aloud, I dreamed my own
dream: the Dead Sea, the Amazon, the Parana! One day . . .

Pete disturbed the reverie. "Well, Tristan, what if we get
our gear ashore? We can have a few beers before the ferry for
Majorca leaves this evening—give the place the onceover.
You know, this is a real hotspot. Tourists from all over the
place—Swedes, English, Yanks. The place is crawling with
crumpet."

He made for the ladder and disappeared below, and I followed him. Soon we were shaking hands ondeck in the early
morning sunshine with Deaf Henry and Closet and making
promises to meet them again in a few weeks.

"So-long, mates!" called Closet.

"Cheers, Closet! SO-LONG, HENRY!"

I never saw Henry again. He and Closet moored *Fanny
Adams* against the wall in Formentera and went inland to see
their friends at the Fonda Pepe. Three nights later a howling
gale blew down from the north and *Fanny Adams* battered herself to death on the rocks after breaking her lines. When I

called in Formentera a month later, all that was left of a legend was a rusty keel in the clear, calm waters of the sun-drenched port.

Henry's friends, mainly Americans, heard of his plight and passed the hat round, raising his fare back to England. His aunt died a few months later and Henry inherited enough money to buy a cozy little sailing sloop. The last I heard of him, he was living onboard, in England, on the calm River Itchinor, near Southampton. Still dreaming of sailing up the Nile to see the Pyramids.

The next time I saw Closet was in St. Thomas, in the Virgin Islands, 11 years later. I had just sailed through the so-called Devil's Triangle in the 38-foot ketch *Sundowner*. Closet was a passenger on a Russian liner taking him to New York on his way to San Francisco to assist the Save the Whales campaign.

Pete and I wandered around the hippy-ridden town of Ibiza, sipping brandy outside the Hotel Montesol on the main square, watching the parade of drugged soul-searchers clutch their self-pity to themselves, imagining they were the lost children of a failing culture, prating, prowling, and prancing among the fishermen and peasants, the latter solidly implanted in the world of natural reality. We sat watching the parade of childish exhibitionism, fear, and doubt.

"They look a bit like they've just rounded the Horn," said Pete. "All that long hair and torn jeans—except for their soft hands."

"More like they've been dragged through a hedge. Jesus, look at those lasses." I ordered another drink.

"Mostly Americans . . . they can get pot cheap here. It's run in from Morocco."

"Well, don't get any ideas, Pete; the only thing I'd ever run in from there is a cartload of monkeys."

"Good money in running pot."

"Yeah, but look at the bloody result. Look at this collection, with their flamin' worry beads, traipsing their neuroses around. Look at that girl, Pete—eyes like pissholes in the snow. Looks like a sheepdog with its throat cut . . ." It was my first close look at a new generation.

Pete frowned. "They're not too bad, Tris, just mixed up. Most of them don't know what it's all about."

"Don't know what *what's* all about?"

"The world . . . Western civilization." Pete laid a hard hand on the table.

"How'd they get here, Pete?"

"The ones I've met came by plane, but some of them have been wandering around Europe for a couple of years."

"How do they travel?"

"Hitch-hike, mostly. Some of them have been as far as India, and even Nepal."

"What for?"

"A lot of them are interested in Buddhism and Hinduism; and the Europeans, mostly, are existentialists—very Marxist and anyway, they can get drugs out there without too much bother. L.S.D. from Switzerland, but they reckon their main interest is Eastern religions as an alternative to Western ways."

"Is that so?"

"Yeah, and in the States the youngsters are kicking up a stink right now. They want to change everything."

"To what?"

"Oh, they're starting up collectives and trying to take over the universities. You know, general shitstirring."

"India, eh? Well, Pete, if they're so taken up with Hinduism why don't they do what the old Brahmans do and *walk* there? If they're so sick of Western ways, why do they travel the Western way, by plane and car? If they want to reject the West, the good as well as the bad, why the hell are they lined up outside the post office every day waiting for a check from dear old daddy? If Hinduism or Buddhism is the answer to the world's woes, why do I have to climb over a couple of thousand starving or dead bodies every time I want to get ashore in Bombay or Calcutta?"

"But you yourself are living outside the mainstream of civilization."

"The hell I am, mate. On my boats I use the products of

Western industry. I use stainless steel for the rigging. My cooking stove was made by some poor sod who gets up at 6 a.m. on a foggy winter's morning to cycle to some factory. My charts are the results of a continuing effort by Western man over the past two centuries to make some sort of sense where none existed before. Even the clothes I wear—yes, and the clothes *they* wear"—I gestured at a trio of *djellaba* and jean-wearing hippies—"even the clothes they wear are made by some *worker* somewhere."

"Well, Tris, you yourself have seen some of the pollution of the sea."

"Pollution?" This was a new word for me.

"Yeah, you know—all that trash and bits of oil on the sea."

"What about it?"

"Well, they're kicking up about that, too."

"So they should, and so should a lot of other folk, but I'm buggered if I can see how you're going to stop oil tankers carrying oil by trudging around with a guitar and strings of beads. Especially when the planes and cars they're traveling in are the *reason* for the oil tankers."

"Yeah, I never thought of it that way." He sipped his brandy.

"If you ask me, Pete, it's part of the postwar baby bulge. Look at 'em . . . what would you say their average age is?"

Pete thought for a moment. "Say 20 to 25."

"Right. Now that means they were born around, say, 1945 to 1950."

"O.K."

"And so they think they are living in an overcrowded world. Their school classes must be crowded—and you know what happens when man or any other kind of animal is crowded: he starts playing up holy shit, right?"

"Guess so." Pete grinned at a passing *guru-nik*.

"O.K., so is this lot. And don't forget, Pete, they're *our* lot, too. Well, it's like a great bulge on a line. As the bulge moves up the line—in other words, as this crowd gets older—it will be the predominant group and insist on making itself heard. And youth has always been rebellious. In a lot of instances quite rightly, but about some things it's a load of cod'swallop, because half the time they just don't know what they're talking about. They don't have the age and they don't have the experience to know why some customs or restraints are as they are. But you wait 10 years, mate; wait till this lot's in their thirties. Wait till they start having kids of their own and owning property. But my heart bleeds for *their* kids, poor sods."

"This crowd owning houses, getting married? You must be joking."

'I'm not joking, Pete. Wait 10 years and you'll see 'em wearing suits and creeping back to Jesus. A fat lot of good Hinduism'll be to them then! Wait . . .you'll see the French 'philosophers' giving old Marx the deep six!"

"What about when they get even older?"

"God help those that come after, because they are going to have to *support* a lot of these buggers. The birth rate will go down, and there'll be fewer people paying into the old-age pension funds. Socialism . . . the phony welfare variety, will die of old age."

Pete finished his drink. "And these bulge babies, when they get old, are going to be in the majority, screaming for more and more money from a diminishing work force?"

"Dead right, mate. Many of 'em are going to be so bloody narcissistic you wouldn't believe it. And here they are, getting busted out of their skulls on the same stuff which has kept Asia and Africa in poverty-stricken misery for centuries. Putting their faith into the cant of whirling dervishes and medicine men."

"What about the communists among them . . . I mean the French lot?"

"Anyone or anything that threatens a Frenchman's dinner table is as dead as a dodo—will be—and that goes for Sartre as well as Marx. But it will take a shock to make them ditch Marx—probably something or someone from the communist countries—probably an artist or a writer . . . a sort of 'star in the east.' They'll never listen to anyone else. And of course the rest of the world will follow France—it always does, eventually."

"You wouldn't want to be born right now, in 1967, Tris?"

"No, if I had my choice I'd wait until at least 1997, so that most of this generation"—I nodded my head at the passing show—"would be dying off by the time I would be twenty. Otherwise I'd spend most of my life supporting this crowd, and the older they get the more demanding they'll be. That's the same as it's always been, but there's a difference with this generation . . . there will be diminishing resources, and so the older they get the more they'll move to the right. The next 30 years are going to be very tricky . . . that'll be the day . . . that'll be the time to be alive! Holy Moses, what I wouldn't give to live my life a hundred years hence! To rise up there amongst the stars and stick my dick into the nebulae! How I wish I could be born after 2000!"

"So you reckon all this lot is caused by the population explosion?" Pete asked, to calm my Welsh exuberance.

"Of course. That and . . . the coming expansion into space . . . it was the same in Europe in the thirteen and fourteen hundreds. There were a thousand different sects starting up, and people dancing crazy in the streets, and finding drug mushrooms and shaky bread yeast which sent them off their rockers. It seems to happen in history before the great voyages of discovery. But the real world has always been in ferment . . . thank God the Edwardians didn't have the atom bomb . . . they were the craziest of the lot."

"And now?"

"It's before the reach for space."

"How do you mean?"

"It's because people are aware that something is happening and they're not quite sure *what*. Fear's involved, of course. It always is whenever we become introspective, and that bloody German . . . Nietzsche, hasn't helped."

"So you think the Yanks will succeed in getting someone onto the moon?" Pete asked doubtfully.

"If they don't the Russians will, and if the Russians don't someone else will, sooner or later."

"Then you think it's inevitable that we're going to the stars?"

"As sure as God made the oceans, as certain as the dawn."

"Do you think it'll do any good?"

"First you'll have to tell me what 'good' is. I mean, for me, our little trot with Deaf Henry and Closet has been, in some ways, good. For you, it's probably been a slow purgatory. Going into space will be the same. But we must go. There's no-one else . . . no little green men . . . only humanity . . . and the sooner we face up to it, the better we'll all be, Pete; it's a case of shit or get off the pot . . . and if we get off the pot—there's nothing. If humanity abdicates, we shall betray God!"

Pete passed me another brandy. "Cheers, Tris. You're a funny bugger; I've never met anyone quite like you before."

I laughed. "Ah, come on, let's head for Wauna's Bar. Might be some crumpet. The wind will outlast the oil. We sailors can wait . . ."

At dusk, we left Ibiza for Majorca on the overnight ferry and arrived at Puerto Andraitx the following afternoon.

"Yoo-hoo!" bawled Sissie as we trundled with our seabags along the jetty in the sunshine. I saw Nelson wearily raise his head and pant.

"Yoo-hoo!" she shouted, waving in her paint-spattered blue gym slip and brogue boots, paint pot in hand. "*Dahlings*, I'll have tea and bikkys ready right away!"

"Jesus Christ!" murmured Pete, pointing his chin at *Tea Pot*, mouth open, eyebrows raised.

"What's up, mate?"

"Look!" He dropped his seabag. "Look at that, Tris!"

Tea Pot was completely repainted from bows to stern. Her mast, which a month before was blistered and gray, was now pristine in several coats of gleaming varnish. *Cresswell* lay immaculate, with all her brass shining like the Queen's state barge.

"Good old Sissie!" said Pete.

"Amen to that!" I replied, as I caught the sound of Nelson's tail thumping the deck.

Tiger, tiger, burning bright
In the forests of the night,
What immortal hand or eye
Could frame thy fearful symmetry?

In what distant deeps or skies
Burnt the fire of thine eyes?
On what wings dare he aspire?
What the hand dare seize the fire?

And what shoulder and what art
Could twist the sinews of thy heart?
And, when thy heart began to beat,
What dread hand and what dread feet?

What the hammer? What the chain?
In what furnace was thy brain?
What the anvil? What deep grasp
Dare its deadly terrors clasp?

When the stars threw down their spears,
And water'd heaven with their tears,
Did He smile His work to see?
Did He who made the lamb make thee?

Tiger, tiger, burning bright
In the forests of the night,
What immortal hand or eye
Dare frame thy fearful symmetry?

William Blake, "The Tiger"

22

Love Me, Love My Dog

Pete sailed away in *Tea Pot* next day, bound for the south of France, where he hoped to find work as a sailing instructor.

"So-long, Tristan, and thanks for the trips!" he called as his mainsail went aloft in the morning sunlight and caught the breeze.

"So-long, mate! Don't forget to drop me a line at my London address."

"Right! See you. See you, Sissie. Thanks for the paint job!"

"Bye-Bye, Petah dahling. Give my fondest love to deah, dahling Robin Maugham!" Sissie called out, balancing on the bowsprit.

"Yeah, and the bloody Aga Khan, and Princess Grace . . . and Norah Docker," I muttered, turning to go below. I fondled Nelson's head as I went through the companionway, but the old boy hardly moved.

That afternoon, Sissie received a letter at the post office. When she got back from her shopping trip her face was aglow.

"Now what?" I murmured to Nelson as she tramped purposefully back to the boat along the dusty jetty, followed at a distance by three admirers.

"Tristan, dahling, I shall have to leave you here and catch a ferry to Ibiza. You see, my bank—what dreadful fumbling *peasants!*—have sent my allowance, a whole six months of it, but they've sent it to the bank in Ibiza. What jolly rotten luck! But it will only take me a couple of days to go over there and get back; then I can pay you for what I owe . . ."

"What the hell are you going on about, Sissie? What do you mean, catch a *ferry?* We can sail *Cresswell* to Ibiza in eight to 12 hours. Save you the fare, and anyway I want to go there." I thought of Deaf Henry and Closet. "I've friends over there, the blokes who gave me a lift up from Gib."

"Oh Skippah, will you reahlly take me theah in jolly old *Cresswell?*" She hopped from one foot to the other, grabbing the starboard shrouds with a sunburned fist, her brogues clomping on the deck.

"Of course. And for Christ's sake, stop wearing out the deck paint." I started to unship the awning. "We'll sail as soon as the sun's a bit lower. Get the headsails out, Sissie."

"Hey ho, hey ho, it's orf to work we go . . ." she hummed as she crashed through the hatch in one bound.

Nelson hardly moved his head, despite all the sudden noise and activity. His one eye was dull and bleary. I bent down to wipe it for him and stroke his neck, as he slowly panted. "We'll be off to sea shortly, old son," I told him quietly. He licked my wrist.

Soon we had all sail bent, and Sissie was hauling with all her might on the long, slimy anchor chain while I gently motored the boat over the anchor to loosen it from the sandy harbor floor. Once the anchor was onboard, I topped up the gaff and hauled in the jib sheets, the sails filled, and we were off in a slight breeze from the north. Within a minute we were outside the harbor, watching the play of the evening sun on the golden foothills of Majorca, the olive trees about the small white-washed cottages ruffling as the wind passed through them.

To the north, as *Cresswell* lifted gently to the swell, the great hump of Dragonera rock lifted out of the blue, blue waters, shining golden boulders toward the sun, deep blue shadows on its shady side. Above, a few wispy clouds trailed away to the south, and to the southeast the pale yellow, creamy shadow of the island of Cabrera floated above the dancing wave-lets. Soon, having brewed a kettle of tea and produced a plate of sandwiches, Sissie joined me in the cockpit as I lounged in the sun, one toe on the wheel, the other fondling Nelson's collar. He liked that.

"What will you do when we reach Ibiza, Sissie?"

"Oh, I'll stay onboard tonight, go to the bank tomorrow, pay you what I owe you, and then buy a jolly old ticket for Morocco. I'm going to meet deah, dahling Willy there. Then we're orf to take pictyahs of the Kasbah in Tangier and that simply *droolingly* beautiful place in Fez. Hope to spend about six weeks there. Then it's back to jolly old Southchester for me. Oh, *what* a bore; just imagine, another blawsted wintah in England!"

Nelson slouched aft, onto the poopdeck, from which I had trailed two fishing lines from each end of the boathook, laid athwartships. This kept the fishing lines from fouling the rudder or the propellor. In these waters there was always a fair chance of catching a fish of one kind or the other, if the basking-sharks didn't break the lines.

The afternoon wore on, with the wind gently playing on the sails, *Cresswell* nodding along in the slight seas at around three knots: a desultory passage, like a thousand others before and since. As the sun lowered over distant Ibiza and the island slowly rose above the horizon, Sissie and I talked of her plans.

"You want to watch those bloomin' Berbers," I joshed her. "Full of tricks, especially with pretty English tourist-school-teachers. They'll have you in a harem before you can say Jack Robinson."

"Then I shall bash them with the jolly old hockey stick, Skippah!"

"Well, anyway, good ol' Willy can look after you, no doubt."

Again, Sissie went below to wash the tea things and I gazed dreamily into the distance ahead, while the boat jiggled and tripped lightly over a feather-light sea.

I turned to look astern. Nelson was guarding the fishing lines, his one front paw lying over one of the lines, the gentle breeze ruffling his coarse black hair. As I turned to look at him again, he looked at me, direct in the eye. He panted, lifted his paw slightly, gave a great sigh which wracked his whole body, then slumped over, his head lolling to one side. I jumped up and thew myself over the afterdeck toward him. I felt for a flutter of a heart beat, then stroked his head and called his name again and again. He was gone—just like that! And it seemed to me that, in that moment, my heart also stopped.

I grabbed his body and lifted it, as gently as I could, into the cockpit, remembering in flashes all that we had been through together, and his love and his loyalty—his strong, true loyalty even at times when the very turn of the world and the tricks of time had been against me, when fate had turned her face away from my puny struggles and had seemed to leave me lost and abandoned, with only the prospect of a bitter, lonely, cold, unknown death ahead. But Nelson's loyalty had never flinched for one minute.

And they'll say: He was just a dog; how could he know. I thought as I stroked his head. "They'll say he was only a dumb creature," I said aloud to Sissie. "But he knew, Sissie, he *knew*, and he was steadfast, and he feared when I feared, and he laughed, in his own way, when I laughed. And he loved so purely, without asking anything back but a bloody bowl of burgoo . . . Oh Christ!"

"Oh, Tristan, dahling," she said as she laid a heavy hand on my shoulder. I tried to hold back my tears.

"Sissie," I said, trying to keep a steady voice.

"Yes?" A great tear dropped from her cheek.

"Get my Arctic parka. It's in the forward foot locker, starboard side."

She emerged from the cabin bearing the moldering, damp, caribou-skin jerkin. She slapped it with her small handbrush to dislodge the green fungus. Then she laid it on the sidedeck, gently, reverently, as if afraid it would fall to bits.

"And my black oily-trousers, the old pair. They're in the same locker."

She brought these up, moldy too, and beat them so they

were once again black-gray instead of bright green. I said nothing, but I could see the patched rents in the leg where my old friend had hung on to me when I was knocked unconscious on the way up to Iceland.

I wrapped the old boy in the jerkin and the pants, tied tightly around him with nylon line so the fishes would not get at him. Then weighted the lot down with the crowbar I'd used to moor onto the ice floe, so long ago. "So long, mate," I said and lowered him over the side.

As his body sank into the emerald waters, a dolphin slashed in a pearly arch of spray not far away, and I watched through tears as his shadow faded into the dark green depths.

The rest of the voyage to Ibiza was made in almost complete silence, with me remembering Nelson and Tansy, my last living links with the age of working sail.

Cresswell eased her way into the shining, wide bay of Ibiza in the late afternoon, 10 hours out of Andraitx. Ten sad, sad hours. I did not go ashore, not even when Sissie left. Everywhere I looked on the boat I could see Nelson, and I didn't want to leave him.

In her tweed suit, her droopy hat and feathers, her brogues —the tennis racket, hockey stick, and the great leather explorer's bag resting on deck—she fussed in her pocketbook for money. I pushed her hand away when she offered it.

"That's all right, lass, you'll need that where you're going. And anyway I owe it to you, for painting *Cresswell* and *Tea Pot* and looking after me and Nelson."

Tears started through the smile in her eyes. "Bye-bye, Tristan, my deah. Oh, how I shall *miss* you! I've enjoyed myself so absolutely, so perfectly *thoroughly*, my pet." She plonked a kiss intended for my cheek, which missed and hit the end of my nose.

"So-long, Siss. Make sure and write now and again."

"Oh I *shall*, nevah *feah*, old cheppie!" she called back as the cabby hefted her baggage and implements into the waiting taxi. When she got in, she opened the window and waved at me, as she nodded at the puffing *taxista*. "*Splendid* little chep, what?"

"Sissie!" I called as the taxi started over the rough stones.
"What, my pet?"
"Thanks a lot for everything, mate!"
She stuck half her stubby torso out the window and waved
all the way down the waterfront, to the shock and consternation of the Sunday strollers, out with their children in the
calm, starry evening.

Tired and bereft, I descended into the cabin to think about
the future. Away in the distance a guitar sobbed. Gradually,
as the days passed, the presence of Nelson faded, until only
my gratitude for him remained.

The 27-foot sloop *Two Brothers*, built in Holland, was for sale in
Vigo, northwest Spain. She had been fitted out for a world
cruise by a German who had now changed his mind. I knew
her for a sturdy boat, having seen her in the Netherlands.
With the money from the delivery of *Antoinette*, plus what I
might get for *Cresswell*, I determined to try to buy *Two Brothers*.

I went to Vigo overland and inspected *Two Brothers* and her
gear. Then I returned to Ibiza and sold *Cresswell*, lock, stock
and barrel (except for the logs and documents) to an English
businessman. He paid me $2,500 for her.

A week after she was sold, he anchored *Cresswell* in San Antonio Bay, on the north side of the island. During the night a
tramontana wind blew up, heavy and strong. She dragged her
anchor and was cast on the sands. I was all set to move my
gear, within the hour, up to Vigo and take over *Two Brothers*,
but as soon as I heard the grapevine alarm about *Cresswell*, I
got a lift to San Antonio and set about rescuing her (with the
permission of the new owner, though I'd have done it anyway). I got her off the sands and patched her up, though she
had again broken her mainmast. The businessman, dishear-
tened, then sold the boat to an English actress, who promised to care for her if I sailed the boat to the mainland, to
Arenys del Mar, where she had a villa. This I did, using a jury-
sail rig and losing valuable time. But I could not knowingly
leave *Cresswell* abandoned and lost. So I made sure she was
cozy and looked after.

I walked away from her in Arenys without looking back. I couldn't bear the thought of Nelson not being with her, panting and wagging his tail. I headed for the train and Vigo.

I was not sorry to be on the Atlantic coast of Europe. There had been a thousand and one adventures in the Mediterranean, some epic, some hilarious, some tragic, for it is the bitch sea, changeable without warning, unreliable, beautiful at times (when she wants to be), downright treacherous at others. Which leads me to wonder if the climatic condition of an area has a direct bearing on the characteristics of the human inhabitants. Steady weather, steady people; and so on.

Once I was settled into *Two Brothers*, which, though shorter than *Cresswell*, was much more roomy and comfortable, I made plans to do something I had wanted to start for some time. To get to the highest navigable water in the world, Lake Titicaca—high up, three miles up, in the wild Andes Mountains of South America.

I spent about two weeks in Vigo, hurrying to get ready for the trip. It was September 1967, and the ideal time to make a trans-Atlantic crossing east to west. I had made three ocean deliveries while the negotiations were going on to sell *Cresswell* and buy *Two Brothers*; so, when the ship's stores for two years were onboard and the food supplies for five months stowed, I had $1,800 left in the Banco de España. I would leave it, and send for it when I reached the West Indies.

Two Brothers was a real ocean vessel. She had a deep keel and a high aspect-ratio sail rig; so she was a witch going to windward. She was constructed of finest Indonesian teak on oak frames, with her planking carvel built. She had a host of refinements never seen in *Cresswell*: plenty of cupboards, an oil-skin-hanging locker, even a head (lavatory) in a small compartment, but I ripped it out and used the space for storage. A bucket is far less troublesome and much more hygienic in the ocean.

All the gear was sound. The German who had owned her was a most careful sailor. He was so thorough that he never got beyond the first stages of planning the ocean voyage, even though he had been applying the metric system to it for four years. But he sure had the vessel shipshape, with not a pin out of place. At first it was like sitting in a boarded-up furniture shop window, but after a week or two I soon had that right, with a nice homey ambience, soot over the galley and a picture of the Queen on the forward bulkhead.

The engine was a French Couach diesel, and it had a miraculous electric starting device, though it could also be swung by hand. The sails were almost new and looked unused, meticulously folded into Prussian regimental squares with Teutonic precision. Of course, no ocean sailor would ever do that with artificial or synthetic fiber sails, because it weakens the weft where the sail is folded. He just stuffs them higgledy-piggeldy into their bags, and that way the folding strain is not confined to one crease.

I left Vigo early in October and headed for Horta in the Azores, direct. Crossing over the southward-running Portugal Current was rough, with heavy winds, but the boat stood up very well, and I was very pleased with my new home.

After eight days I was in Fayal Harbor on the island of Horta. I had an evening's drinking in the *Bar Sport* with Don Enrique, the ancient owner. Then, leaving that crossroads of ocean voyagers, I headed for Antigua.

At first it was a typical ocean crossing, with the boat rising and falling as she moved ahead on a close reach, day after day, night after starry night. I was skirting the southern edges of the Azores High. Suddenly, four nights out of port, I was becalmed.

The following day there was still no wind. I inflated the dinghy and, tying it securely with a very long line to the gently moving boat, paddled away from her to get some photographs. I took four or five snaps; then, as the wind gently picked up, quickly paddled back onboard.

Because of the light breezes, I decided to leave the dinghy inflated, as I would be able to take more pictures on the morrow, when it was light again.

All night long the boat sailed, heaving gently as the long, long Atlantic rolling seas ran under her forefoot, lifted her, then dropped her again, phosphorous streaming from under her stern.

After several hours on the wheel, I fixed the sheets so that she would steer herself southwest and went below to take a nap. I was soon asleep, or as asleep as I can be in a vessel out in the ocean—which is not the same as being asleep ashore, as I am always conscious of movement and noise. But rest enough for weary bones.

The bang came with a shock, a judder, a crash, and a smash that threw me against the forward bulkhead. Then, with a loud roar of splintering timber, the doghouse roof caved in. There was another explosive bang. The whole craft jumped into the air, then crashed down again. Water poured in.

I do not remember thinking anything. All I recall is being ondeck, seeing a great black tail, at least 22 feet wide, smash the foredeck, then send the mast flying with a great flailing flick. Whoosh! Smack! Bang! Wallop!

I scrambled into the dinghy and let go, paddling away with the oar I had left in its floor. Paddling like a madman. After what seemed an eternity, I looked around. The boat had gone! The sea surface, heaving, was utterly empty, with no sound except the slap-slap of the water against the sides of the rubber dinghy.

The first thing I thought was: Thank Christ this dinghy is fairly new and the valve's unlikely to leak! Then, with a jolt I realized I had no air pump for the dinghy. If it was punctured or started to leak in any other way, it would sink! Then I felt in my pockets. No knife, no line. *Nothing!* Two Spanish five-peseta coins and one Portuguese escudo. And, oh God in heaven, no food. And no *water!*

After a few moments of complete bewilderment I set to, thinking. I knew that the current, the southern edge of the Atlantic Gulf Stream, was setting to the east-northeast, but I had only a vague idea of the rate of speed. The wind was light, in the northwest. I was well off the shipping lanes, but if the current moved me at 25 miles a day, with the wind helping it, in an easterly direction, there was a good chance, if I could manage to survive for 10 days, that I would approach the main shipping lane from the Cape of Good Hope to Europe. The thing to do was to exert myself as little as possible and try to hang on. But I *knew* I was already dying.

I spent the rest of the night thinking of the past, of Tansy, and *Cresswell* and Nelson and even Sissie, wondering how *she* would react to this situation. For a few bitter moments I reflected on how I would never reach Lake Titicaca. But then I comforted myself with the thought that it had been a good try. You can't win all the time (though it's good to think you might).

With daylight, I started to paddle toward where I thought the boat had gone down, thinking that perhaps one of the half-empty jerry cans of fresh water might have escaped the disaster and still be floating. After searching desperately all day, all I found were a few pieces of "beautiful" Indonesian teak, shattered and splintered and none more than six inches long.

For the first three days I kept count of the passing of time. At first, sang softly to myself, then recited what poetry I knew, to keep myself company. By the fourth day my mouth was so parched that I stopped and lay thinking, now and again rising to search the horizon. In the hot noon sun I alternately covered my legs and my upper half with my pants, which were all the clothes I had, to try to stop the torturous sun from burning me, and at night the same, to try to protect my body from the salt spray slopping into my blisters and causing stinging burns. Weakening daily, dreaming hazily, I slept as much as I could.

By the evening of the fourth day I had resigned myself to death, hoping I would drift off soon. I could only breathe through my nose. My tongue had swollen so much that it completely filled my mouth and was hanging out on my beard, like a dog's in hot weather. Then I fell asleep, knowing I would not wake.

I was conscious of noise around me, and painfully opening

one eye found I was in a bright, white room with white-coated figures wandering around. Then an eternity passed, while the stinging burns in my eyebrows became less intense.

I was in an ice cream parlor—clean and bright. No . . . a dairy. That was it: a dairy . . . . A three-century pause for a million stabs of pain . . . . No, in a chemist's shop, or a hospital. Yes, a *hospital!*

Then all went black, with only the slight murmur of a human voice speaking near me as I slid away into a long, black tunnel.

I came to 6 days after *Two Brothers* hit the whale. I could now see straight, and by the uniforms passing the open door I knew I was in a Portuguese warship. The pain was severe. A tube was stuck in my arm and another in my throat. One hand and both legs were suspended in space, on a harness strung above the bed. I was bollock naked and black as the ace of spades.

The captain came into the sickbay on the afternoon I recovered consciousness. A big, energetic man, he exuded purpose and authority. In a loud but gentle voice he spoke in Portuguese, as, delicately, he inserted a pencil in my hand. I shook my head, indicating I was not Portuguese until the pain stretched me rigid. Then he asked me in Spanish what I was doing. Again, I slowly, painfully moved my head sideways. Then he addressed me in good, clear English.

"What on earth were you doing in mid-Atlantic in a rubber raft?"

I scribbled shakily on his pad, the pencil weighing a ton, and he frowned as he tried to make out the wispy squiggles. Then, throwing back his black-bearded head, he roared with laughter and showed the others what I had written:

"Selling bibles."

Farewell and adieu to you Spanish ladies,
Farewell and adieu to you ladies of Spain,
For we've received orders to sail for old England,
And we hope in a short while to see you again.

Chorus: *We'll rant and we'll roll,*
        Like true British sailors,
        We'll rant and we'll roll all across the salt seas,
        Until we strike soundings in the Channel of old England,
        From Ushant to Scilly is thirty-five leagues!

So let ev'ry man raise up his full bumper,
Let every man drink up his full glass,
For we'll laugh and be jolly
And chase melancholy,
With a well given toast to each true-hearted lass!

Seaman's song, eighteenth century
This was the only Royal Navy
"working chanty."

23

"I Don't Know Why You Say Goodbye—I Say Hello!"

The sick-berth attendant in Portuguese Navy fisheries protection vessel guarded me from a continual stream of would-be visitors from the crew, who had heard of my encounter with the skipper. News in a small vessel travels fast, and until the ship arrived at Ponta delgada, in the Azores, I was treated as a sort of mascot.

By the time the vessel finished her patrol around the Azores, plodding along at a slow rate for two more weeks, I was almost completely recovered. I could talk and see, hear and feel and smell, and walk reasonably well enough to be able to descend the gangway on my own account. As I left the ship, in clothes and shoes donated by the officers and the crew, the captain was at the head of the gangway. He pressed an envelope into my hand.

"On behalf of myself and my officers, here is a token of our esteem."

"Thank you very much, *Senhor*. May I look at it now?"

"Certainly, by all means."

I opened the envelope. In it were about $100 in Portuguese escudos and a plane ticket to London via Madrid! "But," I protested, "my consulate would have provided me with a ticket, after they confirmed my nationality." He stopped me, holding up his hand. "We know, but it would take many days. Go and see him with the note I gave you, get your passport, and then you can go home and get back on your feet." He smiled. "And may God go with you."

"Thank you, Captain.

"*Bom sorte*, Tristan, and thank you for the jokes you have told us. We never had such a cheerful trip."

"Nor me, Captain."

There was very little fuss at the consulate, and in two days I had my new passport and was off by air to Madrid. On the flight, I wondered whether it would be better to head for the Spanish coast; after all, there might be a boat there waiting for someone to deliver her to some other place. If not, I could try Gibraltar. Then, if there was nothing and no prospects, I could head for London.

It was late November 1967, and most of the craft which would be heading across the Western Ocean would have left Europe anyway. They would be in the Canaries, awaiting the mild easterlies of December before shoving off for the West Indies.

If there was nothing in the Balearics, I would head for Gibraltar. If there was nothing there, I would have to make for London and make my living, as best I could, until the following spring, when I could again think about another boat.

By the time the plane landed in Madrid my mind was made up. I caught the plane for Valencia, where I ferried across to Ibiza. Another idea had come to mind.

On my previous visit to Ibiza I had sighted a very pretty "Folkboat." Like the *Two Brothers*, she was carvel built (also in Holland), of pitch pine on oak. She was smaller (25 feet long), but she was deep-keeled and fast, and German Willie had whizzed past the stately *Cresswell* several times, and I had noted the seaworthy way she rode to the sea.

German Willie was a sailing instructor at a holiday camp on Ibiza, near Santa Eulalia, and I had heard rumors that he intended to start his own business. Perhaps he would sell *Pancho* to me? I had $1,500 in pesetas, still in the Banco de España. As soon as I arrived in Ibiza I caught a taxi and went to see him.

Three days later, after paying German Willie $1,400, I was the new owner of *Pancho*, which I promptly renamed *Banjo*. Her hull was sound and her gear was good, methodically maintained by Willie. I sailed her from Santa Eulalia to Ibiza town, where I moored her stern to the town wall, without having to pay mooring fees (as long as I was quick enough to slip out every time the harbor master came along the water-front to collect dues).

Banjo was not a very comfortable boat to live in as the head-room in her cabin was at the most three feet eight. Being al-most flush decked, she had hardly any doghouse, but I didn't mind this. It made for less windage when she was in heavy weather and allowed the breaking seas to pass unobstructed right over her. She was even more of a windward witch than *Two Brothers*. Sailing against the wind, she would go as close as 45 degrees off the eye of the breeze before her narrow, high-cut jibsail would luff and flutter. She was so handy that in a flat calm I could get hold of the tiller and, waggling it back and forth sideways to move the rudder, propel the boat forward at a good knot and a half. She had a British Seagull outboard engine, which, with six horsepower, was all I would ever need. It drove her, under power, at six knots.

During November and December I carefully counted the coins, eating cheap dried fish and rice, drinking Spanish wine at 20 cents a bottle, and sending written inquiries around for delivery work. Finally, through a British agency in Malta, I landed one to take an Italian 40-footer to Mexico. I made sure *Banjo*'s moorings were good and secure, left her under the eye of a local fisherman, and took off.

I was away for four and a half months, returning to Ibiza in early May of 1968 with $500. As soon as I was back, settled in *Banjo*, German Willie came to see me.

Excitedly, he told me that a rich Frenchman from Paris had asked him if he knew where he could charter a boat for a week to sail around the island. In the previous year he had chartered *Pancho* (as she was then) from Willie and paid very well. The Frenchman was a good sailor and I need have no fear for the safety of the boat.

The next day the Frenchman called on me, his wallet stiff with thousand-peseta notes. The deal was made, and as *Banjo* sailed out of the harbor with the Frenchman and his son onboard, I was $300 richer. The whole process was painless. I stayed in a friend's boat, the Swedish *Amiga Mia*, until the Frenchman came back at the end of the week, with my boat unscratched and spotless. That got me thinking.

If I could make a few more of these charters—"money for old rope," so it seemed—say five more, I would have enough money to be able to take off in the autumn for South America and Lake Titicaca.

The summer and fall of 1968 I did exactly this. I placed a few ads in the Ibiza bars and waited. I also earned money sailing small groups of people on day charters to the nearby islands of Formentera and Espartel. This paid enough to keep me in food, keep the boat happy, and save a little for the great venture. It also paid enough to hire a deckhand to assist me, it being almost impossible to single-hand a small sailing craft with a crowd of five or six passengers onboard.

My deckhand, Steve, was a Cockney kid, about 16, whose father worked in one of the foreign-owned bars of Ibiza. Steve was an honest, hard-working youngster, and we got on well.

One day Steve came to me, eagerly telling me about an "American film director," and "Loike, 'e wants to char'er a bowt to sail arahnd the island for a week."

"O.K., Steve; tell him that *Banjo's* going for 300 bucks American a week, maximum of four, including himself."

"Nah Skip, 'e aint got now one wiv' 'im, 'e's orn his jack; ownly 'e wants me to gow along, give 'im an 'and loike."

"That's fine by me, as long as he pays your food—if you want to go along."

"Cor, fanks, Skip; I'll 'op along and tell 'im."

"And tell him to bring proof of sailing experience, if he's got it."

I was treading on thin ice, because the insurance of *Banjo* had not been renewed since she left Willie's hands. I'd never been insured, either. Couldn't afford it.

An hour or two later, Steve turned up with the "film director" in tow. A swarthy-complexioned man, about 30 or so, with a heavy mustache. He looked a bit like a young Groucho Marx. He wore an expensive suit and shoes, a gold ring, and a gold wristwatch. He soon had me convinced that he was a member of any number of prestigious yacht clubs on the West Coast of the U.S.A., and he showed me membership cards and a list of clubs as long as my arm.

"I wanna sail around the island and dig the scenery. If it looks O.K., I'm gonna make a film here, an' I'm tellin' you it's your boat that'll be used, and there'll be a lotta dough in it for you." And so on and so forth.

To my eternal shame and chagrin, I allowed him to con me into letting him charter the boat.

"Steve," I called, as they prepared the sails before taking off.

"Wot's that, Skip?"

"Here a minute."

Steve scrambled dockside so I could talk to him quietly. "Yers, Skip?" He flicked his head to clear his eyes.

"Now remember this: whatever you do, don't let him anchor out on the open coast at night. Make sure he goes into harbor. The wind around here—or anywhere in the Med, come to that—can change direction very swiftly, and before you know it you'll be on a leeshore with the wind blowing its balls off." I had already left this proviso, in writing, with the "film director."

"O.K., Skip, I've got it."

Off they went, while I headed for my lady friend's house to while away the week, making a bird cage for her kid's pigeons.

Friday night passed and all was well. Over the grapevine I heard that *Banjo* had spent the night at a cove, safe—tucked in on the northeast side of the island. Saturday passed. Nothing untoward. But I got a message by word of mouth that they had run out of kerosene for the cooker. I sent them some by taxi, right across the island. I took my lady friend into the town to eat, but I felt uneasy, for some strange reason I could not explain.

That night I suddenly awoke with a tremendous feeling of anxiety. Five minutes after I wakened, there was a tremendous rush of wind on the roof, on the northern side.

"What's the matter?" asked my friend, sleepily.

"*That's* the matter . . . the wind's shifted. She's gone! She's gone!"

"Who's gone!"

"The boat! I know it. I can feel it. It's in my bones."

"Oh, don't be silly. Go to sleep. Tomorrow you can go to the north coast and see for yourself that she's all right. Your American friend is a very good sailor, a strong, big man." She put her arm around me. "Go to sleep and stop worrying."

I tried to sleep, but it was no good. After the sudden, violent, 10-minute *tramontana*, the storm had completely quieted. I stared at the moonlight pouring through the window, with the clouds passing overhead. Then I dozed fitfully until the dawn.

In town to check the mail, I was sitting at a pavement-table on the waterfront, awaiting a bus to rumble over to the north coast. I fingered the coffee cup on the red-and-white-checkered cloth. I waited half an hour.

And then I saw Steve. I knew by his walk it was Steve, although he was too far away for me to see his face. As he approached, I saw that his face was miserable; but he walked boldly up to my table.

"H'lo, Steve."

"Wotcher, Skip."

I gestured him to sit down. He was wearing only pants and a life jacket. His blond hair was still damp from the sea.

"She's gone, hasn't she?"

"Lissen, Skip, I did wot I could, but the bloke wouldn't take no notice . . ." Tears welled out of his eyes.

"Where is she?"

"I told 'im not to stay aht on the coast at night and to make for the 'arbor at San Antonio, but the fuckin' bloke wouldn't lissen ter me, and like 'e's a big barstard an' me bein' little an' skinny an' orl . . . like . . . "

"Where is she?"

"An' loike I told 'im the anchor wuz draggin' an' 'e said loike that I wuz imaginin' fings, an' come on dahn back ter bed, and then, loike the next fing I knoo she was loike bangin' on the bleedin' rocks, an' the Yank jumped ashore an' the wind wuz blowin'. Bloody great seas comin' up and the boat pahndin' away. I nipped forward to pull on the anchorline, to pull 'er orf, see, an' there weren't noffink on the end of the line, Skip. The bleedin' anchorline wuz broke, loike . . . "

"Where is she, Steve?" I asked again, slowly.

"An' loike I run back to the stern wot wuz sinkin' 'cos she had a bloody great 'ole in her, and I frew the septic* a line an' it missed 'im by abaht two feet, an' the barstard never even went ar'ter it. 'E just left me to fuckin-well drahn."

I ordered Steve a coffee.

"Look, mate, it's no good cryin' over spilt milk. If she's gone, she's gone. All I want to know, right now, it where she is, so I can go out there and see if there's anything I can salvage."

"Big bay, abaht eight miles from San Antonio. I climbed the bloody cliff; ever so 'igh, it wuz. An' there wuz this little Spanish bloke standin' there lookin' dahn. I tried to awsk 'im where it wuz an' 'e said Ensanada 'Ondo."

"Ensanada Hondo . . . do you know what that means, Steve?" I said, bitterly.

"Wot?"

" 'Deep Bay' . . . bloody . . . 'deep bay!' " I stood up. "Where's Big Daddy [the 'film director']?"

" 'E said like he wuz goin' to come dahn an' see you an' square you up."

With Steve trailing behind like a scared whippet, his skinny ribs showing under the bulky life preserver, I made for the lobby of the Hotel Montesol. "You sit there a minute," I said as I made for the phone. With the Spanish-government-run telephone company's usual alacrity, I was through to the air-

*Septic=septic tank=Yank (Cockney rhyming slang).

port within three-quarters of an hour.

"*Si, si Señor. Si, el Americano he partido . . . Si, no. Gracias.*"

Big Daddy had flown the coop. I never heard from him again. Let's hope he never tries his big-shot film-director, yacht-club-member routine with any other poor uninsured soul.

"He's buggered off, Steve."

"Aww, Skip!" More tears came to his eyes.

"Come on, mate, I'll buy you a beer." I put my arm on his shoulder and he looked at me, astonished.

"Well, Steve," I said, leading him to the bar. "It's not every year of your life you lose two bloody boats and all you own in the world, is it?"

Steve grinned at first, our eyes met, he smiled, then laughed. He raised his beer glass, spilling some on the life preserver. He flicked the foam off the orange cloth.

"Don't worry about that, Steve. It's yours, you can have it."

"Cor, fanks, Skip!"

"Might come in handy when you're out with your next friggin' film director!"

He laughed again. Then he leaned over and said, close to my ear, "Tell you wot, Skip."

"What?"

"When that 'appens I'm goin' to be the first barstard on the bleedin' shore!"

I grinned. "Well, at least it's done some good, if it taught you that."

German Willie took me to Ensenada Hondo in his speedboat. All we found of *Banjo* was the ensign, floating and still secured and whipped to the broken flagstaff. I presented it to Willie to hang on his holiday-camp wall. "A trophy for you, mate; it'll make up for the *Scharnhorst!*"

Willie laughed and clapped my shoulders.

Steve's old man put me up for a couple of nights until I could arrange my passage to London. There was no money to go off searching for a yacht delivery, and I was sick at heart. It was the end of September, still the Atlantic hurricane season. Not a thing would be moving to cross the ocean for at least two months. When my flight was paid (with the help of Steve's old man) I was left with exactly the equivalent of three dollars. I bought Steve and German Willie another beer at the airport.

"*Prosit*," said Willie, looking me straight in the eye.

"*Skol*, mate," I replied, keeping my eyes as dry and hard as Glasgow rivets.

The first thing I did when I arrived in London was head for Harrod's Department Store. Not for the wide front doors, where the dowagers alight from their gleaming limousines —I made for a small side door and navigated my way to the engineering office.

Most of the engineers in the big London buildings are ex-Royal Navy men, and this was especially so at Harrod's. By the time I'd explained my plight to the chief engineer I had a job. I could eat, sleep, and recuperate from the blow to my vitals. I got the job of stoking the incinerator.

At that time, all the fresh food that wasn't sold that day was thrown down a hatch, and that was the last the shop clerks saw of it. However, farther en route, the process was quite interesting. A long, dark chute led deep underground to a pit full of garbage from a hundred different departments. There were bruised oranges, lemons, tomatoes, soggy lettuce, potatoes, day-old meat by the bucketful, loaves of old bread—every kind of castaway food imaginable: tons and tons of it. It was like manna from heaven to a castaway sailor.

Besides food in the pit, there were tons upon tons of old papers from files, as well as invoices, wage lists, supplies-requisition notes, typing ribbons, cartons, boxes, envelopes—all the waste from a great concern employing around 7,000 people in one building.

By the pit, rake in hand, I stood, sorting out good food, which I cooked on the gas stove in the engineer's restroom, where I slept and read when I was off watch.

Shoveling the garbage into the incinerator was the easiest, most pleasant part of the job. Pulling out the glowing ashes and dumping them into yet another chute some yards away was another story. Ash would fly all over the place—a fine,